A SHORT HISTORY OF GOLF

A SHORT HISTORY OF
GOLF

MATT CLEARY

FOREWORD BY GREG NORMAN

NEW
HOLLAND

To the old man, Vinny, who taught me the game, drilled in its etiquette and gave me his golf clubs. And then bought new ones.

CONTENTS

PREFACE

Golf is so old there's a book called *The Early Days of Golf* that was written by poet, Andrew Lang, who was born in 1844. The contents page has only one entry, which reads: 'Golf', and that's it. The rest of the page is blank. Turn the page and there's another blank page that lists only the heading of the one and only chapter. And that too reads, 'Golf'.

And then you get into it. As Lang said in his book:

Golf is undoubtedly incomplete, sketchy, and scrappy, a collection of documents and odds and ends. It is not here, in a single chapter, that the history of golf can be exhaustively written. But we may try to show its relations with other ball games, its connection with foreign forms most nearly allied with itself, and we may lightly trace the antiquities of the sport.

Like Lang's *Early Days*, this book claims to be a short history of golf. It's what one mad golf hound found interesting after lightly tracing (and heavily Googling) antiquities. It's one golf hack's crack at history.

And thus Greg Norman has a chapter (and some more), Moe Norman has a stanza or two, Inbee Park a paragraph, Colin Montgomerie a mention here and there, Billy Casper a sentence and that is all.

Just how things rolled.

It also rolled that Ben Hogan is always 'Ben Hogan'. Ditto 'Bobby Jones'. And 'Sam Snead'. And a few others. It just felt right, for whatever reason, that I should write their full name. It felt funny to call Ben Hogan 'Hogan' or Byron Nelson 'Nelson'. Could be just me.

Similarly, and perhaps counter-intuitively, Greg Norman—whom for me as a boy shared top billing with Superman—became and is the only Shark, The Great White. No need to say Greg Norman. Shark will do. Just how things rolled.

This book is only loosely chronological so read it how you like. Go straight to the part about Moe Norman and back to Old Tom Morris. Bounce from Augusta to Ernie Els to Babe Didirikson Zaharias. Or just keep on truckin' on through as you are.

Either way, I hope you learn a bit, laugh a bit, and forgive the sports writer the odd flourish. As Walter Hagen said, 'You're only here for a short visit. Don't hurry, don't worry. And be sure to smell the flowers along the way.'

FOREWORD BY GREG NORMAN

olf has always evolved. Old Tom Morris made his own golf balls
G and clubs. Today super computers make them. Old Tom and Tom
Morris Junior played for their own money. Today on the world tours,
they're playing for telephone numbers each week. Win the Fed Ex
Cup—you've won the lottery.

Golf has changed dramatically even in my time in the game. It makes
it almost impossible to compare the records of players of different eras.

Ben Hogan, for instance, couldn't win the grand slam in 1953
because the PGA Championship was on the week before the Open
Championship, and people mostly travelled by boat. He only played the
Open once. He mostly chose not to play the PGA either; he preferred
stroke play, and the PGA was match play until 1958.

What we call the 'Grand Slam' wasn't around until Arnold Palmer
and the journalist Bob Drum came up with it in 1960. Bobby Jones's
'Grand Slam' was called 'The Impregnable Quadrilateral'. But it would
likely never be equalled. So Arnold—who had won the Masters and US

Open and was on the way to Britain—suggested to Bob that he recast it.

Bobby Jones created Augusta National and the Masters though he'd effectively retired before the Masters became a major championship. And he'd already won his 'grand slam' which was the Open and Amateur Championships of USA and Britain. He never played in the US PGA because he never turned pro.

So many other things. On the greens, you couldn't mark your ball, you had to putt around—or chip over—your opponent's ball. If a round was cancelled because of rain, everybody's round was cancelled, and they started afresh. Tournament leaders didn't play in the last group.

The amateur guys played because they could afford the time off work. Bobby Jones was a practicing lawyer. Professional players were almost looked down upon. For some tournaments, they weren't allowed in the clubhouse. Walter Hagen was the first to challenge that mindset. He deserves a lot of credit, 'Sir Walter'.

One thing has never changed—the game's always produced great characters.

Gary Player was one of the great pioneers of golf on the world stage; a great traveller and ambassador. When he first went to St Andrews he slept on the beach the night before.

Look at Ben Hogan, one of the best there's ever been, a fierce competitor. I met him once or twice and he was very much everything I'd heard about, read about. He was a very nice guy, very humble. And he was Ben Hogan!

It was the same each time I met Gene Sarazen. I had an acute amount of respect for him. We had this amazing admiration for each other. I don't know who admired the other more, Gene or I.

I'll never forget when I won the Open Championship at Royal St George's in '93. Gene Sarazen came up to me, and the passion in his voice when he said I'd played some of the best golf he'd ever seen in his life, it was so humbling. And coming from him, and how he said it. He was 91!

In the 1976 Australian Open, I shot 80 first round, 72 the second round. Jack Nicklaus and I were paired together and had adjoining lockers. He sat me down afterwards and we had a good chat together and he basically said, 'Look, you have the game, you could play well in America because it's a power game.' He said I would be very successful in the United States. To hear that from Jack!

When I got to the US, Arnold Palmer took me under his wing. When I was looking for a place to live, he invited me to look at his place in Florida. He said the weather's the best, you can practice all year round and you can be a member of my golf club. So, I bought a place in Orlando and became a member of Bay Hill Country Club, and we played probably five days a week. And every day after golf we'd be in the locker room, playing cards, drinking beer. I probably drank more beer with Arnold Palmer than anyone else.

Those moments with Arnold were probably the most precious. Not on the golf course so much but in the locker room. Arnold took me on board, brought me into his inner circle and instilled a lot of values in me.

We had our ups and downs too; it wasn't always a smooth run. I can remember being extremely disappointed with Arnold about the world golf tour that I was about to announce. Very, very disappointed that he talked against it.

But those are the things you learn in life. You're not going to agree with everybody and not everybody's going to agree with you. You learn these things after being in the game for 40 years. And I feel that if I don't voice my thoughts then I'm not responsible for trying to improve the game. You've got to learn. You learn from history.

I hope you learn something from Matt's book.

INTRODUCTION

It's July of 2015 and we're leaning on the old stone wall by the Road Hole on the Old Course at St Andrews in Scotland's Kingdom of Fife. Upon this sandy links land they've been whacking away at the pill for 800 years. Versions of golf were played in China and Belgium and in Holland on ice, and in ancient Greece and in Rome. But they took to it here in Scotland with a vengeance.

Maybe not with a vengeance. It's golf, not *Die Hard III*. But Scotland is where golf became 'golf'. St Andrews is the viral epicentre. It's the undisputed home of golf. And being here to watch *the* Open Championship at *the* home of golf—and leaning on *the* stone wall near *the* Road Hole, no less—well ... for this man of golf, it's just about out-of-body.

People who don't play golf might not understand but when you identify as a golfer, you might become a rusted-on crazy person who wakes each day to watch golf, reads the papers about golf, plays golf, drinks a beer and talks about golf, watches golf on TV again while leafing through a golf magazine and checking the Internet for your club's results and your handicap, looks for golf stuff to buy on eBay before heading into bed torn between *Shark Attack: Greg Norman's Guide to Aggressive Golf* and Nick O'Hern's *Tour Mentality*. I know that's what I do. So, a visit to the Old Course at St Andrews—you just have to do it. It's a thing.

We're here at St Andrews on Sunday of the 2015 Open Championship which is still round three given the wind Saturday would've blown Donald Trump's rough orange bonce off. My pals and I—a 14-man crew on a golf, cricket and beer appreciation tour of Britain—spent Saturday morning playing the nearby Scotscraigh golf course (the world's 13th oldest) and were flogged like so many horse thieves. Play was suspended for the pros on the Old Course while we thrashed away, flayed by heather and angry prickles.

Then we drank rather a lot of beer in Scotscraigh's clubhouse and looked at a board which listed people who'd made a hole-in-one at Scotscraigh in 1822. And there we watched sport on the television — including the Open Championship which we never got to that day — beamed in from around the world. People knock globalisation but you couldn't do that in 1984.

Earlier, in 2011, my brother and I went in the ballot and played the Old Course and stayed in the Old Course Hotel in a room overlooking the Road Hole and the homely little Jigger Inn. We woke from jetlag at 4 am with the sun just coming up, the floor-to-ceiling windows delivering early morning hues of purples and mauves, and highlighting the contours and the promise of the Old Course. Man, it was good.

And playing it, well. You stand on the first tee, short par 4, fairway wider than the plains of the Serengeti, and you think, *how the hell did Ian Baker-Finch miss this?* And then you address the ball and you understand for you worry you're going to miss the ball much less the fairway.

But away you go, and maybe you par the first, as I did, and maybe you par the Road Hole, as I did, and maybe you birdie the 18th, oh yes, as I did. And maybe you walk off 18 holding your hat up to the applauding tourists as I did, and maybe you told people about it many, many times since. Yes again, as I did. And maybe you've just had the most fun round of your golf life, as the old boy who created the joint would've wanted.

The Old Course is by Old Tom Morris out of Mother Nature. The fairways look flat enough on TV but are rolling, bulbous—like a roiling green sea of aqua bumps frozen mid-swell. The fescue and bent grass is short-cut to 8 millimetres. The layout is open, undulating. Hard green moguls feed up to greens you can approach from anywhere you dare.

The ground feels hard and trampoline-like, and your golf ball can shoot off at odd angles. There are wee burns and riveted, fiendish pot bunkers. There are massive double greens and double fairways. The first and 18th fairways are so wide combined, they're like the Straits of Hormuz.

St Andrews, the town, is all old grey sandstone buildings and narrow, winding streets and lanes, little pubs and dainty shops selling knick-knacks and pretty little things that we don't need. There's an 'old European' feel that's appealing for visitors.

On the Old Course's eastern perimeter is West Sands Beach, which is all wet, grey sand whipped hard by salt-flecked rain. Old Tom Morris used to swim in these waters, they say, and somehow lived to 86. Gary Player slept in the dunes before the 1955 Open Championship because he was backpacking on the cheap.

Playing the Old Course is like re-enacting history, a bit like the US Civil War re-eanactment types, dressing up. It's like playing golf on history's stage. I took one shot from the bunker on the par-3 11th that Bobby Jones couldn't get out of at all when playing in the 1921 Open Championship. I took one shot from Hell Bunker on the par-5 14th that in 2000 Jack Nicklaus hit four from. I made par; Jack made a quintuplet-bogey 10. Am I twice the golfer as a then 60-year-old Jack

Nicklaus? I am not. But that hole I was. Cop that, you great Golden Bear.

On the Road Hole, the 17th—where Tom Watson flared a 2-iron in the final round in '84, and Greg Norman made a par after whacking one into the wall, and Doug Sanders made the up-and-down of his very life from the bunker to lead Nicklaus by one in the 1970 Open Championship before three-putting the last green and losing the 18-hole play-off—I drained a 15-footer to make four. Does that mean Greg Norman and I are golfing peers? No. But on that hole? You betcha.

And on the 18th I made a birdie three after knocking an 8-iron stiff. And as I walked up to mark the ball, I had to touch my cap as a dozen tourists applauded. I tapped in and wrote down three for an 81. Rory McIlroy shot 80 in 2010. Are we contemporaries? We are not. The day before Rory shot 63.

So then we ate haggis and a soup called a Cullen skink. And drank Guinness and fine old whiskey. And ate rare roast beef in the hotel's cracking restaurant. And met a bloke from Lancashire who insisted that the natty leather napkin holders looked like the 'cock-ring of Spartacus'.

Four years later we met up with 'Spartacus' to play golf at Lundin Golf Club (Est.1868) in the town of Lundin Links (Est. in the time of druids) and Spartacus, a cracking good bloke, presented each of our 14-strong tour party with a gift: a plastic cock-ring upon which he'd inscribed: '2015 Open Championship at St Andrews'.

And that didn't happen in 1984, either.

The champion golfer of 1984, the Grand Senor of Spain, Severiano Ballesteros Sota once said:

> St Andrews, you see, is unique: the road hole, Hell Bunker, the museum, the hotel, the shops in the town where everybody is selling golf—all of it. I want to spend time with the people there. They want to see me, and I want to see them. It's an appreciation.

Through the magic of television and latterly via YouTube, we can still see Seve on the 18th in 1984, pumping his fist after tipping in a 15-foot birdie putt to win the claret jug. It's a moment of ecstasy frozen in time: Seve in his navy blue woolly jumper with a little white Slazenger cat on the breast, pretending to vigorously hand-milk a cow and throwing a punch to the four corners of the Old Course and to the world. You beauty.

As Seve said:

> I love St Andrews as much as my house. It's like going back home. It's a piece of art; a unique, singular place. I really believe the Open should be there every year.

Back into the glorious present and we're halfway up the 17th, known as the 'Road Hole' because a road runs by the hole. The Road Hole's bunker is called 'Road Hole Bunker' and its old stone wall is called 'old stone wall'. I'm standing 20 metres from Jason Day, out in the left rough, flaunting the rules of my media pass. And here I have a private show of a pure, high, fading 6-iron out from the long stuff, which falls pin-high just off a long green good as perpendicular to him. It's gone maybe 200 metres. It's golf but not as we choppers know it.

Because these pros, they are *ridiculous* at golf. And always have been. From Young Tom Morris to young Justin Thomas, they choose irons from tees and bounce onto greens. They hit low runners or high fades, and stinging, flat little bits of kit that zap low off the tee and bound across the frozen green moguls. They *manage* the golf course. And when there's no wind at St Andrews, these emotion-free automatons can eat the Old Course like a fat plate of kippers.

But it's blowing today, blowing hard like the stinging wet breath of a Norwegian Ice God. And golf's top men battle. It's another thing that makes St Andrews magnificent: Mother Nature is a factor, as she should be in a game played in Mother Nature. Close up I see Dustin Johnson duff one on 18. I see Danny Willett bounce one onto 16. And I see Adam Scott swing his driver like a beautiful machine.

The next day, the Monday, we watch the final round from the dressing room of Kingsbarns Golf Club down the road because rusted-on golf hounds would still rather play themselves than watch someone else. And from there we see Zach Johnson beat Louis Oosthuizen and Marc Leishman in a four-hole play-off. And we continue to gaze upon the Old Course, the Home of Golf, headquarters of the Royal and Ancient Golf Club of St Andrews, the beating heart of the great game with its old grey-stone hotels and houses you'd sell many organs to live in. As old mate Connor MacLeod from the Clan MacLeod said in the movie, *Highlander* (1986): 'it's a kind of magic'.

-CHAPTER ONE-

HOME

Old Courses

Golf wasn't invented or discovered. It didn't come from a madman's garage or slam into Earth like baby Superman in a comet from space. Golf just sort of ... *became*. And we don't know how, exactly, it came to be nor the first person to hit a ball with a stick because they didn't write it down.

We do know this. By 500AD Roman legions had ceased conquering the world and imprisoning people as slaves, which was a good thing. Yet it also meant the Romans stopped spreading progressive things such as sanitation, architecture, the aqueduct, the rule of law, advanced viticulture and so on. And so Europe experienced several centuries of cultural and economic degradation, and life for all but the super-toffs was hungry and poor and grubby.

Today they call these times the Middle Ages or Dark Ages. They didn't at the time; they just thought they were crap. But what were they going to do? Nobody had invented anything useful in one thousand years because they were too busy fighting with broadswords and burning alleged witches and being sucked on by leeches, as history tells us.

And then came the Renaissance and golf turned up in Scotland, somehow. It may have come from the Netherlands—the ball and stick game of 'colf', they were playing that in 1297, on ice. On the land now called Belgium, they played colf until their overlords banned it, with failure to comply resulting in a fine of 20 shillings and confiscation of one's overcoat. Germans played 'kolf', Flemish folk played 'chole'. Greeks, Romans, Egyptians—and you could probably go back to druids and even cave men—played games with sticks whacking pebbles at targets.

Top experts in China point to a game called *chuiwan* which was played during the Song Dynasty (AD960–AD1279). China in those days was the most advanced place on Earth. While Europeans were rolling about in mud and muck, in China they were getting to work in super-fast trains that floated on magnets.

No they weren't. But they did have the best medicine and sculpture and painting and ironwork. They were healthy, clean and fit, as least compared to Europeans who were lucky to make their first birthday. Chinese people invented paper money, gunpowder, the compass, tea drinking and the printing press. Europeans' biggest advance in the period was to ride off to Jerusalem to 'take it back'.

Meanwhile, the Chinese were inventing things, staying fit and playing golf—or at least the golf-like game of *chuiwan*—which had etiquette and rules not dissimilar to those of the modern game.

It's further theorized by top experts that Mongol traders took the game to Europe. By 1644, the end of the Ming Dynasty, there is no record of *chuiwan* in China. In 1889, it turned up back again in the form of golf when the Brits built the Hong Kong Golf Club. Then the Communist Party banned golf. Mao Zedong derided it as symbol of bourgeois excess. In 1984 Arnold Palmer built a golf course in China and thus begat the 'King Dynasty', b-boom.

As Palmer writes in his memoir, *Arnold Palmer: Memories, Stories, and Memorabilia from a Life on and off the Course*, golf's re-entry back into China was not without its challenges. Most of those helping build his course didn't know what they were doing.

> [I] gave this man a golf ball I had in my pocket. He stared at a few moments, then tried to take a bite out of the cover. 'No,' I said. 'You don't eat it.' That's when it dawned on me that the men engaged in the grueling labor of building our course had no idea what golf was. When I explained through an interpreter that this ball would be used to play the course our new friend was building, his eyes lit up and he took the ball from me as if I'd just presented him with the crown jewels of China.

In 1995 China hosted the World Cup (won for the third year in a row by Fred Couples and Davis Love III). In 2015, as part of an anti-corruption campaign and concerned at the rampant construction of golf courses, the Communist Party banned its members from joining golf clubs. Six months later the ban was rescinded. And golf, along with capitalism, has flourished in China, and consumed the land like the purple plague of Patterson's Curse. So there you go.

In 1100 or so, some version of stick-and-ball-whacking turned up in Scotland. And they got right into it. By 1457 it was so popular that King James II banned it because his soldiers weren't attending archery practice and hence not protecting King James II.

But prohibition didn't work because prohibition doesn't, and by 1502 James II's grandson James IV was having his bow-maker forge him golf clubs. Golf was then banned on and off until 1552 when the Archbishop of St Andrews allowed people to play on the links land—the non-arable sand lands between sea and farms—each day except Sunday. It's a tradition that stands on the Old Course today.

In 1592 two men, John Henrie and Pat Rogie, were jailed for 'playing of the gowff on the links of Leith every Sabbath the time of the sermonses'. In 1604 a Robert Robertson played golf on a Sunday and was put in a 'seat of repentance'. And lo, did people line up to taunt him with a topical version of Bob Marley's 'Bad boys, bad boys, whatcha gonna do? Whatcha gonna do when they come for you?'

Club-makers then found a market for 'Sunday clubs' or 'Sabbath sticks' which were a walking stick with a golf head as the handle. When no-one was looking, they could quickly flip it upside down to use as a golf club.

In 1707 Scotland and England formed a union and called it Great Britain, and Scottish ex-pats travelled the Empire taking golf with them. In 1739 a consignment of golf clubs—an assortment of brassies, long spoons, mud spoons, baffing spoons, driving putters, cleeks, mashies and niblicks—as ye olde whacking sticks were known—was sent from an Andrew Wallace, a businessman of Edinburgh, to his brother William Wallace of Charleston, Carolina.

By 1744 the world's first golf club was formed when William St Clair, a hereditary Grand Master mason (whatever that is) formed the Gentleman Golfers of Leith. Soon enough a name change and The Honourable Company of Edinburgh Golfers was born, again. They moved to Musselburgh and then to Muirfield where they wrote up golf's original 13 rules.

In 1754 the Society of St Andrews Golfers became a club. In 1764 they reduced their number of holes from 22 to 18. In 1767 an Edinburgh medical student, Thomas Kincaid, wrote the first golf instruction stuff in his diary advising players to:

> stand as you do at fenceing with the small sword, bending your legs a little and holding the muscles of your legs and back and armes exceeding bent or fixt or stiffe, and not at all slackning them in the time you are bringing down the Stroak (which you readily doe).

Time passed. Golf blossomed. And then it was born again—by Old Tom Morris.

✳ ✳ ✳

The Grand Old Man

Old Tom Morris was the first green keeper to top-dress greens with sand. He was the first to use a horse-drawn mechanical lawn mower on greens. Old Tom Morris invented the tubular metal device that green keepers still use to make the hole a uniform size. Previously holes had been dug out in the morning by shovel. By the end of a day's play, the hole would be bigger than when it started. Smart players would tee off late and take advantage.

Old Tom Morris was the first to widen fairways and introduce tee-boxes. Previously golfers would tee off from a point nearest the previous hole. He was the first to route fairways through hazards that golfers could strategically avoid.

Old Tom Morris was the first to put yardage markers on fairways. He put flags on greens. He put cup liners in holes.

He is, indisputably, the godfather of golf.

Old Tom Morris was born in 1821, the same year Mr James Cheape of Strathtyrum purchased the links land at St Andrews so that farmers couldn't breed rabbits on it. Old Tom Morris's childhood was spent running the streets of St Andrews playing a hybrid golf-hockey-hurling game called sillybodkins.

At the age of 14, Old Tom Morris became a caddie and was apprenticed to—and heavily influenced by—Allan Robertson, the champion golfer of Scotland, the best player of his time and probably the game's first professional.

When Allan Robertson died in 1859, it was decided they should crown a new 'Champion golfer'. And thus was invented the Open Championship.

Old Tom Morris made clubs from beechwood, ash and hickory. He made leather pouch balls hard-packed with goose feathers called featheries. The little pouches would be stuffed with feathers (enough to fill a gentleman's top hat, that was the measure) and then soaked, tightly bound and left to dry to tighten and harden into orbs. Featheries were not very good in the rain, however, which in Scotland was not ideal.

Old Tom Morris worked for and with Allan Robertson for 12 years, the last four as a journeyman or tradesman, until he was sacked on the spot when caught using one of the new-fangled gutta-percha balls, which Allan Robertson feared would threaten his business.

The 'guttie' was invented in 1848 by Dr Robert Adams Paterson, an engineer. His *New York Times*' obituary in 1904 declared:

> Dr Patterson said he was too poor to own or buy a pigskin ball and he experimented with other materials, finally using gutta-percha which had been wrapped around an idol sent from India.

Paterson sourced gutta-percha from the sap of the Malaysian sapodilla (rubber tree). Malays had long made things with the dried-out sap— knife handles, jewellery or anything that needed a rubber-like material that could be moulded in the sun and then would set hard when it cooled.

With their firm, yet rubbery feeling, gutties became the ball of choice. Even Allan Robertson conceded they were cheaper to make than featheries—he could knock out as many gutties in a day as he could featheries in a week. They were easier to form (and re-form) into a ball. They could break in very cold weather, which again in Scotland was not ideal. But when little nicks were cut into the surface by iron play, players realized they actually improved the ball's flight and aerodynamics. Golf balls were on their way to getting dimples.

Golf ball makers would later use a similar material to gutta-percha, using the dried sap of *Manilkara bidentata,* a species of tree endemic to tropical Central and South America. It's common name? Balata.

In 1898, a man named Corburn Haskell patented the Haskell ball—gutta percha wrapped around a bouncy rubber core. They flew better, ran better and players knew an extra 20 yards off the tee. So golfers said: 'I'll have one of them'.

They were cheap to mass-produce and by 1901 they were everywhere.

In 1967 Spalding's ball makers injected a 2-piece guttie with rubber and called it 'The Executive'. In 1972 Spalding made a two-piece 'Top-Flite'. Tiger Woods used a one-piece Nike ball at the Open Championship of 2000, which was popular because Tiger Woods used one. And then Titleist came up with something different again. It was 'a 392-dimple icosahedral design home-grown urethane cover that gave the ball a veneer look and helped transmit a softer sensation to the hands while providing more spin' according to the PGA Tour's website which would know. Titleist called the ball the Pro V1. And, again, just about everyone said: 'I'll have me one of those.'

Back in the 1850s, Old Tom Morris's reputation as a golfer, ball maker, club maker, course designer and all-round good fellow was growing. He was on terms with everyone from royalty to caddies.

Old Tom Morris played golf for money. Gamblers who followed his matches would heckle and jostle one another to put off the players—depending how their bets were going. Things became unseemly. Golf is how it is today because Old Tom Morris insisted golfers and spectators show respect. In doing so, Old Tom Morris may have invented etiquette.

After Allan Robertson died (aged 43 of deadly jaundice), Old Tom Morris kept on playing golf for money, and making clubs and balls and golf courses. He is the father of golf architecture. Old Tom Morris designed or remodelled over 60 golf courses, including Muirfield, Royal Dornoch, Carnoustie, Royal County Down, Prestwick (site of the first ever major championship in 1860) and St Andrews Old Course, New Course and Jubilee Course.

The first Open Championship was contested by eight golfers over three laps of 12 holes in one day. It was won by Willie Park from Old Tom Morris. Prize money was awarded to the three runners-up given it was felt the honour of being crowned 'Champion Golfer of The Year' outweighed mere money. The winner was also awarded a very fine belt, not unlike those awarded to rodeo riders.

By 1864 Old Tom Morris had won his third Open and was also awarded the money. He won again in 1867, aged 46. He remains the oldest man to win the Open Championship, though Greg Norman and Tom Watson nearly surpassed him in recent times. The only older winner of a major is former accountant, Julius Boros who somehow beat Arnold Palmer to win the 1968 US PGA at the age of 48.

Old Tom Morris would play in each of the first 36 Open Championships. He played his last Open in 1896 when he was 75. He was custodian of the links at St Andrews until he retired in 1904. He died in 1908 aged 86. His name marks the 18th hole at the Old Course, St. Andrews.

Fair old legacy.

Wunderkind

The first claret jug was awarded to the Champion Golfer of the Year in 1873 after Tom Kidd won the 36-hole Open Championship at the Old Course with scores of 91–88. But the first name inscribed on the trophy is that of the man who won in 1872, Tom Morris Junior, the Tiger Woods of his time.

Aged 13, he beat his famous father on the Old Course. His father was reigning Open champion at the time and word got around. When the young lad played an exhibition match against another boy in Perth, so interested were folks to see the wunderkind that crowds were bigger for that match than for the tournament featuring Willie Park and Old Tom Morris. Tom Morris Junior won the match and a not inconsiderable sum of 15 pounds. His legend grew.

Tom Morris Junior's first Open Championship was in 1867 when he placed fourth behind his father. A year later, aged 17, he won. He set two course records. His 36-hole total of 154 smashed the previous mark by eight shots. He made the first hole-in-one in tournament golf.

He won the championship the year after by nine shots. Next year he won by 12 shots. In 1870 he set a new Prestwick 12-hole course record of 47 including the unbelievable feat of a three on the 578-yard first hole (holes didn't have a 'par' then, they were just holes.) It is estimated that Tom Morris Junior's 'cleak' (like a 2-iron) travelled 200 yards for the 'eagle'.

The Open Championship wasn't played in 1871 because the sponsor had died and no-one put up a prize. Plus, Tom Morris Junior had kept the belt because he won three on the trot. But they found a sponsor in 1872 and Tom Morris Junior was champion golfer of the year again. He was the greatest player anyone had ever seen.

They say Tom Morris Junior wound up and hit the ball so hard his tam-o-shanter would fall off his head. He hit the ball longer and straighter than anyone else, was more flexible and athletic, taller and stronger.

Tom Morris Junior was the first to use his rut iron—a wedge-like club used to extract balls from the various indentations that balls could find themselves in on the un-groomed fairways of the day. With a full swing, he would loft the ball clear of obstacles and land it softly on the green. Sometimes he'd impart another thing nobody had ever seen—backspin. *Gadzooks! The man's Merlin!* Yes, Tom Morris Junior invented backspin.

He and his father would often contest matches for money with other pairings. They were playing one such match, against the Park brothers, Willie and Mungo, across the Firth of Forth at North Berwick, when a telegram found its way onto the course and to Old Tom Morris.

Tom Morris Junior's wife was having trouble during childbirth, and Tom should hurry home. Old Tom Morris didn't tell his son until they'd finished their last two holes. There were no trains back but Tom Morris Junior took up the offer from a local yachtsman to ferry him across the water.

On arrival, a reverend relayed the terrible news; his wife and child had passed away. And Tom Morris Junior was never the same. He took to drinking and his golf game went south. He died on Christmas Day of 1875, aged 24, they said of a broken heart'. It was sort of right—he'd suffered a heart attack.

'I could cope with them all on the course,' said Old Tom Morris. 'All but Tommy. He was the best the old game ever saw.'

Harry Vardon and the Greats

Harry Vardon once played six consecutive rounds of 68 or better using only six golf clubs. Harry Vardon once advised golfers: 'Don't play too much golf. Two rounds a day are plenty.' It is also said that Harry Vardon once admonished a journalist: 'I'm the best and I'll thank you to remember that.'

And he could make a case. Harry Vardon won the Open Championship six times and the US Open once. He won the Open Championship in 1896, 1898, 1899, 1903 (when he beat his brother Tom while battling tuberculosis), 1911 and 1914.

Harry Vardon was born in Jersey, an island in the English Channel. At the age of 20 he left for England and became a greenskeeper and golf professional. He preached relaxation in the swing, and bent his left arm at the top where others preached stiffness. Harry Vardon was among the longest hitters of his time.

Harry Vardon didn't invent the interlocking grip that still today bears his name. That was amateur champion of Scotland, Johnny Laidley. But he did make the grip famous. One possible reason it's not called the Laidley grip is because Harry Vardon wrote in his book, *The Complete Golfer* that: 'my grip is one of my own inventions'.

Harry Vardon had a narrow stance and an upright swing and seemed to chop down hard on the ball, imparting a counter-intuitively high-ball flight and a funky thing called 'backspin' that Young Tom Morris had invented but that Harry Vardon perfected. He could stop the ball on an ant.

Harry Vardon's contemporaries—JH 'John' Taylor (five Open Championships) and James Braid (five Open Championships)—also used the interlocking grip. They dominated golf from 1896 until the inaptly-named Great War, winning 16 Open Championships in 21 years.

John Taylor was born in North Devon in 1871 and didn't do much at school, leaving aged 11. He did learn a lot at the excitingly-named Westward Ho! Golf Club and became a club maker who was very good with them. He won the first Open Championship held in England in 1894, and followed it up with wins in 1895, 1900, 1909 and 1913.

John Taylor was a founding member of the Professional Golfers Association (PGA) and according to famous golf writer, Bernard Darwin (grandson of Charles), turned a feckless group of pro golfers into a 'self-respecting and respected body of men'.

James Braid came from the Kingdom of Fife in Scotland and worked as a club maker in London until he was 26. He also played golf every day. He was six-foot-three and gave the ball a whack. He was recruited to work as a pro at Romford GC in Essex. He went close in the Open Championship of 1898 (won by Harry Vardon), then dominated the first decade of the 20th century winning in 1901, 1905, 1906, 1908 and 1910.

After his victory in 1908—by eight shots—Braid joined Harry Vardon, Old Tom Morris and Young Tom Morris as four-time winners of the Auld Claret Jug. Dr J.G. McPherson of St Andrews wrote in *The Golfers Magazine*:

> The crowd got what they came for, an exhibition of golf which, at the present time at any rate, only Braid can provide.
>
> He is now in a class by himself—he drives further and putts better than any of the others ... he is the longest driver in the world. The ball goes off like a rifle bullet ... James Braid is a hero unequalled in the modern history of the game of golf.

They called them 'The Great Triumvirate'. And that was apt. It stuck forever.

-CHAPTER TWO-

AUGUSTA DREAMIN'

Bobby Jones

Bobby Jones created Augusta National as a sanctuary. He played in each Masters, as a favor to chairman Clifford Roberts. But he didn't practice and he didn't care. Betting money flooded in on him for he was Bobby Jones and in practice rounds, he would be in hot form. But he never did better than T13 in his first Masters—the first Masters—in 1934.

Bobby Jones was as big as Babe Ruth. He was the Michael Jordan and Pele of golf. He was so famous that hundreds of people would follow his social rounds, and look at him with crazy eyes, as people do.

Bobby Jones called his putter Calamity Jane. It was the most famous putter in the world. After he won the fourth major of his 1930 Grand Slam of titles that was called the 'impregnable quadrilateral', he held the club above his head in triumph. People noted that it was held together by brown leather tape. The shaft had broken through misadventure (not by Bobby Jones snapping it over his knee—he didn't do that). When tens of thousands of replica Calamity Jane putters were sold, they came with a brown leather strap. Bobby Jones' putter strap was the Nike swoosh of its time.

Bobby Jones first played in the US Amateur Championship in 1916 when he was fourteen. He reached a quarter final and was knocked out by defending champion Robert Gardner 4-and-3. They called him Boy Wonder.

Bobby Jones won the US Open four times and the Open Championship three times. He didn't win the PGA Championship because he never turned pro. And he didn't win the US Masters because he'd brushed competitive golf by the time it came along.

In 1921 Bobby Jones went to St Andrews for the Open Championship with 'the face of an angel and the temper of a timberwolf' according to famous sports writer, Grantland Rice. He was the low amateur after two rounds, but the weather got up in round three, and he carded 46 shots on the outward nine. He double bogied 10. Then he couldn't get out of the greenside trap on 11 after four attempts. So he picked up his ball, tore his scorecard into many pieces and stormed off the course.

Locals weren't impressed. 'Master Jones is just a boy and an ordinary one at that,' wrote a local pressman.

Opinions would change. He apologized a lot and with great feeling. By the time he won the Open Championship on the Old Course in 1927, he was chaired off by Scots calling him 'Our Bobby'. In 1958 he was made a Freeman of the City of St Andrews. The only other American to receive the gong (which granted the awardee no privileges other than a whole lot of love) was Benjamin Franklin in 1759.

Bobby Jones won the US Amateur Championship of 1927 carrying 22 golf clubs (the maximum of 14 not being implemented until 1938). His clubs were always hickory-shafted, though the United States Golf

Association (USGA) declared steel ones legal in 1924, the Royal and Ancient Golf Club of St Andrews (R&A) following suit in 1929.

After Bobby Jones was stunningly knocked out of the 1929 US Amateur Championship at Pebble Beach, he had a week to kill on the Monterey Peninsula so he headed to Cypress Point, a creation of the foremost golf architect of the time, Dr Alister Mackenzie. So taken was Bobby Jones with the golf course that he decided Mackenzie should design his private fame sanctuary, Augusta National.

In 1930 Bobby Jones won the 'grand slam' (as it was coined by sports writer O.B. Keeler) after winning the Open and Amateur Championships of USA and Great Britain. The feat was coined the 'Impregnable Quadrilateral' because no-one surely could do it again. And no-one did.

While he was doing all this golfing, Bobby Jones was a practicing lawyer. He'd spend most of his year working, emerging to play golf for about three months of the year, most of which was spent travelling.

By 1930 he was jack of it. He was tired of being looked at by odd-bods with crazy eyes and tired of spending so much time on boats and trains and other forms of transport. And he had won the 'grand slam' of golf; there was nothing more to achieve. So, Bobby Jones quit golf. He was 28.

**

The Tyrannical Mr Roberts

Clifford Roberts was close friends with Bobby Jones and Dwight D. (Ike) Eisenhower. With the former, he built Augusta National, created the Masters and formed a company called Joroberts Inc. that bottled Coca-Cola in South America. For the latter—the hero of World War II and President of the United States of America—he brokered a book deal and put the profit into oil and made our man Ike a very wealthy man.

Ike would play Augusta so often that Clifford Roberts built him a cottage on the grounds near a little lake where Ike could fish. Clifford Roberts spent so often at the White House that he had a room called Mr Roberts' bedroom.

Clifford Roberts' views on race relations would be described as racist today. They were in 1960 too when he ranked human beings, in order of willingness to work as white first, black second, and mixed race third. He described the latter group as 'the most worthless of all in every respect'.

When Bobby Jones contracted a rare spinal disease called syringomyelia and was slowly crippled, bent and confined to a wheel chair, Clifford Roberts told Bobby Jones he didn't want him on stage at the Masters presentation due to the look of him. It made Bobby Jones very sad but Clifford Roberts saw it as pragmatic. Augusta's look and standards had to be upheld.

In 1972 Clifford Roberts told Ben Crenshaw, fresh off his first round at Augusta, to get a haircut. He told Bruce Fleischer to get new pants because he didn't approve of bell-bottomed trousers. He made people working in the concession stands cut holes in their pockets so they couldn't steal the change.

In 1975 caddie Carl Jackson was in the golf shop with Clifford Roberts when Tom Watson and Ray Floyd asked if they could use their regular caddies at that year's Masters. Problem was they were white men. Until then players could only use Augusta-supplied black caddies. Roberts refused. 'As long as I'm alive there will not be a white caddie working at Augusta National,' said Roberts.

On September 29, 1977 Clifford Roberts sat by the little lake he'd built for President Eisenhower, pulled out a rifle and shot himself in the head. He didn't leave a note to say why, though he did leave behind many thousands of pages about Augusta and President Eisenhower and the Masters, observations and thoughts that he stipulated could only be made public 20 years after his death. And so, in 1998 we learned that Clifford Roberts loved golf, loved Augusta—and was a bit of a prick.

Though he did invent the Masters.

Clifford Roberts' innovations for the Masters tournament include roped-off galleries, course maps, pairing sheets and leader boards that would be updated around the course.

'The standards and quality with which he conducted the Masters are unmatched anywhere,' said Jack Nicklaus. 'All of us in golf appreciate what he has done for the game.'

Arnold Palmer was equally glowing. 'Although he was a tough man, he was a person who was truly dedicated to golf and the quality and standards of the game.'

**

The Masters

Within months of Augusta National's formal opening in 1933 members began lobbying for Augusta National to host the US Open. Yet the US Open is a summer tournament held in June or July. Augusta National—according to the original plan of Clifford Roberts and Bobby Jones—would be closed over summer.

So Clifford Roberts came up with the Masters. Bobby Jones didn't like the name, deeming 'the Masters' unseemly, as if they were bragging.

But Clifford Roberts ignored him as did the coterie of supportive newspaper editors who duly wrote his stories. Roberts did cede to Jones that officially the event would be called the 'Augusta National Invitation Tournament'. And that lasted for five years. But they called it the Masters from day dot.

When the club held the first Masters in March of 1934—two months after architect Alister Mackenzie's death as a pauper—there was an open bar and free booze for players, members and spectators called 'patrons'.

The tournament was won by Horton Smith who won the name of the Joplin Ghost on account of him coming from a nowhere place called Joplin in Missouri, and because he was a lanky pale man. Most reporting of the first Masters, however, was on Jones's poor form in his comeback.

Bobby Jones played in each of the first 12 Masters to 1948, even though he didn't enjoy competitive golf. In practice rounds he'd shoot the lights out, playing with his buddies. And money would flow for Bobby Jones in the official pre-tournament Calcutta, hosted by Bobby Jones.

Gene Sarazen turned up to the 1935 Masters after spurning Clifford Roberts' invitation the year before because he thought Roberts wanted to sell him insurance or stocks or something. When the second letter arrived, it had Bobby Jones' name on it. And Sarazen was in.

Sarazen promptly won the 1935 Masters after holing a 4-wood on the par-5 15th hole for a double-eagle or albatross. Grantland Rice coined it 'The shot heard around the world'. Sarazen made pars in the last three holes and tied with Craig Wood whom he beat in a 36-hole play-off.

Byron Nelson won the Masters in 1937 from Ralph Guldahl who gave up a four-shot third round lead. A photo of Guldahl in the *Pittsburgh Post-Gazette* had the caption: 'Ralph Guldahl, loser'.

Nelson won the Masters again in 1942 and was so good they named a bridge after him over Rae's Creek. He gave up tournament golf after World War II but continued playing the Masters where he was always in the last group on Sunday with the 54-hole winner. 'I nursed seven winners home,' said Nelson. The Masters didn't have a cut until 1958.

Writer Herbert Warren Wind first came up with the name Amen Corner to describe the approach to 11, the par-3 12th, the first half of 13. It wasn't until 1965 that the *Augusta Chronicle* first used the term. Then everyone used it.

The *Pittsburgh Post-Gazette* was complimentary to Nelson after his famous win in 1937:

> Blazing over the closing stretch with a spectacular 32, Byron Nelson, gangling Irishman from Reading, Pa [Pennsylvania] clamped a 'full Nelson' on the field today to win the fourth Augusta national golf tournament featuring the annual return to competition of Bobby Jones.

Guldahl, described as 'a big Norwegian from St Louis' by the *Pittsburgh Post-Gazette*, bogied 11 and double bogied the par-3 12th Nelson birdied 12 and chipped in for eagle on 13 and won by two.

The 1938 Masters was won by Henry 'The Hershey Hurricane' Picane with Ralph Guldahl second again. The winner in 1939? Come on down dogged Ralph Guldahl who beat Sam Snead by one.

An amateur has never won the Masters although a few have come second including Frank Stranahan in 1947 who finished second two shots behind Jimmy Demaret. In practice rounds he was warned about hitting two or more balls onto the green. In 1948 the course superintendent accused him of doing the same thing though Stranahan insisted he was only putting multiple balls. Regardless he was met on the 8th by a phalanx of green jackets and kicked out of the tournament.

The green jackets became a thing in 1947 so patrons would know whom to ask about anything. The tradition of awarding the winner a green jacket began in 1949 when one was draped on Sam Snead. On the issue of patrons, they are never called spectators because doing so will warrant a warning; call them a mob and you're ex-communicated as CBS commentator Jack Whitaker was for five years. Patrons, it is then.

Sam Snead reckons it was Ben Hogan who first floated the idea that the winner should get a jacket. Another Ben Hogan idea that became a tradition is that the winner selects the menu for the Masters dinner and picks up the tab.

Sam Snead picked up the dinner tab three times. Snead's first jacket, from his win in 1949, went missing from his locker four years after he received it. Augusta wouldn't make Sam Snead another one so he borrowed Bobby Jones' jacket. Then Bobby Jones died and Augusta made Sam Snead another jacket. Augusta National doesn't hand out many jackets. Multiple Masters winners don't get a new one.

On a super-windy fourth round in 1956 an amateur called George Kunkle shot a record high score of 22-over 95. With no cut in place he would card 52-over for the four rounds and finish last. In second-last place was Masters champion of 1934 and 1936, Horton Smith, who posted scores of 86–84–84–82 for 46-over. A year later the Masters introduced a 36-hole cut.

Arnold Palmer won the 1960 Masters with birdies on 17 and 18. After leading for three rounds, he trailed the amateur Ken Venturi by one shot with three to play. For an hour Venturi was clubhouse leader, waiting for the King to come in.

Then he did—with a vengeance. Palmer's putt on 16 hit the flag (it was permissible to leave it in) and stopped close; Palmer rolled in a 40-foot birdie putt on 17 that just tipped into the hole. And on 18 Palmer stiffed a wedge to four feet and stroked in the winner. Hail, Your Majesty.

After nine holes of the 1988 Masters, Sandy Lyle of Scotland led by four shots from Mark Calcavecchia, a one-time Florida Gator. Lyle had won the Open Championship of 1985, the Greensboro Open (the week before coming to Augusta), and was ranked third in the world behind Greg Norman and Severiano Ballesteros. And then he hit Amen Corner. And his hands went to 'jelly'. He bogied the 11th. He hit an 8-iron into Rae's Creek on 12 for a double. He made par on the two par-5s then again on the 13th and 15th. Coming to 16, he was one shot behind. But a tidy 12-foot birdie putt on 16 and a par on 17 saw him requiring par for a play-off.

Lyle hit a 1-iron off the 18th tee 'to be safe' and found the steep-faced fairway bunker left. Walking up 18, he though it was over. Yet the ball was sitting nicely and his 7-iron from 143 yards was a laser beam, top of the flag. The ball landed just before the crest of the second tier, and began to slowly, inexorably track down towards the hole. The noise from the crowd built to crescendo and told Lyle it was close.

When he stroked in the downhill knee-trembler for a birdie, a Scotsman owned a green jacket for the first time. One admirer was Calcavecchia, who said:

> He's got a great attitude. Just plug it around, 'Cheerio, tallyho and all that rot.' He's 99 per cent unflappable. I'm glad he's going home. I can't wait to get rid of him. No telling how many tournaments he'd win if he was here all the time.

Lee Trevino played the Masters in '68 and '69 but turned down invites from Augusta in '70, '71 and '74. The course didn't suit his flat trajectory, his power fades. McKenzie had built the joint for Bobby Jones' high draw. Trevino also wasn't that happy with the whole racial discrimination thing. He'd grown up as a caddie surrounded by black kids. They slept on his porch near the club to claim early bags. Treating them as servants and worse, patronising them, it didn't sit right. He also knew he wouldn't be allowed in the gates if he weren't a player.

And he wasn't that enamoured with the guy who ran the show. In 2016, Trevino told Memphis newspaper, *The Commercial Appeal*:

> Clifford Roberts was a dictator. He played by his rules and you had to walk on egg shells at Augusta

when you were there. I'm not an eggshell-walking guy. Never have been. I have fun. I do whatever within the law.

Augusta changed their law for the Masters of '75 and allowed Lee Elder to tee off. First black man ever. Charlie Sifford was another great player who was National Negro Champion six times. He played in the 1959 US Open, finished T32. He won twice on the PGA Tour, 1967 and 1969, but he never got an invite from Augusta.

The 1970 Masters, described by Dan Jenkins in *Sports Illustrated* as 'one of the more exciting dramas since Bette Davis invented chain-smoking' was won by Billy Casper (−3) in an 18-hole play-off with Gene Littler (+2). The event was marred by protests against the champion South African, Gary Player, whose caddie, Ernst Nipper had quit in fear after Black Panthers and others threatened violence. Said long-time Augusta caddie, Carl Jackson:

> Gary Player was getting troubles from what's going on with Apartheid back in South Africa, and the NAACP [National Association for the Advancement of Colored People] was picketing out on Washington Road, and they [were] getting death threats. And Nipper got scared, or whatever, and quit.

Player asked Jackson to take the bag. Jackson was quick to respond: 'The NAACP is not going to pay my bills or whatever, you know. So it was a, you know, a yes.'

Player finished third.

As a child, Jackson was fishing with some friends in Rae's Creek when a white Augusta security guard, a 'very mean man who thought he was

John Wayne' according to Jackson, opened fire with a sawn-off shot-gun, hitting one boy in the leg. African-Americans, even kids, had their place in the world, and fishing in Rae's Creek was not one.

In 1990, Augusta National, under pressure from the PGA Tour and government, invited a black man to be a member. In 1997 Tiger Woods shot 21-under to obliterate the field by a record 12 shots.

Broadcasting his first Masters from Augusta was veteran Australian (Channel Nine) journalist, Ken Sutcliffe who said the 'place went berserk'. He continued:

> There's this rarefied air at Augusta National and it's got a chequered past, how they treated certain people, black people. And I saw these girls, they were new to the game, black Americans and they were just jumping out of their skin. They looked like they were going to a dinner dance after the game.
>
> And I thought, at last, something has broken it down and the sport is sport and it's about people and how you treat them. It was a really good moment. I'm not one to rattle cages but it's good to see people treated as human beings, with dignity. To be there when a black man won the big one, in a place that had history of not being very enlightened in terms of black athletes, or blacks in particular. It was great, and I loved how it was special.

Carl Jackson's reaction to Tiger' win was reported widely:

> We were proud to see one of our own come through that day. We were proud that a black man [won]. Very, very happy ...

Things were surely changing.

For Australian golfers, the final day of the 2013 Masters was one to remember. Clubs across the country have a tradition of hosting breakfasts for early-rising members to watch the last round. No need to say there were many happy golfers who watched Adam Scott become the first Australian to win a green jacket. Against Argentina's enigmatic, skilful and Zen-like zone-hanger, Angel Cabrera, Scott holed a putt on the second play-off hole prompting thunderous roars around the nation. Men hugged who don't normally hug, they cheered and roared. It was just past 9 am. And they were very good times.

***

Augusta National: Genesis and Nemesis

Bobby Jones was the first man to play Augusta National. On 26 August 1932, he shot an even-par 72. Augusta chairman Clifford Roberts convinced Bobby Jones to play in the first Masters tournament of 1934 even though Bobby Jones no longer wanted to play competitively.

Dr Alister Mackenzie, who worked with Bobby Jones to develop the course, died broke in January of 1934 waiting for Augusta National to pay him. He'd led a high life of roast beef and whiskey on the Monterey Peninsula, and hadn't saved much before the Great Depression.

Mackenzie wrote letters to Bobby Jones and Clifford Roberts asking, begging really, for $500 of his promised $5,000 fee. He'd earlier asked for $2,500. He didn't get a cent.

A year earlier at the opening of Augusta National, Clifford Roberts and sixty members of Augusta's 80-man membership—lawyers, investment bankers, presidents of companies such as Coca-Cola—boarded the latest in Pullman steam engine trains from Penn Station in New York City for the 18-hour trip south to the heralded new golf course. There were games of bridge and servants pouring whiskey (Prohibition was a month from repeal) and much carousing.

Mackenzie and Bobby Jones spent months on the site of Augusta National, a former Civil War indigo plantation, planning where to put things. Bobby Jones would stand on a potential tee box and hit a shot. They'd walk out to where the ball landed and Bobby Jones would hit another one. Mackenzie would plan the hole thus, routing it around Jones's high draw.

Bobby Jones had a vision for Augusta based on the golf he'd found at St Andrews, which had interesting answers to seemingly simple questions. Bobby Jones understood and liked the questions that St Andrews asked. He had this to say about the Old Course.

> I think it was not long before I began to see her as a wise old lady, whimsically tolerant of my impatience, but ready to reveal the secrets of her complex being, if I would only take the trouble to study and learn.
>
> The more I studied the Old Course, the more I loved it and the more I loved it, the more I studied it. There is always a way at St Andrews, although it is not always the obvious way.

As with the Old Course, Augusta isn't smothered in bunkers. At both courses you need a super short game. At both it's not just miss-the-green-take-lob-wedge. There are angles, knolls and bowls, and the ball can be rolled and bounced as much as flown. On several of Augusta's greens, Mackenzie created undulations that—like the par-3 11th at St Andrews—would enthuse BMX bike riders.

Tom Weiskopf, who finished runner-up in the Masters four times, once said:

Back in my hometown of Columbus, Ohio, alone there are four courses ... as good as Augusta. You can go elsewhere, too, and find other courses that play as challengingly without having to resort to putting the pins on slopes and knolls.

Another golfer who commented on the course did not wish to be named lest Augusta National green jackets ex-communicate him as they did Garry McCord who, in 1994, said on television that Augusta's 17th green was 'bikini waxed' and that if players go long they're 'out with the body bags'. McCord hasn't worked the Masters since. The unidentified golfer said of Augusta's greens:

The first is a mine-field. Three and six are brutal. The seventh and ninth have the most slope of the front nine. The 14th slopes back left to front right and would have the most slope of any green on the course. And then you've got the greens on the 10th and 18th, which aren't kind either. The greens at St Andrews are fairer because they'd run about ten on the Stimpmeter. Augusta can push 14.

In the 1988 Masters, leading players Lee Trevino, Fuzzy Zoeller and Ben Crenshaw were critical of the ice-like speed. As Zoeller said at the time:

If you've got a downhill putt, you're just touching the ball and hoping you can make the 10-footer coming back. If that's golf, I'm in the wrong damn league. Golf is supposed to be fun. This wasn't fun. It's a joke out there. You don't hear the roars from the crowds at Augusta anymore. It's like a morgue. If they don't start listening to the players, they're going to be sitting around here looking at themselves and saying, 'Where did we go wrong?'

'There may not be anything living on No. 11 green,' said Crenshaw. 'They need to call the Augusta fire department on that.'

Fred Couples finished four shots from winner Sandy Lyle and said: 'You can't hit the putts soft enough.' Masters champion from 1971, Charles Coody, shot 78–74, and called it 'goony golf'.

When Seve Ballesteros was asked to describe a four-putt on 16 he said: 'I missed the hole. I missed the hole. I missed the hole. I made it.'

Nick Price shot the course record 63 in 1986, afterwards concluding that, 'Bobby Jones held his hand up from somewhere and said, 'That's enough, boy'. Greg Norman equalled Price's record in the first round of 1996.

Ah, Greg, you'd think the golf course could've given him one jacket. Jack Nicklaus didn't need a sixth one. Nick Faldo didn't need a third. Jose Maria Olazabal can't wear two to a dinner party. You only ever get one anyway. Yet for all the tempest and travails, Norman says he loves Augusta National and its iconic tournament, the Masters. Even if they've beaten him up over the years.

On Augusta from Greg Norman:

Do I feel like Augusta has beaten me? No, not at all. Augusta is a great golf course. It's one of my favorites of all time. I do love the establishment of Augusta. I love the discipline, the principles, the ethic they conduct themselves with. Some people don't, I do. I truly love that.

Does a part of me wish that I'd won Augusta? Absolutely! Of course! I'd be telling a big fat lie if I said it didn't really bother me. But at the same time,

I really feel like I'm part of the Augusta National. I have a lot of wonderful memories there. When I go back there occasionally to play with some members, I remember all of the staff; the guys that were there in my day. When we get together, we talk about how much they remember and how much they felt for me. And how much I remember sitting in the locker room and they'd bring me a drink, and just leave me alone or just talk to me. I feel like I'm part of the club, to a degree. One day, do I have the dream of maybe wanting to be a member there? That would probably be the feather in the cap.

And thus yet another use for an Augusta National green jacket: a gift idea for the Shark who has just about everything.

CHAPTER THREE

DIASPORA

The Von

It's folklore in the Cleary house that Mom's uncle Oswald 'Ossie' Short beat Norman Von Nida in a match play event in 1938. Then came World War II and both men joined up. Ossie was killed in Libya at the Battle of El Alamein. 'The Von' survived and went on to be one of the greats.

Von Nida was born in Sydney Australia and grew up in Brisbane. He worked as a caddy and left school aged 14 to work in an abbatoir. At the age of eighteen, he won the Queensland Amateur. At twenty, the Von borrowed £50 and beat Gene Sarazen in an exhibition match at Royal Queensland in Brisbane. Von Nida was a caddie, stood five-foot-five. Sarazen was thirty-four years old and in his prime, had won six of his seven major championships and had skipped the first ever Masters to be there. Von Nida beat him 2-up, and shot 67.

Over a beer in the clubhouse later Von Nida asked Sarazen, 'Mr Sarazen, do you think that one day I will be a player like you and travel the world playing golf?'

'Little man,' replied Sarazen. 'Who did you just beat today?'

'You, Mr Sarazen,' replied Von Nida.

'That's right,' said Sarazen. 'And I am the best in the world.'

After World War II, Von Nida travelled to Britain in one of British Airways' converted Lancaster bombers. From 1946 through 1948 he won 24 times in Europe and Australia. He finished T4, T6, T3 in the Open Championship. He'd turned up with 17 pounds. He left with pockets full.

Watching at home in Australia was a young Peter Thomson who later said:

> Had he not been the one to leave Australia and try to make a living playing golf tournaments, then I wouldn't have gone after him and I wonder where we would be today. Norman Von Nida is really the hero.

Von Nida had just two starts in the US Open (T59, CUT) and never played the US PGA Championship. In 1950 he was invited to take the place of Bobby Jones (by Bobby Jones) in the Masters at Augusta National. In five starts he didn't do better than T27.

In 1948 Von Nida was involved in a fistfight with US Ryder Cup player Henry Ransom that resulted in Ransom's disqualification from the Lower Rio Grande Open and suspension from the PGA Tour.

Von Nida alleged that on the first hole, Ransom had made an annoyed swipe at a very small putt which Von Nida alleged had tapped the ball. Then he tapped it in. Ransom wrote a four on his card, not a five. Von Nida told the man scoring Ransom's card, Frank Strazza, that he should not sign Ransom's card.

Ransom was incensed. 'You mind your business, you son of a bitch,' said Ransom.

'It is my business,' replied Von Nida.

In *The Argus,* Von Nida wrote:

> Ransom became heated and said he would like to punch my head in. I walked away. He followed and struck me. I naturally hit him back. They were the only blows struck.

Von Nida later wrote of the incident in his book, *The Von*. He said that as a boy working in the abattoir he had developed extremely strong hands and wrists.

> I would break open the heads of sheep after their skulls had been partially split by a machine. My forearms, hands and fingers became incredibly strong. I was unbeatable in an arm wrestle against anyone my size.

And thus, when Ransom came at him, Von Nida felt well equipped.

> As I stumbled back I managed to grab him by the throat and closed my fingers on his windpipe. My fingers were still like steel bars after my time at the meat works and Ransom was turning blue before the police arrived to break it up. I was so worked up. I couldn't let go of him and a sheriff had to bash my forearm with his hands a few times to make me loosen my grip.

Von Nida's big beef was with the PGA Tour's 'winter rules' which allowed players to pick up their ball, clean it and place it on a nice lie. Von Nida felt a man should play the ball as it lies. And he was not backward in coming forward with this opinion.

He wrote that Ransom's alleged cheating was 'typical of many occurrences in the last two days that have made this the worst tournament in the history of the PGA'.

'Many pros are openly violating the rules. In my opinion, Lloyd Mangrum, who is leading with 196 [and who would go on to win] should have been disqualified three times already,' wrote Von Nida.

Such unvarnished honesty didn't endear Von Nida to US pros who reckoned the foreigner's sentiments were just sour grapes. Harlingen Golf Club professional, Tony Butler, said that Ransom had told him he was sick of Von Nida talking down American golf and its golfers.

'After three hours, he was sick of it,' said Butler. 'The little Australian is angry because everyone over here doesn't bow and scrape to him. And because he hasn't been shooting very good golf,' he added.

Harvey Yale, sports editor of Harlingen, Texas *Valley Morning Star* told Australian Associated Press (AAP) that:

> The consensus of opinion of several touring professionals is that Von Nida, failing to hit his stride since the winter tour began at Los Angeles on January 2, has been ill-disposed toward his fellow golfers and conditions in United States golf.
>
> It seems that Von Nida, as a leading money-winner in England in 1947, resents the lack of attention shown him. His complaint is that Bobby Locke, the South African, has received all the acclaim.

Henry Ransom would soon retire from golf because of an allergy to grass. Norman Von Nida would mastermind the breeding of the outstanding Australian racehorse Kingston Town (that won over $1.6 million AUS) and continued to play golf into his mid-80s off a handicap of five—while legally blind. He died in 2007 aged 93.

The Travellin' Man in Black

When Gary Player was sixteen he declared that he would be the world's number one golfer. When he was twenty, he wrote down six things he would win: the US Open, the British Open, the US PGA, the US Masters, the PGA Tour money list and the PGA Tour's 'Vardon trophy' for the lowest stroke average.

And people thought, well, he's a confident little chook, isn't he? And then they watched as he ticked them off.

He won the Open Championship at Muirfield in 1959, the US Masters in 1961 and the US PGA at Pennsylvania's Aronomink Golf Club in 1962. In 1965 he arrived at St Louis's Bellerive Country Club for the US Open, set to become only the third man in the history of golf, after Ben Hogan and Gene Sarazen, to claim a career 'grand slam' of golf's major professional titles.

With four holes to play in the 65th US Open, Player led Australia's Kel Nagle by three shots. Then a US Golf Association official, a man perhaps not well versed in sport's unwritten rules pertaining to mock or hex or 'shut the hell up', sidled up to Player and said, 'Well, you've got it all locked up now'.

Thanks for that, champion! thought Player, or thoughts to the effect, and double-bogied 16. Nagle birdied 17. And it was all square.

And thus, Player stood on the tee at 18 and wondered if he was destined to be like famous Sam Snead who won all the majors except the US Open. (Others might've just been nervous; Player was thinking of destiny, legacy, a place in the annals of history.)

In typical fashion the South African banished negative thoughts. A true believer in Norman Peale's *The Power of Positive Thinking*—the book that 'changed my life', according to Player—he smoked his drive, stiffed his 5-iron and watched his 15-foot putt for the championship roll straight at the hole and—fall inches short.

After four holes of the 18-hole play-off, Player led Nagle by one. On the fifth tee Nagle hooked his drive hard and angry, the ball socking a woman right on the head, knocking her out. Blood shot from the wound. Nagle rushed over. 'Jeez, sorry Luv.' Player did his best to comfort the Australian. 'Not your fault, man. Not your fault.' But Nagle was inconsolable.

Nagle's next shot was a snap-hooking worm burner—thin, low, hot and ugly. It scuttled along the turf and whacked into a woman's ankle, and dropped her. Thankfully it was not the same woman. You could say Nagle's mind was not on the job from there. He made double-bogey on five, bogied seven, bogied 10. Player birdied 8. And won by three.

And with that, Gary Player had won everything that he said he would. He wasn't thirty years old.

✶✶✶

Son of a Miner's Son

Gary Player was born in 1935 in Johannesburg, South Africa, the son of a gold-miner and the youngest of three. His grandfather, Horace Ferguson, once of Glasgow, died when Player was six. His mother died of cancer when he was eight. Five operations. Terrible times. A 'black emptiness enveloped me,' wrote Player.

One day he met his father as the old man came out of the mine after a shift. His dad took off his boot and poured water out. Player asked him where the water came from. 'It was perspiration,' Player told *Golf Digest* later.

He told me how men died like flies in those mines.

He said a miner's best friend was the rat, because

when the rats took off running, it meant a cave-in
was imminent. Every day the workers gave the rats
bits of their sandwiches as tribute.

With his father working so hard, his sister Wilma taking a job and his
brother Ian away in the Army, young Gary spent many lonely hours after
school waiting for his people to come home.

Yet he grew strong. His father always drilled into him that it wasn't
adversity that shaped a man, but rather how one responds to it. Gary
once worried that his height may stop him being a golfer. 'Rubbish,' his
father boomed 'It's only what's in your heart!'

Player took that to heart. He dedicated himself to physical and
mental fitness. He was forged hard by his brother, Ian, who joined the
South African Army and served in Italy in World War II when only
sixteen. Ian's idea of bonding with his nine-year-old brother was to take
him on five-mile runs. Ian rigged up a 30-foot rope from the tallest
branch in their backyard and had Gary climb it each day. There was
boxing, weight-lifting, running, swimming, rugby, cricket. Every day.
He became a champion springboard diver and athlete. Ian and his
younger brother competed at everything. By the time Player got to
high school, he may have been the fittest 12-year-old in South Africa.
As he recalls:

> Ian was several years older so naturally I wanted to
> follow his lead. He was very fit and active, which
> was lucky for me. My outlook could have been
> completely different if he was lazy!

One day Ian whittled his little brother a golf stick and taught him how
to swing. In Gary's first round with his father, a 2-handicapper, he made
par on the first three holes. And that was it—golf had him.

At fifteen, Player was challenged (in the way that boys do) to leap into a giant compost heap near his school. The pit was filled with dried leaves and decomposing matter. Other boys had leapt in feet first. But Player went one better, and pulled off one of his swan dives.

With great symmetrical poise, he leapt outwards and downwards and went in inverted, arms out stretched, head first into the leaves, hit the ground, knocked himself out and broke his neck. He was in a brace for months and didn't play golf for a year. And all the while he ached for the game like a junkie.

He got out of plaster and practiced every day. He took lessons from his local club professional and dated the man's daughter, Vivienne. He turned pro when he was seventeen. He set out to be the best in the world.

'You have to believe in yourself,' says Player.

> I thought about becoming a world champion every
> day. My father instilled a hard work ethic in me. I
> had to face adversity head on when my mother died
> of cancer when I was eight years old. Believing in
> myself was natural.

Norman Peale's *The Power of Positive Thinking* solidified what Player felt.

> Reading that book, it was as if a light went off in my
> mind. And I knew that to be successful I simply had
> to adopt this position with everything I tackled in
> my life and career. I continue to read it to this day.

People lined up to say he wouldn't make it. 'Too short,' they said. 'Swing's no good,' they said. 'Too many muscles,' was another thing they said. He told his mates he would have to travel to Britain to play links golf if he wanted to be the world's best. They laughed and said, 'Mate, you can't win here. How can you win there?'

But Player knew he could play. He had discipline, fitness, focus. And he was infused with belief. He joined the South African tour. In his first pro tournament, he placed second behind his hero, Bobby Locke. He finished the season T12. Members of his club had a whip-around to fund an overseas tour. And Gary Player boarded his first aeroplane.

He won the Match Play Championship of Egypt. It helped fund a five-month tour of Britain. He played all over. He did it on a shoe-string budget. To save tipping porters, he carried his luggage from hotel to train to hotel, wearing a hole in his golf bag. He never left a tee in the ground. He once slept on the beach where they filmed *Chariots of Fire* (1981). Not coincidentally it's the same flat slab of sand that borders the Old Course at St Andrews, where he would play the 1955 Open Championship.

> There was not a lot of money in golf during the 1950s, and I had only been a pro for a couple of years. The first night in St Andrews I couldn't find an affordable hotel. So, I put on my waterproofs and slept in the dunes of the beach. Luckily the next day I found a place in my budget.

A year later he finished fourth in the Open Championship at Royal Liverpool, five shots behind Peter Thomson. He spent the last of his funds on a flight home. He had no money to marry Vivienne.

At the invitation of Australian pro, Norman Von Nida, he flew to Melbourne for the Ampol Tournament, which was running in conjunction with the Melbourne Olympic Games (1956). The prize was £5000, five times more than the Open Chmpionship. Player won by seven shots. He walked off the 18th green and sent a telegram to Vivienne: 'Buy the wedding dress. We will be married immediately.'

On 19 January of 1957 the happy couple walked under an honour guard of golf clubs. On their 10-day honeymoon they, blissfully, played golf every day. Vivienne was a 2-marker.

Player's father sent a letter to US Masters Tournament Chairman, Clifford Roberts. Clifford Roberts sent one back inviting the boy to play at that year's tournament. And Player made his first trip to the United States—46 hours from Jo'burg in South Africa to Augusta National in Georgia USA.

In a practice round of the 1958 US Open, Player had a hit with the great Ben Hogan, a taciturn and serious man not given to encouraging his fellow pros. After the round Ben Hogan said to Player: 'Son, you're going to be a great player one day.' Player says it was the 'greatest compliment I ever received'.

> It filled me with pride, appreciation, confidence. My hard work was leading me on the right path. But the key was to work harder. Something else he told me was perhaps more significant. One day he told me, 'Son, the secret is in the dirt'. It meant practice, practice, practice.

With 36 holes to play at Muirfield on the last day of play (a Friday) in the 1959 Open Championship, Player was eight shots behind. He shot 70–68 and won by two. Dressed in a white suit and a red tie, he was seated at the presentation 30 minutes before anyone else.

Rain washed out the fourth round of the 1961 US Masters which meant all scores were wiped clean. This meant Player again had a four-stroke lead over Arnold Palmer. Player birdied the first and second. Palmer came back, inexorably, at him. After 10 holes Player's lead was two. Then Player was snagged on Augusta's infamous Amen Corner.

His drive on 13 went into the woods right. His iron shot out was hot and ended in Rae's Creek. His fourth hit the green. He took three putts to card a double-bogey 7. Player was all square with The King, Arnold Palmer.

When Player bogied the par-5 15th, Palmer led by one, a lead the great man maintained as he stood over his ball on the 18th fairway after a typically straight, strong tee shot. A seven-iron and two putts for par would win him the championship.

Player, watching on television from Clifford Roberts' apartment, thought it was over. Everyone did. Palmer was defending champion. He just had to hit the green and pull on the jacket. Yet Palmer's approach up the hill was blocked into the bunker right. The lie wasn't great. Palmer thinned his next one over the green, through the spectators and down the slope. His fourth shot skipped past the hole, leaving a 15-footer to force a play-off. Player was still sure Palmer would make it ... and watched the putt slid by. Double-bogey six for The King.

And 25-year-old Gary Player of South Africa had $20,000, a green jacket, and half the grand slam.

**

Rabbit, Skins and Black Panthers

Alfred 'Rabbit' Dyer grew up in America's south and caddied from the age of nine. The first bag he carried in a pro match was Ben Hogan's, playing an exhibition with Sam Snead and Fred Haas. He would later caddie for Arnold Palmer and Gary Player, as his father had. Player once said: 'Rabbit is the best caddie I've ever had. He knows distances and he knows me.'

Prior to the 1974 Open Championship at Royal Lytham & St Anne's, Dyer, the first black caddie in an Open Championship, amused the British press by saying of Player: 'My man complains a lot. I just stick some paper in my ears, and say, "Don't gimme no jive, baby," and I make him laugh, loosen him up.'

After 70 holes, Player led by six. He'd played superbly on a course that *Sports Illustrated*'s Dan Jenkins described as 'funky'. And then his approach shot on 17 went left into very thick grass. Walking up to the ball Player wasn't sure it could be found. He went down on his hands and knees. He had spectators and marshals looking for the ball, which had landed about 10 metres from the fringe of the green and pin-high to the flag. He asked the marshal to put him on the 5-minute clock.

With a minute left, another marshal found Player's ball. Player chopped it out as best he could and made a bogey. And thought little enough of it.

In the days that followed, however, a story—most likely apocryphal, certainly never proven—began bubbling about the ball that Player hit out of the thick rough was not the one that he hit in. The tale went that someone—his caddy, Dyer, they reckoned—had dropped a fresh ball into the thick grass.

Another (unproven, apocryphal) thread of the yarn goes that the original ball was later found and now sits in a safe, somewhere, the 'truth' waiting to be set free.

Player called the story 'bullshit' at the time and many times since. 'There are certain things that are possible and certain things that are impossible,' he told *The Independent* in 1996.

> First of all, they had the TV cameras on during the whole incident. For anybody to say that Rabbit dropped a ball is dreaming. I would put my life on the fact that he wouldn't do something like that. It's impossible. The grass was so thick.

In 2003 Player said:

> That accusation was directed at my caddie, Rabbit, the first black man to caddie in the Open. People would shout at him 'Hey darkie, get out of our country'. What they were saying was very cruel and

an attack on Rabbit, because we had a six-shot lead. Is there any common sense that says Rabbit would do anything like that with a six-shot lead?

On the 18th, Player's ball came to rest against the clubhouse which was ruled an integral part of the course, hence no drop. He backhanded a putter onto the green. Made a two putt bogey. And won the '74 Open by four.

In 1983 he won the princely sum of $170,000 in a 4-man Skins match with Tom Watson, Jack Nicklaus and Arnold Palmer. For reference, the winner of that year's US Open, Larry Nelson, won $72,000.

On the 16th hole, with $120,000 up for grabs, Player removed a leaf from behind his ball. Watson declared that it was not a loose impediment and therefore could not be moved. Player replied that it was a loose impediment and that it was within the laws to move the leaf.

Microphones picked up Watson saying: 'I'm accusing you, Gary ... you can't do that ... I'm tired of this ... I wasn't watching you, but I saw it.' Player was heard replying: 'I was within the rules.'

Player explained later. 'Tom thought that I'd moved a leaf that I shouldn't have but I told him I didn't and he accepted that. And that's the way we left it.'

Not really. Watson complained later and the issue dragged on. Player noted that Watson had played with non-conforming clubs in the Open Championships of '75 and '82. If you come at The King, you better not miss.

In the late '60s civil rights activists, the Black Panthers and the National Association for the Advancement of Colored People [NAACP] protested against South Africa's Apartheid system of racial segregation by taunting Player at tournaments.

At the 1969 US PGA at Dayton, Ohio, Player was paired with Jack Nicklaus in the third round when a program the size of a telephone book was thrown at Player. Golf balls were rolled between his legs on the tee. Spectators coughed as he putted. A man threw a cup of ice in his face and called him a 'damn racist'.

A large man emerged onto the green just as Nicklaus was about to putt. Nicklaus drew back from the ball, and drew back his putter. The man was intercepted before Jack buried his club in the man. In a see-sawing final round, Ray Floyd shot 67 and beat Player by a shot.

Player said of that event:

> That was the toughest round I've ever played. I honestly thought I might get shot because of South Africa. It was unbelievably difficult to concentrate out there. I'm no racist. I want everybody to understand that. I love all people—white, black, yellow.

By 1970 Player had security guards. Player's caddie, Ernest Nipper, a black man, quit the Masters in fear. A man called Carl Jackson took the gig, reasoning that the Black Panthers didn't put food on his table.

Player says:

> It was very frightening indeed. At one point police officers stayed in our rented houses at various tournaments. People quite literally wanted to kill me even though I had protested against racial oppression a decade earlier and continue to do so today.
>
> I love my country and am a proud South African. It was a dark time for our nation, but fortunately we have moved forward thanks to great leaders like Nelson Mandela.

Player had moved forward too. In 1965, aged 30, he said: 'I am of the South Africa of Verwoerd and Apartheid', referring to Hendrik

Verwoerd, the South African Prime Minister known as the 'Architect of Apartheid'. Yet as he travelled and matured and changed, and the world changed, Player saw things differently. He worked out that Apartheid was against the teachings of the Holy Bible.

In 1974 Player played golf in South Africa with Lee Elder, the first black man to play in the Masters. Player's caddie was Rabbit Dyer. It created waves in South Africa. By the late '80s, Player was an outspoken advocate for scrapping the regime.

> My views began to change, particularly as I travelled around the world. The injustice was so obvious and the implications quite chilling. I am now quite convinced that I have played a significant role in trying to eradicate apartheid. It was a terrible system.

Eventually activists realized Player was neither racist nor an effective target for protest. Gary Player wasn't pro Apartheid. He was just a man doing his best. He wished people would love each other. He preached fitness and food, God and golf. He was a pain in the arse for some people. 'Too preachy' some said. But he meant well.

In 2004 when black man Charlie Sifford became the first African American inducted into the World Golf Hall of Fame, he chose Gary Player to present him for induction.

As James Erskine, Player's manager at IMG said:

> Gary Player is fantastic, a charming man. I remember we were at the German Open and he had a contract to model a winter range of clothing. I'd forgotten about this shoot, and it's summer, a hundred degrees in the shade.
>
> So, I told Gary about it and he said, 'Fine, let's shoot it on the practice range before the first round'.

So, there he is, changing into all these cashmere sweaters, hitting his golf balls, sweating. And never once did he say 'You blithering fool'. Then he shook hands with everyone, put his golf shirt on and wandered to the first tee.

Player's generosity with his time was cemented following a phone call with his friend and idol, Ben Hogan. The great man made his own clubs, steel-shafted beauties named after, of course, Ben Hogan. Player rang the man to ask some advice.

Ben Hogan listened to Player's question then asked what equipment Player was using. Player replied that he was using Dunlop. 'Then call Mr Dunlop,' replied Ben Hogan and hung up.

'Hogan was tough and not really prone to handing out free advice to anyone,' says Player.

The thing is, I love people. I love my fans. I've spent time with royalty and with the poorest of the poor. And it's important to treat everyone with respect. And from this experience I am happy to share advice with the young pros today if and when asked.

In the preface of his autobiography, *Gary Player, World Golfer*, Player estimated he'd travelled four million miles around the world. That was published in 1975. He later claimed to be the most travelled man in history. He reckons he's travelled more than pilots. Perhaps he has. Who's travelled more? The Pope?

Player today is still a world traveller. He believes that travel is the university of the world.

Immersing myself in different cultures around the

world through golf has been a blessing. I will be in debt to the sport long after I am gone.

Player is the only man to win a major championship in three decades. He contested the US Masters at Augusta a record 52 times. His last Masters was in 2009 when he shot 78 and 83. He was 74. At 80, he started most days with '1,300 sit-ups and pushing 300 lbs on a leg machine a day ... when I'm 90, I'll still play golf and I'll still break 80'.

As always, Gary Player *believes*. All power to him.

✳ ✳ ✳

Old Muffin Face

Arthur D'Arcy 'Bobby' Locke was born in 1917 in Germiston, a city in the East Rand of Gauteng in South Africa. Aged 18, he won the South African Open. At 21 he turned pro and won the South African Open again, along with the Irish and New Zealand Opens.

Bobby Locke won the South African Open nine times and the Open Championship four times. He won the Dutch Open, German Open, French Open, Mexican Open, Swiss Open, Australian Open and Egyptian Open. He won the Canadian Open six times. He won the All American Open and and had five top-5s in the US Open. He won 15 US PGA Tour events and 94 professional tournaments all up.

Bobby Locke was a superb putter of the golf ball. His short, 'jabbing' style was much copied by the players of the day, including Gary Player, who says Locke is the 'best putter the world has ever known'.

Peter Thomson gives an insight into Locke's character in his book *Golf My Way*. Thomson writes:

> Bobby Locke was a very fierce, mean character on the course. He didn't enjoy any popularity with his

fellow players. They called him 'Old Baggy Pants' and 'Old Muffin Face'.

Thomson reckons Locke almost went out of his way to irritate others.

Bobby Locke flew bombers for the South African Air Force in World War II and retuned home to continue winning golf tournaments. He was invited by Sam Snead to compete in a series of exhibitions in the US. Locke won 11 of the 14 matches. Snead encouraged him to play on the PGA Tour. Locke won eleven times in 59 starts in America.

Bobby Locke won the 1949 Open Championship at Royal St Georges but on returning was barred from the PGA Tour. Ostensibly it was because he had violated some rule or another about appearances. But his success and brusque manner hadn't endeared him. He was allowed back in later years, but he never again felt welcome.

And he kept on winning. He won the Open Championship in 1950, 1952 and 1957. That last one, unfortunately, comes with a caveat. Locke was on the 18th green and leading when he was asked to move his marker by playing partner Bruce Crampton. Locke made the putt but hadn't replaced the coin. He signed his card, was awarded the claret jug and the newspaper men wrote history.

In the days that followed, Australia's Norman von Nida and Henry Cotton of England asserted that the jug should be awarded to second-placed Peter Thomson. This did Thomson no favors at all in Locke's eyes, according to Thomson.

Thomson had never agitated for the result to be reversed but it scotched their friendship forever. 'He was very contemptuous of me, very angry,' wrote Thomson in his book. 'But I can honestly say that the storm wasn't my doing.'

Bobby Locke was a particularly 'meticulous' character on the golf course, according to Thomson:

I think the realization he had made this terrible mistake in etiquette destroyed him and he took to drinking. He was a beer drinker and he started drinking a lot of it.

Bobby Locke's life nearly ended in 1960 when, on the way to see his wife who was in hospital in labour, he ran into a train at a level crossing. He sustained many broken bones and ended up in the same hospital as his wife and new born. He never played competitive golf again. He died in lonely circumstances in 1987 aged 69.

✳ ✳ ✳

Aussies, Aussies, Aussies

Jack Nicklaus once described the Australian Open as 'the fifth major'. Media magnate Kerry Packer wanted to stage the tournament at his home club, The Australian, each year just as the Masters has a home at Augusta. And he pumped his considerable wealth into the sport to make it happen (and naturally own the broadcast rights in perpetuity).

But the powers that be in Australian golf wouldn't go for it, didn't like the brash tycoon owning 'their' sport. And thus there are four majors and 'The Aussie' is a bit of a blip on world golf's radar when it may have been quite big.

Ivo Whitton won the Australian Open five times between 1912 and 1931. For reference, Gary Player won it seven times, Jack Nicklaus six times and Greg Norman five times.

Australians were doing well outside Australia too.

Jim Ferrier won the 1947 US PGA Championship, which was 36 holes of stroke play followed by match play for the final 64. Bruce Devlin won eight times on the PGA Tour and made 51 cuts in 61 majors. Graeme

Marsh won 70 times around the world and was runner-up to Gary Player in the 1970 world match play.

Jack Newton was runner-up to Tom Watson at Carnoustie in '75 and chased Seve Ballesteros home at Augusta in 1982. Wayne Grady won the '86 US PGA, Steve Elkington won it in 1995. Bruce Crampton finished runner-up to Jack Nicklaus in four (4) major championships.

Kel Nagle won the Open Championship of 1960, the Canadian Open of 1964. His record in Open Championships in the 1960s (including ties) reads: 1st, 5th, 2nd, 4th, 45th, 5th, 4th, 22nd, 12th, 13th, 9th.

Joe Kirkwood was born in Sydney 1897 and left home aged 10 to walk 600 kilometres (370 miles) to work on an outback sheep station. He helped the owner make a three-hole course, built his own clubs with snakeskin grips and learned to play golf.

Kirkwood won the 1920 Australian Open. He travelled to Britain and beat Harry Vardon. He travelled the world with Walter Hagen and Gene Sarazen putting on trick shot shows. He had 29 hole-in-ones, two in the same round. According to historian Andrew Crockett, Kirkwood popularized the use of wooden tees. The Kirkwood Cup is the prize awarded the winner of the Australian PGA Championship.

Jan Stephenson is famous for a photo of herself in a bath full of golf balls. She told *Playboy* magazine in 1983:

> I love to sweat and heave and breathe and hurt and
> burn and get dirty. There's something good about
> getting all dirty and grimy and nasty and then
> showering; you feel twice as clean.

It may have taken focus away from her golf a tad, which is a shame because Jan Stephenson won three LPGA major titles. She won 16 LPGA tour events and twice won the Australian Open.

And she was Australia's best lady pro until a girl from North Queensland won pretty much everything.

***

Rare Ayr

Karrie Webb came from Ayr, not far from Greg Norman's home town of Townsville in north Queensland. She has won 57 professional tournaments, the most recent in 2014 when, aged 40, she beat Lydia Ko, Stacey Lewis and Amy Yang in the JTBC Founders Cup.

Twenty years before that event, she went on the Futures tour in the US and won something called the 1995 Golden Flake Golden Ocala Futures Classic. Her second win on tour was the British Open. She was the youngest ever champion.

She beat Laura Davies in the 1999 du Maurier Classic, a major. She won the 2000 Nabisco Championship, a major, by ten shots. She won the 2001 US Women's Open by eight shots. In the 2006 Nabisco, she birdied the first extra hole to beat Lorena Ochoa in a play-off then surprised all by leaping into the drink (water hazard).

From 1999 to 2002 Webb won at least one major a year. In 2000 and 2001 she won two majors. By the age of 25 she was in the World Golf Hall of Fame.

***

Thommo

It was 1945 when Peter Thomson was invited by Norman von Nida to his room at Sydney's Aaron's Hotel. Thomson was a prodigious talent from the Victoria Golf Club on the Melbourne sandbelt, Von Nida was the greatest Australian player of his time. The Von wanted to pass on some tips. He wanted to show off his clothes.

'The wardrobe was so full of trousers you couldn't see past them,' wrote Thomson in *A Life in Golf* in 2013. 'He had more sets of slacks than any department store.'

Von Nida's lesson was that a golfer should look the part, should 'dress for success' as they say, and thus make one's opponent believe, even subconsciously, that he was the lesser player. Sam Snead dressed well. Ben Hogan dressed well. Walter Hagen was as dapper as Dapper Dan. They looked cool. And played accordingly. Belief was half the battle.

The Von also took Thomson to a barber's shop, told him to look after his lustrous head of hair. 'A head of hair like yours,' said von Nida, 'will be priceless where you're going.'

Where was he going? Everywhere. In thirty years of tournament golf between 1947 and 1977, Peter Thomson won tournaments in India, Hong Kong, the US, Canada, New Zealand (he won the NZ Open nine times), England, Scotland, The Philippines and Japan.

Peter William Thomson was born in Melbourne in 1930, the son of Arthur, a sign-writer and cricketer for Brunswick City XI, and Grace, who was his mom. Thomson's first golf club was a left-handed hickory 'cleek', like a one-iron except harder to hit. Thomson batted in cricket left-handed but soon realized he was a right-handed golfer. (Left-handed batters David Warner, Brian Lara and Adam Gilchrist are the same.)

Thomson finished school in 1945 and joined Spalding's ball- and club-making factory. And he tested out all the kit. He quickly came from a 20-handicap to scratch. Four years after picking up that left-handed cleek, he was asked to join the Victoria Golf Club. Today there's a statue of him out the front.

After finishing T2 in the 1949 Australian Open as an amateur, Thomson went professional, and to Britain. First crack at the Open Championship at Royal Portrush in 1951 he finished T6. He nearly won a tournament in Yorkshire. He headed home with pockets full of money.

The South African champion, Bobby Locke took a shine to Thomson and invited him to spend a few weeks playing golf at his home. Thomson's biographer, Tony Walker wonders, a tad cynically, if Thomson's exhibition value wasn't foremost in Locke's mind. The pair would play 63 rounds in nine weeks. By the end, Thomson had begun to beat him.

In 1952 Thomson finished second in the Open Championship at Royal Lytham & St Anne's. In first place was Bobby Locke.

But from there on it was Thommo Time. Only Harry Vardon (with six) has won more Open Championships than Peter Thomson, who shares second-place with James Braid, John Taylor and Tom Watson.

Thomson's record at the Open Championship in his first nineteen Opens reads: 6th, 2nd, 2nd, 1st, 1st, 1st, 2nd, 23rd, 9th, 7th, 6th, 5th, 24th, 8th, 8th, 24th, 3rd, 9th and 9th. He wasn't cut until 1974. He didn't play from 1980 to 1983, came back in 1984, aged 55, to be farewelled on Swilken Burn Bridge. And he was. And then he was cut.

Peter Thomson loved the Open Championship because he enjoyed it. The seaside 'links' style of golf suited him because he liked to use various clubs in various ways. And he liked to keep things simple. The plan was: see target, hit target.

Counter-intuitively, he didn't particularly enjoy the 'target golf' courses of America.

Thus his record is criticized by some—and his ranking above Greg Norman as Australia's greatest player debated—because he rarely played, much less won in the United States. Thomson's PGA Tour record of six wins includes five Opens and the 1956 Texas International (now the AT&T Byron Nelson).

The lack of run on the lush ground, how the courses were designed and setup, how the ball was most often in the air, didn't particularly appeal to him. He described US courses at 'Cadillacs with wings' meaning flashy but lacking substance. And all those trees …

He could play that way—in the air. He won on the Seniors Tour several times. But he didn't really think it was much fun. And fun was why Thomson played. Fun was scooting the ball around the place in many and various ways.

His record in the United States precludes him from some conversations of the greatest players of all time. Yet Peter Thomson is among the very best there's ever been.

***

The Dog

David Graham left Australia for the United States in 1969. Ask him why and he'll tell you 'I really don't like that question'.

> I didn't leave Australia because of 'Australia'. I left Australia to play in a country that had an established tour. If I had stayed in Australia, I would have finished up being a club pro or playing in Asia. I did not want to do that. I was following a dream. It had nothing to do my leaving Australia. So that's really an offensive question.

Wasn't meant to be. Just wanted to know why he left.

World golf in the sixties was a very different beast from what it is today. Outside the US PGA Tour, there weren't organized tours with big prize money. Players would head overseas to contest a national open and a regional tournament either side.

As Graham says:

> You went all over the place trying to make a living. You travelled to different countries. But the

only structured tour was in the United States. I came here and was lucky; in my first year I won a tournament. So instantly I knew I was a reasonably good player.

So you get your exemption and you just keep playing and playing and playing, and instead of flying around the world, you just go from [US] state to state. It was completely different to what it is now.

Graham was accepted by pros in the US. He was of a generation just removed from Peter Thomson and Bobby Locke whom American players resented for winning 'their' tournaments. But Australians Kel Nagle and Bruce Devlin had made livings on tour, as had the great Bob Charles of New Zealand. It was Devlin who convinced Graham to make the move. Graham again:

Bruce had come over here and settled. He had tried to commute for a couple of years and found that to be impossible, and financially not viable. So he raised his kids here and bought a house here, and when you've got kids getting into school and you have roots on the ground, it's hard.

I stayed in America because that's where the money was. And this is where the best players were.

I didn't want to go every January and February and play in Asia. I wanted a life. I wanted to play where the best players were. And I wanted to play where the most money was.

The money was there because things were just getting exciting. IMG and television had created a 'big three', Nicklaus, Palmer, Player.

Golf was entertainment and these were the stars. It was all so new and modern. And it was on color TV. Graham wore flared red trousers. He was along for the ride.

'You think about what Jack, Gary and Arnold did in the early '70s and their contribution to golf is incredible,' says Graham.

> And not just on the US Tour. They went all over the world. Think about the type of aircraft that were there, and the places they went. They weren't non-stop jumbo jets.

> In 1973 Jack Nicklaus flew all the way from Florida to Hobart, Tasmania for the Australian Open. He got from Palm Beach to California to Hawaii to Fiji and across to Sydney, connected to Melbourne and then down to Hobart. Took a couple of days.

Graham won the 1979 US PGA Championship with a final round 65 that was flawless for 17 holes.

> I knew I was playing the best golf of my life, I couldn't do anything wrong. I didn't realize what I was doing until the 18th tee. On my backswing there, I said to myself, 'My God, where am I?' Then I woke up in a playoff.

Irritated by hecklers pulling for Ben Crenshaw and photographers clicking shutters, and tightening up some under the strain, Graham double-bogied 18. He went into the sudden-death play-off with the game's best putter. And out-putted him.

As second-placed Crenshaw said:

> I don't like second worth a damn, but I shouldn't have been in the playoff. David will be remembered

as a man who shot a 65 on the last day of a major championship—with a double-bogey. And that's incredible.

Graham recalled the significance of his win:
> If I'd have lost the playoff, no telling what would happen. You look at that Frenchman that lost the British Open—he never played well again. When you lose a major championship, especially if it's your first one, I can't imagine what that's like and I'm glad I never went through that. It kind of all ended well for me. It was wonderful. I was blessed. I was very fortunate.

Graham won the 1981 US Open at Merion closing with a peerless 67. Afterwards he received a call from Ben Hogan who had won the 1950 US Open on that same course, 16 months after a car accident that almost killed him. Hogan said of Graham's win; it was 'one of the best rounds of golf I've ever seen'.

'He was very nice to me,' says Graham.
> He was a wonderful gentleman. We had lunch together many times. I only knew him in the latter stage of his life but he for some reason cottoned on to Bruce Devlin and he cottoned on to me. I actually spent some lovely time with him.

David Oswald Graham (DOG) is one of only six golfers—with Gary Player, Bernhard Langer, Hale Irwin, Justin Rose and Laura Davies— to win professional golf tournaments on six continents. He says he was 'born' an international player by dint of being Australian.

I went through the Asia tour, went through the European tour, went through the South American tour, the Japanese tour. It was common for people of my generation to travel the world to play golf. Gary Player pioneered that whole thing. He doesn't get enough credit, or all of the players of that generation.

You look at Sam Snead, came to Australia to play golf. Byron Nelson. Bobby Jones. Norman von Nida. Look at Peter Thomson in the 50s and early 60s. Flying to England on DC6s, changing three or four times. Now you can go on a plane and take a sleeping pill and a glass of wine and you get there non-stop.

Graham says he's perfectly happy to have won two major championships without receiving the acclaim of Norman, Thomson, or even lesser-credentialed Australians such as Wayne Grady or Steve Elkington.

I'm perfectly happy with my life and perfectly happy that I've raised a wonderful family and that I've won two major championships. I'm happy I've never relinquished my Australian citizenship, nor would I ever do that. My children are Australian citizens.

I just made a decision to come here [to the US] because I love to play and this is where the top players were. I don't need to be compared. If you talk about putting anybody on the map, you could bypass everybody and the first name that comes to my mind is Peter Thomson.

People grow up in eras. The kids playing golf in America now are all 'Tiger Woods, Rory McIlroy'. You don't hear the kids talking about Hogan and Snead, they didn't even know that they played golf. And that's understandable. So I never thought about [being compared].

Well, he did a bit. World Golf took rather a long time to induct him into the Hall of Fame considering that Jumbo Ozaki (one tour title outside Japan), George H.W. Bush (President of the USA) and Bing Crosbie (singer, actor) were inducted ahead of him.

Without rancour Graham says:

I wondered why a certain few people were already in the Hall of Fame who had not as accomplished career as I had. When you see people inducted you think 'Why him and not me?'

On Graham's behalf, Jack Nicklaus, Arnold Palmer and particularly Gary Player lobbied for Graham's inclusion. They set about restructuring qualification for the Hall of Fame. A new category of 'Male Competitor' was created. And Graham was in the pantheon.

✳ ✳ ✳

'What A Stupid I Am!'

Roberto De Vicenzo won the Open Championships of Argentina, Brazil, Peru, Mexico, Chile, Uruguay, Colombia, Panama, Venezuala, Belgium, Holland, France, Germany and Spain. He won the Open Championship in 1967 at Royal Livepool and would have been in a play-off at the 1968 US Masters if he'd signed his card correctly and not been disqualified.

As De Vicenzo said:

> I play golf all over the world for 30 years, and now all I can think of is what a stupid I am to be wrong in this wonderful tournament. Never have I ever done such a thing.

De Vicenzo is the greatest player to come from South America. He won 230 tournaments around the world including 131 times on the Argentine Tour. His first tournament victory came aged 19 when he won the 1942 Argentinian tournament, Abierto del Litoral. His final trophy was the 1985 Argentine PGA Championship, which he won when he was 62.

✳ ✳ ✳

World Gamers

The first non-Brit to win the British Open Championship was Frenchman Arnaud Massy, who shot 76-81-78-77 at Royal Liverpool in 1907. The first American to win this championship (known as '*the* Amateur Championship') was Australian-born Walter J. Travis, who did so in 1904 aged 42. Travis, a highly-successful hardware salesman, had first picked up a golf club at 35.

Chi Chi Rodriguez of Peurto Rico learned golf by hitting tin cans with a branch from a guava tree. He joined the PGA Tour in 1960 and won eight times. He was famous for putting his porkpie hat over the hole when he made birdie or eagle. On hearing that this annoyed his fellow professionals, Rodriguez pretended to be a bull-fighter who would use his putter as a sword to defeat the hole (bull).

Rodriguez represented Puerto Rico in the World Cup and the USA in the 1973 Ryder Cup alongside Jack Nicklaus, Arnold Palmer, Lee Trevino and Tom Weiskopf.

Masashi 'Jumbo' Ozaki was another world gamer so to speak. He won 94 times on the Japan tour and once outside it—the 1972 New Zealand PGA. He played on the 1996 International President's Cup team alongside Greg Norman, Ernie Els and Vijay Singh. He won all three of his matches in the Internationals' 16.5 to 15.5 loss.

Isao 'Tower' Aoki, another Japanese golfer, won 51 times on the Japan Tour, once on the European Tour (the 1983 European Open) and once on the US PGA Tour (the 1983 Hawaiian Open). In 1978 he won the World Matchplay at Wentworth when he beat New Zealander Simon Owen 3 and 2.

In the US Open of 1980, Aoki (nicknamed 'Tower' because he is 6 feet tall) was paired with Jack Nicklaus all four days. The pair went head-to-head in the final round until Nicklaus made birdies on 17 and 18 to win by two.

'I realized there was a player in the world who could play far better than I ever imagined,' said Aoki.

> I kept telling myself [that] no matter how perfect he is, he will make a mistake in 72 holes in four days. But I was wrong. Jack did not make any errors until the end of the tournament.

As Brent Kelley wrote:

> Aoki's 274 was the second-lowest total ever posted in a U.S. Open, and it still shares the tournament record for lowest score by a non-winner.

Just before Nicklaus made his final birdie putt on the 72nd hole, Aoki honoured him with a bow.

Nick Price is from Zimbabwe and holds a British passport. He won 49 professional golf tournaments including 18 PGA Tour titles and three majors—the '92 and '94 US PGA, and the '94 Open Championship. In 1988 he went head-to-head over the last 18 with Seve Ballesteros in the Open Championship at Royal Lytham & St Annes. It was brilliant theatre: Seve the freak, imperious; the Zimbabwean–Brit clinging to his leg like a pig-dog on a hunk of osso bucco.

In the third round of the 1986 Masters, Price shot a course record 63 and was paired in the last group with Greg Norman. He shot one-under 71, finished fifth behind Norman, Seve Ballesteros, Tom Kite and the winner Jack Nicklaus who'd smoked 65 aged 46.

A month later at the PGA Championship at Southern Hills Country Club, Price shot 11-under 269, 67–65–70–67, and won by six shots. It was the lowest ever total in a US major. It was the first tournament that featured all the world's top 40 ranked players. And Price beat them all. And was crowned World No. 1.

Renowned coach David Leadbetter described Price's ball-striking as 'the best-sounding strike in golf—if you watch and listen to him hitting iron shots, the ball comes off the club head like a bullet'.

Ben Crenshaw described Price's play at Southern Hills as:
magnificent to watch. He's a man in full flight. He's so strong. That's one thing that's often overlooked. In striking the ball he's as good as anyone since Ben Hogan.'

Thailand's Thongchai Chaidee (sometimes spelt Jaidee) has won the Malaysian Open, Indonesian Open, European Open, French Open, Korean Open, Indian Open, Myanmar Open, Cambodian Open and the Masters of Asia, as befitting a master of Asia. He's never won the Thailand Open but he has twice won the Bangkok Open.

Thongchai Chaidee grew up playing soccer and was good enough to play for his province. He'd play barefoot, mostly, because he couldn't afford boots. A splinter in his foot put paid to his soccer career. However, he lived in a shack without running water near an army base that had a golf course. He found the head of an old 5-iron and attached it to a length of bamboo. That was his first golf club. He found balls and whacked them. He did it every day.

He became a paratrooper. He was dropped into jungles and told to 'Bear Grylls' his way out. He spent 14 years in the army. He kept playing golf. He turned pro when he was 29. He is the first Thai to play in all four major championships. His best finish is four shots shy of Stewart Cink and Tom Watson in the 2009 Open Championship. He beat Rory McIlroy in the 2016 French Open.

Inbee Park of Korea has won seven major titles including a grand slam. She won the US Open in 2008 aged 20, the British Open in 2015 at 27. She won gold at the Rio Olympic Games. She probably deserves more space in this book than being wedged in between the Thai paratrooper and the 'most interesting man in golf'.

In the US Open at Pebble Beach in 2000, Miguel Angel Jiminez finished in a tie for second (with Ernie Els) and a score of 3-over, fifteen shots behind Tiger Woods. A year later in the Open Championship at Royal Lytham & St Annes, he finished equal-third four shots behind David Duval who was in the middle of the most purple patch.

Yet the cigar-smoking, calisthenics-practicing Spaniard once called the most interesting man in golf makes this stanza because, as he told Alan Shipnuck in *Golf*, those who criticize him for smoking and drinking can 'stick their tongue up their ass and let the rest of us do what we want to do.'

*** *

Zimbabwe's Jackie Robinson

On 30 December 1992, on his seventeenth birthday, Lewis (Lewie) Chitengwa, an amateur golfer from Zimbabwe beat Tiger Woods by three shots in the Orange Bowl World Junior Championship in Miami. Chitengwa went into the final round tied with Woods and Gilberto Morales of Venezuela. But his even-par 71 proved enough to take the title from Woods whose putter Woods said 'let me down every day'.

'I don't know if it's mechanics or something else,' said Woods who was also 17. 'It must be the youngest case of the yips recorded.'

A year later Chitengwa turned up at East London Golf Club to contest the 1993 South African Amateur Championship. At the front gate, he was told caddies had to enter through the back. He insisted he was a player. He was told to take the back entrance regardless.

After he'd beaten Rory Sabbatini en route to becoming the first black man to win the South African Amateur title, he politely shook hands with the man who'd barred him, and thanked him for the hospitality. Apartheid had only been abolished a year earlier. Chitengwa's win has been described as the equivalent of Jackie Robinson breaking baseball's color barrier.

Chitengwa joined the University of Virginia and was two-time All-American. He turned pro and was the first black Zimbabwean on the Buy.com Tour. He played two PGA Tour events, the '96 Vancouver Open and the '99 St Jude Classic.

On 30 June 2001, while playing on the Canadian tour, tragically Chitengwa contracted meningitis and died aged just 26.

'I guarantee you, he would have been a tournament winner on the PGA Tour,' Nick Price told *Golf Digest*. 'He had determination and intensity, and he had a great short game. Guys with great short games win golf tournaments.'

In *Sports Illustrated,* Price wrote:

> No matter what Lewie could've done as a pro, his most significant achievement would've remained winning the '93 South African Amateur. He was the first black to take that event, and he did it only two years after apartheid had been abolished. I jumped for joy when he won. Here was a kid reared in the same junior program as I was, yet he had the chance to influence an entirely different, and much larger, audience.
>
> Lewie had impeccable manners and was humble and generous. He gave every penny away that he didn't need to support himself, sending money to numerous charities in the U.S. and back to Zimbabwe for his brother's schooling and to help his parents. He was a special young man, and I want him to be remembered.

On 17 August 2003 on the Stoney Creek Course at Virginia's Wintergreen Resort, Nick Watney posted his first professional victory on the Canadian tour—the Lewis Chitengwa Memorial.

CHAPTER FOUR

GOD BLESSED AMERICANS

❖◄►❖ ❖►

The Hawk

Ben Hogan invented practice as we know it. Most professionals of his time—that is all golfers around the world—didn't see the point. Most felt that playing golf was the best way to hone a man's game, and give one the feel needed to play a course. Ben Hogan was the first golfer to get out on whatever field he could find and repeatedly beat balls. It follows that Ben Hogan invented the range.

Ben Hogan would arrange balls in a pyramid and start whacking away—bang, bang, bang and repeat until they'd whistle out into the ether, pure, strong and straight. And his muscles developed 'memory' as he honed a tight, fluid, ever-repeatable swing.

'All I know is I've seen Jack Nicklaus watch Hogan practice,' said the Texan Tommy Bolt. 'I've never seen Hogan watch Nicklaus practice.'

Ben Hogan practiced before a round, which was highly unusual, and after a round which was unheard of. What *is* he doing? He shot 64 in the

1941 Rochester Open and headed out to practice. 'What are you trying to do, man?' remarked his friend and fellow pro, Jimmy Demaret. 'You had ten birdies today. The officials are still inside talking about it. They're thinking of putting a limit on you.'

They called Ben Hogan 'The Hawk' in America and the 'Wee Ice Man' in Scotland. His countenance was of focus and steel-eyed will. He didn't say much on the golf course. He would go an entire round or a tournament without talking to fellow players. Change rooms were the same. Once, when overhearing talk of greens and speed, slope and grain, he said: 'Anyone can putt on fast greens.'

And that was it. Righto then. Thanks, Ben Hogan.

In 1942 journalist Shirley Povich wrote:

> Sam Snead dropped into a Washington recruiting station and joined the Navy the other day, and when he did a sizeable hunk of color went out of professional golf. In a profession populated for the most part by grim, poker-panned young business men whose golf shots represent their only sparkle, Hillbilly Snead was a refreshing character.

She didn't mention Ben Hogan. Though the inference was clear. Sam Snead remembers Ben Hogan this way.

> Ben would never speak. He wouldn't say 'good shot', 'bad shot'. He didn't give anything and he didn't ask anything. He'd say 'good luck' on the first tee. On the green, he might say 'Sam, I think you're away'.

> While I'm playing I have little or no sense of humour,' said Hogan. I wish I did have. But I'm no Bob Hope and I tell a very bad story. I would like to appear as a happier

fellow. I *am* actually happy. But while playing golf I give the best I can give it. I love to play golf. That's what I'm there to do—I'm not there to tell funny stories.

William Benjamin 'Ben' Hogan was born in Dublin Texas in 1912, and grew up a dead ringer for his dad, Chester, a blacksmith. The pair would hunt rabbits in the snow and ride around on Chester's horse until Chester died when Ben Hogan was nine years old. It wasn't known for many years that Chester had put a shotgun to his chest. Ben Hogan's biographer, James Dodson suggests that young Ben was in the room when it happened. Ben Hogan never spoke about it either way. His wife Valerie didn't know how his father had died for a decade after they were married.

To help his mom, nine-year-old Ben and his brother sold newspapers. A friend told him there was a golf course nearby, Glen Garden, that paid caddies 65 cents for 18 holes. For four hours work he would make twice what he was making selling papers until midnight each night.

Ben Hogan walked the seven miles to the course to find more caddies than golfers. The other caddies, older boys, didn't want Ben Hogan taking their jobs and turned him away. The next day he pretended to be another caddie's brother. But the ruse was found out and Ben Hogan was put in a barrel and rolled down a rocky hill. The boys came down the hill with sticks and gave him a beating.

Ben Hogan came back up the hill. The boys took off his hat and threw it back down. He came back up again. He was tried and found guilty in a kangaroo court. As punishment–initiation, he was made to fight a bigger boy. If he won, he could be a caddie.

'After selling newspapers for a couple of years I was pretty handy with my fists,' said Ben Hogan. 'I gave this boy a rough time. And I got to be a caddie. And after that they left me alone.'

Each day he'd set off before dawn on the seven-mile walk to Glen Garden. Then he'd play golf. Then he'd caddie. Then he'd walk seven miles home.

Every time Ben Hogan earned enough money, he'd visit a store in Fort Worth and pick a club from a big barrel of cheap ones until he'd amassed a set of wooden-shafted clubs with bad grips.

In 1927 he played in the final of Glen Gardens' Christmas Caddies Tournament. He lost in a play-off to another handy local youngster, Byron Nelson.

Ben Hogan turned pro in 1931 because he couldn't afford to get around the country just to play amateur events. He didn't win often. He'd lose his savings. But he kept trying, working, funding little trips. All through the 1930s he kept at it. He was driven. As he told *Golf* magazine editor George Peper in 1987, 'One, I didn't want to be a burden to my mother. Two, I needed to put food on the table. Three, I needed a place to sleep.'

And he improved. He knew his swing wasn't pretty like Sam Snead's. But it was his. Through beating balls and shifting dirt he 'dug his golf swing out of the ground'.

Ben Hogan worked out that his low draw wasn't suited to the courses he was playing, and that high fades were better into receptive greens. He tried to eradicate his hook. 'I hate a hook,' he said. 'It nauseates me. I could vomit when I see one. It's like a rattlesnake in your pocket.'

He made a change to his grip and hit the ball so well word got about he'd found 'the secret' to perfect golf. He never really let on what it was.

In 1940 he won the North and South Open at Donald Ross's Pinehurst No.2. He won it again in 1942 and was the leading money-winner for three years, 1940 to 1942. Some of his prime golf years were taken away by serving as a pilot during World War II, but he came back as pro golf's dominant player.

He won the 1946 PGA Championship, the 1948 US Open and the 1948 PGA. Former PGA Tour player and World Golf Hall of Fame inductee David Graham met Ben Hogan several times in the 1970s. For some reason the great man had taken a shine to Graham as he did to fellow Australian, Bruce Devlin.

Says Graham:

> You think about playing professional golf in the United States straight after the war, tournament first prize might be $300. They made their money with exhibitions. They played because they loved the game. They didn't play for the money because there wasn't any money.
>
> Hogan, when he missed a putt for $100, that was a lot of money. There are stories about Mr Hogan, about how he didn't have any money to feed himself, how he played on an orange the last day.

In 1948 Ben Hogan won 10 tournaments. And the US public—who previously thought the man aloof at best given the perception of him as unsmiling automaton—warmed to Ben Hogan.

In February of 1949, Ben Hogan and Valerie were driving home on an icy road in thick fog when they had a head-on collision with a Greyhound bus. Ben Hogan threw himself across his wife, saved her, and probably himself—the steering column ended driven through the driver's seat. But he broke just about everything: collarbone, hip, pelvis, ribs, ankle and ruptured bladder. There were blood clots. They flew in a surgeon on an Air Force plane. Friends heard he was dead. The surgeon saved his life, though his family were told he might never walk again.

Authorities used his mangled wreck of a car for road safety awareness. A sign read: 'This is the car Ben Hogan was driving when struck by a bus near Van Horn, Texas, on February 2 1949. In the crash, Mr and Mrs Hogan were seriously injured.' People came to look at it.

For three weeks he was in near full-body cast. First day out of the cast, one lap of the bed. Next day, two laps. He walked a lap of the room. Then two laps. He walked the grounds and then the block. At one time when his wife came to visit, she found him out in the rain, streets away.

Within a month of the accident he was discharged. He was 37 and would never be free from pain. But 'golf was my life and I didn't want to give it up,' he said. 'So I went to work.'

Letters and cards poured in. Hogan thought the US public believed him a cold fish. 'It did something to me I can't describe,' said Ben Hogan.

> I was always known as a 'mom' fellah. But this gave
> me an insight on life that I never thought existed.
> I didn't know that many people knew me. And I
> wanted to come back and play and win again.

It would take 11 months before he could play again. In March of 1950, in cold and rainy weather, his legs heavily bandaged, Ben Hogan stiffly teed off in the Los Angeles Open. And the people flocked to see him. Incredibly, after 72 holes he was in the lead. Sam Snead birdied two of the last three holes to tie to force a play-off over 18 holes.

Snead won the play-off. But Ben Hogan was back.

✳✳✳

Merion and Other Miracles

There's a cracking, iconic photo taken by sports photographer Hy Peskin of Ben Hogan hitting a one-iron on the 18th hole at the 1950 US Open at Merion. He's frozen in time but you can see, even *feel* the balance and poise of his finish. The rhythm and tempo and purity of the strike are encapsulated in the finish. Thousands line the fairway and ring the green in the distance. It's a magnificent shot and a wonderful shot that recorded a famous moment.

The 1-iron found the green and The Hawk two-putted to force another 18-hole play-off. He'd just limped around 36 holes (as they played on the last day in tournament golf) in so much pain that his playing partner, Cary Middlecoff, a dentist, marked his ball on the green for him.

Ben Hogan shot 69 in the play-off to beat Lloyd Mangrum (73) and George Fazio (75). They called it 'The Miracle at Merion'. The car accident had nearly killed him 16 months previously. And yet there he was, bandaged up, clearly in pain, hobbling stiffly about, and winning the US Open. People wrote books about it. Tiger Woods read them.

Ben Hogan won the Masters in 1953 and Augusta named a bridge after him. He won the US Open the same year, at Oakmont, leading all the way and winning by six shots from Sam Snead. Walter Hagen, aged 60, rang him, talked of a legacy unfulfilled unless he won the Open Championship. Ben Hogan had never been to Britain.

But away to Carnoustie he went, to battle the winds, and the locals' perception that you weren't any sort of golfer unless you'd played golf in Scottish winds. On the first hole in practice rounds, he hit driver, 9-iron to the green. By the week's end it was driver, 2-iron, and he'd end up short.

On the last day (a Friday so that pros could go back to work on the weekend at their clubs), he was two back. After 54 holes, he was tied with the brilliant Argentine, Roberto de Vicenza, with Peter Thomson one back. In the last round, battling the flu and the cold weather, his injuries bothering him, Ben Hogan made birdie on 18 and hobbled off to huge cheers from Scots who coined him 'The Wee Ice Man'.

'I'm happy but so very, very tired,' said Ben Hogan. 'Don't even mention the possibility of a play-off, I don't think I can make it.'

There were players still to come in. But none got close, and he won by four. By year's end, he was in a convertible waving at the people of New York in a ticker-tape parade.

Tiger Woods once said that only two people have 'owned' their golf swing, Ben Hogan and the enigmatic Canadian, Moe Norman. Gary Player said of Hogan, '[He] was the best striker from tee to green and the best golf swing I saw'.

Player remembers asking for Ben Hogan's advice on perfecting the golf swing. Hogan replied that it was about practice, nothing else, just practice. For Hogan, it was about beating balls until your calluses bleed. It was about shifting dirt.

'The secret,' said Ben Hogan, 'is in the dirt.'

✳ ✳ ✳

The Big Swinger

The 1959 Sam Snead Festival golf tournament at The Greenbriars, where Sam Snead was the pro, wasn't an official PGA Tour event. And that's why Al Geiberger's 13-under 59 in the 1977 Danny Thomas Memphis Classic is known as the first official sub-60 PGA Tour golf round.

Yet Sam Snead's 59 in the third round of his own tournament, replete with 10 birdies, an eagle and 25 putts, was good enough that *Sports Illustrated* described it as 'the greatest ever round in competitive golf history'.

Snead shot 31 out and 28 back. His last seven holes needed just 21 shots. He might have shot 58 had he not missed a four-foot putt on 17. The next day Queen Elizabeth sent Sam Snead a telegram.

Sam Snead had a flowing, graceful yet powerful golf swing. 'He was the most athletic man to ever play golf,' reckons Gary Player. 'He was like Gumby!' Player once compared Ernie Els to Sam Snead; the size of the men, their grace, that 'effortless' power.

In an interview with *Golf Digest* in 2010, Sam Snead had this to say.
The sportswriters started calling me 'Slammin' Sam'
in the late 1930s, I never liked it very much. I really
preferred the nickname I got when I first joined the
tour: 'Swingin' Sam.' That was the name that showed
off my true strengths: smoothness and rhythm.
Somehow people liked 'Slammin' Sam' better.

They said he had a 'natural' swing. It peeved Sam Snead, much as Ernie
Els is occasionally peeved with 'The Big Easy'. As Sam Sneed told Guy
Yocom in *Golf Digest*:
They thought I wasn't a hard worker. But when I
was young, I'd play and practice all day, then practice
more at night by my car's headlights. My hands bled.
Nobody worked harder at golf than I did.

Sam Snead came to Australia and was described as 'a good style of
a bloke'. He wore a trademark porkpie, straw hat much copied by men
of the day. The author John Updike once described Sam Snead as
'swaggering around the range like the sheriff of golf county'.

Sam Snead won every tournament on the PGA Tour at least once,
except the US Open in which he was runner-up four times. In 1939 at
the Philadelphia Country Club he needed birdie on the 72nd hole to
win but made triple-bogey. In the first US Open to be televised, 1947,
he led by two shots with four to play in the 18-hole play-off with Lee
Worsham but bogied 17 and 18.

Sam Snead won the 1946 Open Championship at St Andrews by three
shots. He didn't like the Old Course when he first saw it. 'What the hell
is this place?' he remarked, thinking it was an abandoned golf course. In

the immediate post-War years, the Old Course wasn't at its best, having been cared for by German POWs. There was an Allied airstrip near the 12th. Snead considered everywhere but America 'camping out' including the Old Course in Scotland.

He was here because Walter Hagen (and a deal with Wilson Sporting goods) convinced Snead to play. Thus, the big fellow teed it up on the Old Course, drove the ball great distances and hit powerful long irons under the wind, and won by four shots from Johnny Bulla and Bobby Locke.

Sam Snead won the Greater Greensboro Open eight times. The first time was the inaugural event in 1938. The last time was in 1965 which also marked 25 Greater Greensboro Opens for Sam Snead. It was the last of his eighty-two PGA Tour victories.

The field at Greensboro in 1965, held a week before the Masters, sported Jack Nicklaus, Gary Player, Billy Casper and Julius Boros. Sam Snead shot 68–69–68–68 and won by five shots. He was 52. He remains the oldest man to win a PGA Tour event. Carson Bain, a future mayor of Greensboro, awarded him a lifetime supply of McDonald's hamburgers and a hunting rifle.

Sam Snead won the 1957 Texas International (now the AT&T Byron Nelson) with a score of 20-under. The record stands today. In 1972, aged 60, Snead finished T4 in the US PGA, three shots behind Gary Player. In 1973 he finished T9 in the US PGA, seven shots back of Jack Nicklaus. In 1974 he became the oldest man to finish Top-10 in a major when he ran equal third in the US PGA, three shots behind Lee Trevino. Five years later, aged 67, he made the cut in the 1979 US PGA, the oldest man ever.

Sam Snead won seven majors, placing him fifth on the all-time win list with Bobby Jones, Arnold Palmer, Gene Sarazen and Harry Vardon. His 82 PGA Tour event wins are more than Tiger Woods (79), Jack Nicklaus (73), Ben Hogan (64) and Arnold Palmer (62).

Sam Snead's last major was the 1954 Masters that he won in a play-off with Ben Hogan, a man he considered a 'blood brother'.

> Some people didn't understand that, because Ben and I never socialized and rarely talked. But we were like brothers, because we both made the other guy better. A lot of blood brothers can't say that.

Sam Snead was pals with King Edward VIII. As son, Jack Snead told the *Naples Daily News*:

> [The King] would always bring Dad a gift. It was always something to do with golf. I remember one year he brought Dad two feather balls. They were made back in the 1700s. One year, he gave Dad one of Tom Morris's playing clubs that he [Morris] had won the first British Open with.

Sam Snead was a friend of President Dwight Eisenhower's, who in 1961 had a nuclear weapons-proof bunker built under The Greenbriar. The bunker remained an official US government secret facility until 1992. Today it hosts tours.

In 1983 *Sports Illustrated* pointed out to Sam Snead that he had won golf tournaments in six decades. 'Is that right?' replied Snead. 'How long are decades nowadays?'

In the second round of the 1979 Ed McMahon Quad City Open (now the John Deere Classic) in Coal Valley, Illinois, Sam Snead shot his age, 67. In the last round he shot 66.

Sam Snead was the US Masters ceremonial starter at Augusta National for many years. On occasion, when he felt like it, he and Gene Sarazen would tee the ball off and just continue on their way, playing the golf course ahead of the field. One time after nine holes, Sam Snead was 2-under. It was 1991. He was 79.

***

Iron Byron

Byron Nelson changed his golf swing when steel shafts replaced hickory. They named the mechanical ball-whacking machine 'Iron Byron' after Byron Nelson. Jack Nicklaus called Byron Nelson the straightest driver of a golf ball he's ever seen.

An engineer named George Manning began working on 'Iron Byron' in 1963. For three years he studied film of thousands of golf swings. Manning found that only one golf swing produced the same results time and again, Byron Nelson's.

As Manning says:

> We were looking to have a very efficient swing and what I mean by efficient is a minimum amount of energy for a maximum distance hit. What we discovered when we went through the pictures is that Byron Nelson had an extremely repeatable and efficient swing. We designed the machine to copy that swing.

Ben Hogan—who with Sam Snead was born within six months of Byron Nelson (born 2 February 1912)—is acknowledged by top experts as the greatest of his time. Yet there are those who make a case for Byron Nelson coming in above Ben Hogan. And they can mount a fair case.

Byron Nelson won five majors before the end of World War II. Ben Hogan won all his majors after it. Ben Hogan began winning when Byron Nelson retired from full-time golf. Ben Hogan never beat Byron Nelson head to head.

In 1945 Byron Nelson won 18 of 35 tournaments played, and finished second in seven others. He won 11 tournaments in a row. His 'Vardon' average score of 68.33 was the lowest of all time until Tiger Woods bettered it in 2000. Byron Nelson owned the cut streak record of 113 until Woods set a mark of 143. A 'cut' in Byron Nelson's time meant that he'd earned a cheque by finishing top-20. Which means Byron Nelson finished top-20 in 113 consecutive professional golf tournaments.

In the first round of the 1937 Masters Tournament at Augusta National—only the fourth Masters ever played—Byron Nelson's winning score included a course record 66, which stood for 40 years until Ray Floyd's first round 65 in 1976.

Byron Nelson was one down with three to play against Sam Snead in the 1940 US PGA Championship (when it was match-play) and began stiffing irons at flags. He birdied 16 and 17 and won 1-up.

Byron Nelson won the 1942 US Masters after an 18-hole play-off with Ben Hogan. Byron Nelson double-bogied the first, birdied the second, bogied the fourth and was three shots behind. And from there he unleashed: birdie on 6, eagle on 8.

'That eagle on the 510-yard uphill eighth broke little Ben and gave Lord Byron his margin,' reported *The Pittsburgh Post-Gazette*. The article continues.

> Coming up one stroke short of Hogan after whittling two from Hogan's lead on the short sixth, he whipped a perfect spoon shot uphill and to rest a bare six feet beyond the flag. He was down with one putt while Hogan chipped to the green over a mound and took two putts for regulation five.

Byron Nelson birded Amen Corner, 11, 12 and 13, and led by three. In eight holes he was six-under. Ben Hogan came back, got within a shot after three straight birdies on 13,14 and 15. But a bogie on 16 left him two down, two to play. And that was the match.

Ben Hogan described Byron Nelson's play as his 'greatest golf'. 'Playing that well, six or seven under over the last 12 holes at Augusta is something to behold,' said Ben Hogan.

Byron Nelson played his last US Open and Open Championship in 1955 but played every Masters until 1966. For many years after he'd 'retired', he teed off in the last group as a partner for the leading player. In 1958, Augusta National named a bridge after him.

* * *

The Squire

Gene Sarazen once said he invented the sand iron but that isn't true, exactly. He did perfect his niblick or 'scoop' club—the 9-iron-like weapon golfers used to extract balls from bunkers—by 'soldering various globs of lead along the sole of his niblick until he arrived at a club that had an exceptionally heavy, abrupt, wide, curving flange,' according to golf historian, John Fawcett.

The original inventor of the sand wedge was Edwin MacClain who in 1928 patented a heavy, weird-looking thing with a concave face like a giant soup spoon. Marketeers then put Walter Hagan's name on it and several pros put one in their bags.

Horton Smith, who won the first and third US Masters, used one of MacClain's Hagen-embossed soup ladels when he beat Bobby Jones in the 1930 Savannah Open. He gave the club to Bobby Jones and the great man carried it along with 21 other clubs (the bag limit of 14 not yet being imposed) in all four events that he won in 1930 on the way to his 'impregnable quadrilateral'. Yet Bobby Jones used the club only once in anger—and only once in his entire career—when he famously extricated himself from a tough lie in a bunker in Britain.

The R&A outlawed MacClain's soup ladel in 1931—there was a propensity for the club's concave face to double-hit the ball. And then

Gene Sarazen got to work. He unleashed his sand iron on the world in the 1932 Open Championship and won by five.

On winning the 1922 US Open, 20-year-old Gene Sarazen told reporters: 'All men are created equal. I'm just one stroke better than the rest.' A year later Sarazen was playing Walter Hagen in the final of the (match play) US PGA Championship. On the second hole of sudden-death, Sarazen nearly drove out of bounds. He inspected his lie, decided it was okay, and said to the gallery: 'I'll put this one up so close to the hole, it will break Walter's heart'. He did and it did.

On the 15th fairway at Augusta National in 1935, Walter Hagen was getting antsy. It was cold and wet and Hagen was on his way to a 79. He didn't see the point in finishing second much less well down the leaderboard. He wanted to get into the clubhouse and get a drink into him. But Gene Sarazen was conducting all due diligence.

Sarazen was three shots behind the leader in this final round of the Masters, and trying to decide on his second shot. He was middle of the fairway but was in between four-wood and five, high cut or long draw.

And Hagen was in his ear.

'Would you hurry up, please Gene,' said Hagen.

Sarazen smiled. He took out his 'spoon', the equivalent of a four-wood, stood over the ball, gave a little waggle, and whacked it 220 yards onto the green and watched it roll into the hole for a double-eagle two. Sportswriter Grantland Rice said it all in *The Spokesman-Review*.

> Millions of stars and duffers have played billions of golf shots in the 500-year history of the ancient game. But Gene Sarazen played one in the final round of the Masters' tournament at Augusta that holds all records for all time.
>
> Standing in the middle of the 15th fairway, 230 yards from the cup after a 255 yard drive, the stocky,

swarthy Italian was three strokes back of Craig Wood, the leader, with only four holes left to play. A mere miracle would be of no help. The big New Jersey blond had posted his 282 with a brilliant finish and his looked safer than a dozen Gibraltars.

Sarazen lined up and took his time, swapped an iron for a spoon, wound up and had a whack and 'the ball left the face of his spoon like a rifle shot,' wrote Rice. The ball went straight at the flag, bounced into the bank in front, rolled up onto the green and tracked straight into the hole. Rice called it 'The Shot Heard Around The World'.

**

Sir Walter

In 1913 English golf writer, Henry Leach wrote of American golfers:
> I am sure that we are appreciably better than their best, and I believe we shall always be so because the Americans have to play the game under inferior conditions and such as hardly permit of their developing the finer shades of skill. The Americans play a rather plainer game than we do. The country may and probably will produce an occasional golfing phenomenon, and it may win our Championship again, but it will never be really superior to us at golf.

And then came 1920 and American players won 12 of 14 Open Championships up to 1933.

Walter Hagen won the Open Championship four times. Bobby Jones won three times. Tommy Armour won in '31. Gene Sarazen won in '32 with his funky new club, the sand iron. Jimmy Barnes won in 1925 at Prestwick—site of the first ever Open Championship in 1860—with a score of 16-over. They called him 'Long Jim' on account of his lanky, 6ft 4in frame and long-hitting. He won the US PGA Championship (when it was match play) in 1916 and 1919, and the 1921 US Open by nine shots.

Herman Densmore 'Denny' Shute won the Open of 1933 after tying with fellow American, Craig Wood after 72 holes and beating him by five shots in the 36-hole play-off.

Hagen won the 1922 Open Championship at Royal St George's by a shot. He set the course record in the 1929 Open Championship at Muirfield with a third round 67 that he called the round of his life, and won by six. In 1924 he won at Royal Liverpool after storming home the last seven holes and casually slamming in a six-foot putt. Asked if he knew the putt was for the win Hagen said: 'Sure, I knew. But no man ever beat me in a play-off.'

They did. Though not often.

Walter Hagen won 11 majors before they'd invented the US Masters. He was the 19-year-old resident pro at Rochester when the 1912 US Open came to town, and Hagen fancied his game against the best. In 1914 he won the US Open. He won the Western Open five times—it was one of the biggest tournaments of the day. Some will argue worthy of major status. His last was the 1929 Open Championship at Muirfield. He won the PGA Championship for the first time in 1921 beating Jimmy Barnes 3 and 2. In the PGA Championship of 1923, he ran second to Gene Sarazen after 38 holes. Then he won the PGA Championship four years in a row.

Walter Hagen played hundreds of exhibition matches. His fame rose so that he was asked to put his name to 'sets' of golf clubs. Before then clubs had been individual 'cleeks', 'spoons', 'niblicks' and so forth. But the 'Walter Hagens' came as a set.

There was a time that some country clubs in the United States—being particularly private and elitist—would not allow professional players into their clubhouses. Professionals were seen as employees of the clubs, there to teach the members how to play. That was their place.

In the 1922 Open at Royal St George's (that Hagen won), he hired a limousine and parked out front of the clubhouse because he wasn't allowed to enter. He changed clothes in the car and took his meals in it. He hired a butler to bring him bottles of champagne.

Hagen would show up to tournaments in a tuxedo, as if he had just come from a party. He would drink 'Scotch' on the tee, though often it was tea with ice. It made opponents think. It was part of the show. He wrote:

> It pleased the public to think I lived the easy, carefree life, the playboy of golf. Frankly, I was happy to support both those illusions since I was making money out of the showmanship.

Hagen could be erratic off the tee and elsewhere, but knew great calm on the course. He knew he could get the ball on the green and salvage par. If he duffed three and holed the fourth, he'd remind people that 'three of those and one of them still count four.'

In his autobiography he wrote about his game.

> I set up shots the way a movie director sets up scenes. I hooked and I sliced them into the rough off the fairways, but how I clobbered that little white ball when the chips were down, the gallery tense and my opponent either overconfident and/ or sick with apprehension.

Hagen considered his greatest win knocking over Bobby Jones in a 36-hole challenge match in 1926. It was considered a heavyweight world championship to decide the best of the day. Hagen won 12 and 11. Afterwards the normally gracious Bobby Jones remarked: 'When a man misses his drive, and then misses his second shot, and then wins the hole with a birdie, it gets my goat.'

***

Patty Berg

There is no doubt of Patty Berg's ranking in golf's greater schema—she is one of the greats.

Patty Berg won 15 major championships and founded the Ladies Professional Golf Association (LPGA) in 1950 along with twelve other women golfers including Babe Didrikson Zaharias, Louise Suggs and Marilynn Smith.

Patty Berg grew up playing American football, played quarterback for the 50th Street Tigers. Her teammate was Bud Wilkinson, famous coach of the University of Oklahoma Sooners.

Aged 13 her parents convinced her to try golf. By the time she was 17, she lost in the final of the US Amateur against the leading player of the time, Glenna Collett Vare. At 19, she won it. She represented the USA in the Walker Cup and won the Titleholders—dubbed the 'women's Masters'—played at Augusta Country Club. She turned pro in 1940 and toured giving exhibition matches and hosting clinics.

Patty Berg was 5 feet two inches tall but long off the tee, and a surgical iron player. Wilson Sporting Goods made Patty Berg golf clubs and they sold in large numbers.

Patty Berg did her bit in World War II joining the Marines in 1942 and serving as a lieutenant. In 1946 she won the first US Open. She won the Western Open (a major) five more times. She won three more Titleholders and was three-time leading money-winner. As men played for the Vardon Trophy, women played for the Vare. Patty Berg won that three times too.

In 1950 after founding the LPGA Tour, Patty Berg became first president. But she never won the LPGA Championship. She was the player of the 1950s. Associated Press named her Athlete of the Year in '55. She shot a 64 in 1952 that smashed records.

Patty Berg survived stomach cancer in 1971. After years of golf, she had hip surgery and back surgery. She died in 2006 at the age of 88.

Earlier that year she'd been in the gallery of the US Women's Open. 'Look at all these people,' she exclaimed. 'In my day, we had six professionals playing for $500.'

'She had a simple golf swing that never changed,' said Mickey Wright in *The Illustrated History of Women's Golf.* 'She had the club square. She hit the ball solidly, she hit the ball high. She knew more golf shots than any other women before or after.'

*** *** ***

The Good Doctor

According to Bobby Jones, Cary Middlecoff was a 'voluntarily unemployed dentist' who took time off work to win the US Open in 1949 and 1956, and the Masters in 1955. Middlecoff sits tenth on the list of all-time PGA Tour winners with 40, two behind Phil Mickelson, one ahead of Gene Sarazen.

In the second round of the 1955 Masters, Middlecoff had four straight birdies on the front nine to card a record 31. He made steady pars through the bend in Amen Corner and came to the 13th tee five-under for his round.

Watching on was *Sports Illustrated*'s Herbert Warren Wind (who would coin the phrase 'Amen Corner') who noted that:

[Middlecoff] can rarely play a shot without working up to it with several tugs at the vizor of his cap, a brief exploration of the territory stretching before him, a long gander at his target, a movement of repose as he hikes his trousers, a little unloosening of the neck muscles, a pause to dry his right hand on the seat of his trousers, another tug at the vizor, another brief exploration, and so on—all this accompanied by a frown of furious concentration.

Beneath the parade of gestures there is the complete absorption of a high-strung, intelligent, emotional individual playing an extremely nerve-racking game. And it is this abiding intensity, of course, that Middlecoff communicates to his galleries and which explains the charged atmosphere he creates when he is pouring it on.

Middlecoff's drive landed right side of the fairway. Middlecoff approached his ball and called for his 'spoon', a lofted, 5-wood-like club. As Wind wrote:

There was an absolute hush the length of the gallery—stretched out some 300 yards along the roped-off fairway—as Middlecoff went with his spoon on his second. He hit a fine, solid shot, and as the ball cleared the creek and landed on the green and rolled to the back edge, a series of shouts went up the length of the line of spectators. These salvos bounced off the pines on the ridge across the fairway and the area reverberated with a sound not unlike artillery fire on a distant battlefield.

The pin position this day was right front. Middlecoff landed back left. The distance was reckoned at 82 feet, over a ridge and into a valley. Middlecoff 'inspected, sighted, scrutinized and deciphered the line,' wrote Wind. Then he set it free. Wind said it best.

> ... and no ball ever looked whiter than this one did
> as it ghosted its way just below the centre folds of
> the shadow-strewn green and rolled and rolled and
> slowed down and then crept off a final slight break
> and fell into the hole. And then, those salvos again.

Middlecoff shot 65 for the round and won by seven.

✶✶✶

The Joplin Ghost

Horton Smith came out of the Ozarks in Missouri and caddied at Oak Hill Golf Club. He was six feet one inch tall, long and thin and had a fluid, graceful swing. The sports writer O.B. Keeler said Horton Smith had 'the best grooved swing I ever saw'. Keeler should know. He was a personal friend and confidante of Bobby Jones whom Bobby Jones described as 'the greatest golf writer there's ever been'.

Horton Smith was also known as 'the greatest putter who ever lived' because he won the first and third Masters at Augusta. As previously mentioned, he was also called the 'Joplin Ghost' because he was long and pale, and came from a place considered to be nowhere, Joplin, Missouri.

'I really don't see why he ever misses a shot, except that he is human,' wrote Keeler. 'But if ever there were a perfect mechanical golfer, Horton Smith is it.'

Aged just 21, Horton Smith won eight tournaments. He played in five Ryder Cups and never lost a match. In 1930 he placed fourth in the

Open Championship and US Open, both won by Bobby Jones.

Horton Smith played in the first thirty US Masters until 1963 when he died aged 55 of Hodgkin's Lymphoma.

**

The Greatest Game Ever Played

In a field featuring the greatest professionals of the time, Britons, Ted Ray and Harry Vardon and a relatively unknown local pro called Walter Hagen, a 20-year-old amateur, Francis Ouimet—a former caddie from working-class roots described by *The New York Times* as 'barely a stripling'—won the 1913 US Open at The Country Club in Brookline, Massachusetts. Ouimet grew up near the Country Club's 17th green and with his brothers had built a three-hole course in his backyard featuring a gravel pit, swamp and buried, upturned tomato cans as cups.

He played there every day and became good enough to win the Massachusetts Amateur Championship. He entered the US Open because it was being played near his house and because his boss, baseball team owner, George Wright, gave him time off.

Ouimet's regular caddie, 12-year-old Jack Lowery, wasn't allowed to caddie because a truant officer said he needed to be at school. Ouimet turned to his next best option, Jack's 10-year-old brother, Eddie, who had escaped the truant officer's clutches.

After three rounds Ouimet was tied with Vardon and Ray. With six holes of the championship to play, he was two behind. On the par-4 17th, the hole across the road from his house, Ouimet made the tying birdie.

Into the 18-hole play-off with Vardon and Ray and 10,000 fans came to watch, the most ever seen at a golf match. On the first tee Ouimet smashed his driver down the middle. In the first round his ball hadn't gone 40 yards. But he was on today, and led Vardon by one after ten. It was a lead he maintained to the 17th tee. Vardon gambled, and hit his ball in a bunker, Ouimet made birdie on 18 and won the US Open by five shots.

And America had a hero.

It's estimated there were 350,000 golfers in the US in 1913. Ten years later as Hagen and Bobby Jones followed Ouimet's heroics, there were two million.

Disney made a movie in 2005 about the US Open called *The Greatest Game Ever Played*, starring Shia Lebouf as Ouimet, Stephen Dillane as Vardon and Josh Flitter as Eddie Lowery, Ouimet's caddie.

Francis Ouimet never turned professional though his amateur status was rescinded when he opened a shop that sold sports gear. Eddie Lowery became an accomplished player, sports writer and multi-millionaire car salesman—and a friend of comedian, Bob Hope.

✳ ✳ ✳

Tommy Five Times

Thomas Sturges (Tom) Watson was born on 4 September 1949 and almost won the Open Championship 59 years after that.

Almost won, but not quite. When he couldn't make par on the 72nd hole at the Ailsa Course of Turnberry Resort, golf folk around the world were sad, for it would've been a fairytale up there with Leicester in the Premier League and Buster Douglas whooping Iron Mike Tyson in 1990 (one of the most sensational defeats in boxing history).

The 18th was playing downwind that Sunday in 2009 at Turnberry. Stuart Cink hit a fine approach that finished pin-high, fifteen feet. He rolled in the birdie putt, raised his putter and punched an imaginary dwarf on top of the head. He finished 2-under. He was stoked with his 69.

Standing on the 18th tee, leading by one, Tom Watson couldn't swallow. Still, he hit a perfect tee-shot dead centre, the ball rolled and rolled, and left him 187 yards in.

Eight-iron or nine-iron? Eight-iron or nine-iron? That was the question. The wind was up his clacker. It was a back pin. What to do?

Watson chose the 8-iron. Hit it pure. Said aloud 'I like it'. It was the shot he wanted to hit. What else could he do? Watson always had something of the philosopher about him. Dr Bob Rotella used him as a study case. It was Watson who first said 'golf is not a game of perfect'.

His shot was not perfect. It was hot and didn't land soft, and rolled through the back. He may have softly chipped from the back, but chose his putter. Jack Nicklaus said it was the right option. But gee, that lie, there was a couple billiard tables between fringe and flag.

And so, Tom Watson putted from the fluffy flange and went hard-ish at it so he wouldn't be short, and gave himself eight feet coming back. He stood over his putt for the championship with millions mentally urging it in ... and hit it weak, effete. The ball fell away limply and didn't reach the hole. Worst putt of the week. And off he went with Cink for a 4-hole play-off, watched on by Lee Westwood who'd attacked 18 feeling he needed birdie but made bogie when par would have done. Such has been Lee's luck and lot.

And then, right then on the tee of the first play-off hole, Tom Watson looked like a 60-year-old playing against a big buck pro in his prime. He chunked a five-iron. He blocked an approach. He hooked his drive on the third play-off hole into the wild wheat. Cink finished birdie-birdie. And harpooned Bambi in the heart.

'This ain't a funeral,' exclaimed Tom Watson in the media centre after, and everyone laughed with him. But they were still sad. Even hard-bitten hacks because what they love most of all is a story.

Asked to describe his round, Watson said: 'It's your job to write the story. It's my job to make the story.'

And what stories Tom Watson made.

He duelled in the sun with Jack Nicklaus in '77 three months after winning the Masters by two shots from Jack Nicklaus. He won the 1981 Masters by two shots (from Jack Nicklaus) and he won the 1982 US Open by two shots from, yes, Jack Nicklaus.

He won five Open Championships in '75, '77, '80, '82 and '83 and nearly won in '84 succumbing only to Seve Ballesteros's famous tilt at the title. Only Harry Vardon (6) has more Open Championships.

He was second in the Masters in '78 and '79 (after a sudden death play-off won by Fuzzy Zoeller) and '84. He was second in the US Open in '83 and '87.

He never won the US PGA Championship but did have ten top-10s and a T2 in 1978 when he lost in a sudden death play-off to John Mahaffey Junior, a bigger journeyman than Moses.

But eight major championships, 71 wins around the world, PGA Tour Player of the Year six times (only Tiger Woods has more with 11), four Ryder Cups, induction into the World Golf Hall of Fame in '88, and acclaimed as one of their own by golf fans either side of the Atlantic—the sum total places Tom Watson right up there in the pantheon with Vardon, Nicklaus, Palmer, Player, Hogan, Tiger, the best there's ever been.

After his final tilt at a sixth Open Championship at Turnberry, Tom Watson said:

> One of the things I want out of life is for my peers
> to say, 'That Watson, he was a hell of a golfer'.

Few golfers are peers of Tom Watson. But peer or otherwise, anyone with the barest knowledge of golf can attest: Tom Watson, he was a hell of a golfer.

***

The Rest of the Best

Johnny Miller won two majors. He won the 1976 Open Championship at Royal Birkdale by six shots over Jack Nicklaus and Seve Ballesteros. His previous major win was the 1973 US Open at Oakmont when he fired a slashing 63 in the last round to beat John Schlee by one shot.

Schlee's 4-under 280 in the championship would have won 69 previous US Opens and made the play-off in six others. Schlee was tutored by Ben Hogan but said his good form came because 'Mars is in conjunction with my natal moon'. Schlee would go to sleep with his hands taped together in a perfect Vardon grip. In spite of this, Schlee didn't win many.

Ray Floyd did. He won the 1969 PGA, 1976 Masters, 1982 PGA and 1986 US Open when he was 43. Hale Irwin won three US Opens, and tournaments on six continents. Larry Nelson won three major championships. So did Billy Casper.

In 1997 Casper shot 94 in the Masters and later received a letter asking that he not play in the Masters anymore. Casper defied the letter, turned up and shot 104, though he didn't hand in his card. Thus, amateur Charles Kunkle's 95 in the final round of the (cut-free) 1956 Masters remains the tournament's highest score.

Mary Kathryn 'Mickey' Wright won 13 major championships. She's the only woman to hold four majors at once. Louise Suggs won 13 majors and 61 LPGA Tour titles. Kathy Whitworth won 88 LGPA Tour titles, more than anyone else. She also won six major titles. And if there are male golfers (yes, you Johnny Miller) complaining about under-representation in this book, read this paragraph again.

Jimmy Demaret won three majors. So did Ralph Guldahl. Julius 'Moose' Boros won the 1968 PGA Championship at the age of 48, eclipsing Old Tom Morris as the oldest man to win a major championship.

Boros was an accountant and spent his twenties practicing and playing amateur golf. He turned pro at the age of 29. Three years later he won the 1952 US Open. Ben Hogan, trying to win three consecutive US Opens, was five shots back.

About Boros, *Sports Illustrated* journalist, Herbert Warren Wind wrote:

> Julius was the most relaxed guy. He seemed to have no nerves, and that made him very dangerous. I also remember that Julius was one of the few players who could stand up to Hogan. He was never scared by him, and at that time, that was pretty hard not to be.

Boros also won the 1963 US Open beating Arnold Palmer and Jacky Cupit in a play-off. Talking of his relaxed approach and quick setup over the ball, he said, 'By the time you get to your ball, if you don't know what to do with it, try another sport.'

Juli Inkster won seven major titles. Pat Bradley won six. Nancy Lopez won the LPGA Championship in 1978, 1985 and 1989. In 1978 Nancy Lopez won five LPGA tournaments in a row including the LPGA Championship, which she also won in '85 and '89.

Tom Kite won the '91 US Open and had nine top-5 finishes at the US Masters. Only Jack Nicklaus (15), Tiger Woods and Phil Mickelson (both 11) have more. Tom Kite has as many top-5 Masters finishes as Ben Hogan, Arnold Palmer, Tom Watson and Sam Snead. From 1975 through to 1986 Kite's finishes at Augusta read: T10, T5, T3, T18, 5th, T6, T5, T5, T2, T6, cut, T2. He was fourth in 1994 and would have won in 1997 had Tiger Woods not shot 18-under and won by 12.

Tom Weiskopf won the 1973 Open Championship at Royal Troon by two shots from Johnny Miller and Neil Coles of England. His 276 tied Arnold Palmer's Open record, also set at Troon.

Weiskopf says of his win:

> It was the best I've ever played, even though I still don't like the course and can't figure it out. Two guys really gave me some confidence. Tony Jacklin called me and said, 'Lad, if you can keep your concentration and play your game, the greatest championship in golf will be yours'. Later I saw Nicklaus, and Jack said, 'Whatever you do, don't play Miller. Play the course'. And that's what I did, concentrate and play the course.

Weiskopf was runner-up in four Masters: 1969, 1972, 1974 and 1975. He was third in the US Open of 1973 and followed up his Open Championship victory with T6 in the PGA Championship. His US Open record from 1972 reads: 8th, 3rd, T15, T29, T2, 3rd, T4, T4.

In four rounds of the 1980 US Masters Tom Weiskopf took 20 shots at the par-3 12th hole including a decuple-bogey 13 in round three after plopping five balls in Rae's Creek. Gary Player once said, 'Tom Weiskopf was a better golfer than Jack Nicklaus, but he didn't fulfil his promise for reasons only he knows about.'

Perhaps that's true.

CHAPTER FIVE

THE KING OF TV

The King

Arnold Palmer won the 1958 US Masters after shooting 82 in the first round. He had played with Ben Hogan (71), their first competitive round together. When Palmer had the green jacket on, Ben Hogan was heard to remark, 'How the hell did *that* happen?'

Palmer won the Masters again in 1960. After three rounds of that year's US Open at Cherry Hills he was behind by seven shots to Mike Souchak. Palmer mused to journalist Bob Drum what might happen if he shot 65. 'Nothing,' replied Drum abruptly. 'You're out of it.'

Palmer was infuriated. He smashed his drive on the par-4 first onto the green. He birdied six of the first seven holes. He shot 65 and beat an amateur called Jack Nicklaus by two and Souchak (75) by three.

Nursing a drink on a flight over the Atlantic for the 1960 Open Championship, Palmer said to Drum (the pair were old friends and confidants) that the 'Grand Slam' that Bobby Jones had won (the US

Amateur, US Open, British Amateur and Open Championship) would be very hard if not impossible for an amateur to win again.

So Palmer suggested that the term 'Grand Slam' be re-applied to the Masters, US Open, Open Championship, and US PGA Championship. Drum liked it and ran with it, effectively lobbied for it. And thus each year, golfers contest and shape their years around the four 'major' grand slam events.

Former IMG man, James Erskine says:

> Palmer single-handedly changed the Open Championship from a big event in Britain to what it is today, which is probably the biggest and most international tournament of all.
>
> There's more hype over the Masters—and of course Palmer helped that tournament, too. But if I had to vote for which was the most important tournament of the year, my money is on the Open Championship. And golf can thank Arnold Palmer for it.

And Arnold Palmer can thank Bob Drum for creating 'Arnold Palmer'. Like Bobby Jones had sports writers, O.B. Keeler and Grantland Rice, to add lustre to legend, Palmer had Bob Drum. He'd always had him. Drum had been writing about the boy since high school.

Drum asked *Golf Digest* in 1987:

> Do you know how many Arnold Palmer stories I wrote? Five thousand, quoting him in every one and half the time I couldn't find him. Palmer still thinks he said all those things.

But if Drum had made the legend, it was Mark McCormack who made it pay. When Palmer shook hands with the young Cleveland lawyer in 1960 to agree that McCormack should look after Palmer's business affairs, it was effectively the invention of sports management. There had been athletes who'd played for money, of course. Professional golf had been around since Allan Robertson, the mentor to Old Tom Morris. Sam Snead appeared in advertisements for Valvoline and pork pie hats. But nobody had managed sports stars the way Mark McCormack did it for Arnold Palmer.

The timing was perfect. There were televisions in most homes. People had money. Golf had been perceived as a sport for the idle rich, not far removed from polo. To an extent, it was. But then Palmer turned up in his pleated pants and open-necked shirt—this well-formed and cool all-American dude—and suddenly golf was exciting, aspirational. McCormack formed International Management Group (IMG). Palmer was a phenomenon. And his brand went global.

Says James Erskine whom McCormack employed in 1976:

> [McCormack] realized that sports were international, that you could have events in America that were huge in Japan and Britain. And Arnold was willing to travel. Golf owes Palmer a huge debt of gratitude.

Palmer spent months of each year in Europe and Australia. He had an extensive business in Japan. He was an earlier version of Seve Ballesteros, a swashbuckler. And he won and won. The man's magnetism enthralled America and the world. And McCormack knew it.

McCormack was the first to realize, and convince others, that golf was entertainment, and that the players were the stars of that entertainment, just as actors and musicians were stars. McCormack convinced the golf establishment—and it took a while—that tournament golf was a show, hence show business.

Televised golf needed a hero. Arnold Palmer was to be it, golf's first TV star. He was golf's first millionaire. He was golf's first King. Palmer's biographer, James Dodson, (*A Golfer's Life*) said this.

> He was the perfect figure for television because of his athleticism, his good looks, the way he played the game. He created the excitement that TV symbolized. It was immediate, it was fresh. It could take people right to the scene in ways media had never done.

And TV was good for Palmer too. He went from earning $60,000 to $500,000 per annum within two years of meeting McCormack. By 1967 Palmer's businesses were generating sales of a massive $15 million ($100 million today).

As Palmer's rival, Jack Nicklaus, once said:

> Arnold is the reason golf enjoys the popularity it does today. He made golf attractive to the television-viewing public. There never has been anyone like him before in the game of golf, and there probably won't be another like him again.

Palmer was exciting and people wanted him to win. James Erskine first met him at Royal Birkdale during the Open Championship of 1961, the year Palmer won. Erskine was eight. When Erskine was 25, he was introduced to Palmer by McCormack. 'I was quite in awe,' recalls Erskine.

> I always remember he stood up at the table. And it was like, 'Oh my, here's Arnold Palmer standing up to meet 25-year-old me. But a lovely guy, very humble. In the early '80s I was at an event in Venice

and there was Arnold Palmer's wife Winifred, Tony Jacklin's wife. Barbara Nicklaus, Vivienne Player, Bob Charles' wife Verity. And we're having dinner one night and I asked them, 'Why are your husbands all so normal?

And Winnie Palmer came up with this line, she said: 'James, when they win the US Open on Sunday, we make them put the garbage out on Tuesday.' And we had a great laugh.

In business, Erskine remembers Palmer was:

very exact about what he wanted to do, and very single-minded. I've never met a successful person in any field who didn't have that, didn't have a large selfish streak in them.

The world of golf lost the great man on 25 September 2016, the same year as Muhammed Ali with whom Palmer once shared Most Famous Sportsman in the World status. When his final tally was done, he'd won seven majors and 95 professional tournaments around the world.

In the first round of the first tournament of the 2016/17 PGA Tour season, the Safeways Open in October, 25-year-old Australian Brett Drewitt hit a pure wedge over some trees, pitched the ball past the hole and sucked it back in for an eagle, much to the acclaim of the beer-infused sales reps in the adjacent corporate tent.

The PGA Tour put footage of the shot on their website as a 'Shot of the Week' as did the Golf Channel, and Drewitt knew a little fleeting fame Internet-style. And there, on his lapel, a stickpin that his girlfriend Brianna had just reminded him to affix, a memento commemorating the life of Arnold Palmer.

The Ayatollah of Golf Broadcasting

Frank Chirkininan is known as the father of golf broadcasting. While the Masters had been filmed for TV prior to Chirkininan producing the TV event, Chirkinian made it accessible and personal for viewers. He gave the Masters its look.

Chirkinian produced the Masters at Augusta for 36 years. He popularized the concept of players being 'under par' or 'over par', 2-under or 5-over, for example. Previously leaders only recorded a four-round score of 280 say, or 290, and that was the number to beat. Chirkinian put plus or minus numbers on leaderboards and on screens. He didn't invent 'par' but he re-cast it.

He had multiple cameras shooting from different angles. He put a camera in a blimp. He sent cameras out with reporters to bring the action to the viewer. He put white paint in golf holes so viewers could see them on TV. Chirkinian put microphones around the green so people could hear the players, the crowd. He put microphones on the tee-box so people could hear the pure strike of Persimmon wood on Balata ball.

He is as responsible as anyone for the characteristic, and strictly regulated, 'look' of The Masters. You never see a camera on the broadcast from Augusta National. You never see anyone inside the ropes who shouldn't be there. Chirkinian thought of Augusta as 'the greatest theatre in sports'.

As Tom Watson put it:

> I give credit to where we are today to Arnold Palmer and television together. And Frank Chirkinian was in the mix right there. He understood the game of golf. He understood the camera angles. He understood what people wanted to see.

What people wanted to see in 1960 was Arnold Palmer. As Chirkinian said of Palmer's TV appeal:

> My first experience with Arnold was in 1959, my first Masters. The camera is strange—it's all-revealing. It either loves you or hates you, and it loved Arnold. And it has ever since.

And as Palmer said of Frank:

> [He] could make the game of golf interesting even when it wasn't interesting. He would say to me, 'Are you planning on doing something different today,' or 'What's your objective?' I would kid him back and say, 'Frank, my objective is to win the golf tournament.' And he, of course, liked that.

They called Chirkinian 'The Ayatollah' for his autocratic style. He quite liked the moniker. In the operations booth he'd say, 'This is not a democracy'. Peter Kostis admits to fear. David Feherty admits to great respect and intense dislike. Nantz said he was 'tough-loved to death' by Chirkinian.

Chirkinian did his first broadcast in 1958, the PGA Championship. He impressed CBS who poached him because they didn't know anyone else who could broadcast golf and thus entertain and inform a growing middle-class audience of SpaghettiOs consumers.

In the early 1980s Chirkinian found another man the camera had a fondness for, the Great White Shark of Australia, Greg Norman. And America fell in love with the Shark too. How could you not? Those piercing blue eyes, the shock of white-blonde hair, the hooked nose, the very shape of him, clothes hanging off his shoulders. As Jarrod Kimber wrote in *Sports Illustrated*:

The godfather of TV golf had found his Mad Max, his Crocodile Dundee, and he put him front and center as often as he could. At times, such was the coverage, you could almost sense Chirkinian's man crush through the lens. Other colorful golfers existed, but Norman was his man. He had his Robert Redford with a club, and he showed him as often as he could.

When Norman folded at Augusta in '96 and Tiger Woods won by 12 shots at Augusta a year later, the baton of compelling all-action man of televised golf passed seamlessly from one man to another. Woods was a good-looking, well-formed African-American kid from Los Angeles with a golf game from another world. The camera loved him as it had loved The King. Ironically Woods's victory in '97 was the first broadcast in 38 years that Frank Chirkinian wasn't involved in. As he said:

> It was the first time in my adult lifetime that I was sitting in front of the TV set watching the Masters from a foreign place: my den. I asked, 'What am I doing here?' I was wallowing in pity.

Yet CBS's cameras remained true to Chirkinian's direction. They captured Woods' every toss of grass, every shirt tug, every dimple on the ball before it was bludgeoned by a low stinging 2-iron. The cameras zoomed in and sucked us all in with them.

Thus was the Way of the Ayatollah, Frank Chirkinian, the man who changed how golf is watched.

CHAPTER SIX

GOLDEN BEAR MARKET

Big Jack

Jack Nicklaus was a big lump of a bloke with a high-pitched voice who could hit the golf ball a country mile. And when he started beating Arnold Palmer in the 1962 US Open at Oakmont—and by dint of that, everybody else—Arnie's 'Army' of Pittsburgh steel workers were loyal to their man and their bets.

'Hit it in the rough, Fat Jack,' they yelled. 'Hit it out-of-bounds, Ohio Fats.'

Palmer looked cooler, more muscular. His clothes were better, fit better, his hairstyle that of a matinee idol. He had that cool squint with his eyes, a Clint Eastwood thing going on, the thousand-yard stare. Nicklaus looked like a tubby farm boy. But that husky kid from Ohio would not be denied. He was bombing drives 30 yards past Palmer off the tee.

And when that US Open came down to an 18-hole play-off, it was Nicklaus who prevailed. And golf's firmament shifted. And the soldiers in Arnie's Army—many locals from Pittsburgh near Palmer's home town who'd been boisterously rooting for their man and their bets thereon— worked it out: this Nicklaus kid (recently coined 'The Golden Bear' by Australian sports writer Don Lawrence) could really play.

They didn't know the half of it.

Since golf began, there's been conjecture over who is the greatest player there's ever been. Yet it's impossible to compare Old Tom Morris with Bobby Jones with Gary Player with Tiger Woods. Equipment, rules, conditions, money; golf has always evolved. But you can compare golfers by numbers. And on statistics alone, Jack Nicklaus is the greatest golfer there has ever been. Consider said numbers.

Nicklaus won 18 major golf championships and was runner-up 19 times. He ran 3rd nine times. He had 56 top-5s and 73 top-10s. In almost half his majors, he was top-10. Read that again: he was on the leaderboard, a contender in half of the majors in which he played.

And that's using data from tournaments Nicklaus was playing as a boy-amateur, and well into his dotage. Narrow it down from 1962 when he won his first major, the US Masters, through to 1986 when he won his 18th, again the US Masters. During this time Nicklaus played an even 100 major championships.

So Nicklaus' winning percentage in that time is 18 per cent. In those 24 years he won one in five major championships. In the same period his top-3 percentage is 42 per cent. So in four out of every ten major tournaments, he was top-3.

His top-10 percentage at major championships in that 24-year period is 67 per cent. So again, in two-thirds of the majors Jack Nicklaus played between 1962 and 1986, he was deemed a good enough chance to win that they put him on the leaderboard.

Narrow the numbers again. In the 1960s he played 36 majors. He won seven of them, again about one in every five. He had eight 2nds and four

3rds. He finished Top-10 23 times. In 36 tournaments he's top-10 in 23.

He was better in the 1970s. owned the '70s. He played 40 majors, every one there was to play. He won eight of them. Again, 20 per cent, one in five. He finished top-10 thirty-five times in 40 major championships. Thirty-five times! Meaning he finished outside the top 10 just five times in 40 major tournaments featuring the world's best players.

In 1971 he was top-5 in all four majors. Same in 1973. In 1972 he won two majors, ran second in another and T13 in the other. In 1975 he had two wins, a T7 and T3.

For 24 years from 1960 through to 1983—let's call it his prime— Nicklaus finished T6 or better in at least one major a year.

He turned 40 on 21 January 1980, and there were pundits speculating if it would signal the start of his decline. He ran T33 in the 1980 Masters, his worst result at Augusta since '67. And pundits mused afresh: is this the end?

Jack Nicklaus answered by winning the 1980 US Open and 1980 US PGA and ran fourth in the 1980 Open Championship. He shot a final round 65 to win the US Masters at Augusta aged 46.

He won the US Masters six times, the US PGA five times, the US Open four times, the Open Championship three times. He was the best putter there's ever been, certainly inside 10 feet. He was long and strong off the tee, immensely so for his time. He'd out-drive Arnold Palmer, himself something of a brute.

On the final hole of the 18-hole play-off with Doug Sanders in the 1970 Open Championship at St Andrews, Nicklaus took his Persimmon wood and belted the ball through the green, a blow of 360 yards.

He won the Masters in 1965 and 1966 and hit the ball so long Augusta National's members lengthened the 18th.

He won his 13th major in 1972, the US Open. The wind blew most everyone off Pebble Beach that year, only Bruce Crampton (who would finish runner-up to Nicklaus in majors four times) and Arnold Palmer got close. He'd already won the 1972 Masters and headed to Muirfield with everyone, including Nicklaus, thinking Grand Slam. He ran second to Lee Trevino. And T13 behind Gary Player in the PGA.

He did win the PGA the next year, though. And in 1975. And in 1980. So there was plenty to console him.

*** *** ***

Big Mac

Mark McCormack invented appearance money. Yes, Tom Morris Junior would demand to be paid up front for turning up. But McCormack was the first to say to tournament promoters that if you have Player X—say, Gary Player or Greg Norman—then you will generate Y money for your tournament through gate takings, sponsorship and television ratings. And thus you should pay the player for turning up.

Normal today but preposterous and unthinkable before McCormack. For the players—and Seve Ballesteros and Greg Norman were vocal about it at the time—it was a no-brainer. As Greg Norman said:

> Appearance money was going on before me. It went on during my time and it goes on today. It goes on in all sports. I got appearance money in Australia, I got appearance money everywhere I played in the world, to tell you the truth, even the United States, even though paying appearance money was against the PGA Tour rules.

Norman would be paid to speak at a lunch or a dinner. It wasn't called 'appearance money', but he was paid to appear.

And rightly so, Norman argued:

You're an independent contractor, you have the right to earn a living any way you want to earn a living. So the restrictions put on us were a little bit suffocating to some degree, because they were against our right to earn a living. Seve and I were really staunch about it. We'd say, 'Hey, we are independent contractors. We can go where we want to go, play where we want to play, get what we wanna get.'

Norman suggests that the PGA Tour and golf administration in general should have been more transparent.

They didn't seek the advice of the top players, who were the ones putting bums on the seats, pulling the TV rights, the TV deals. The players were the ones bringing in the sponsors in. I can name eight or 10 of us, it wasn't just me. There were ten of us that really carried the game. And I think we didn't get a fair whack of it to tell you the truth. We did well because we played well and won our prize money. But at the end of the day I think that the distribution of wealth was a little bit skewed.

Yet golf—and by golf one means the establishment (what might today in these fractious modern times be termed 'the elites')—remained aghast. One can hear the protests: P-p-ay players for turning up? We invite them. It should be for honour. We put on the show. They are but minstrels.

But honour never paid a bill. And capitalism, like love, found a way. And McCormack found Arnold Palmer. And that was all she wrote.

Through the enduring popularity and the two champions who

competed with him, Gary Player and Jack Nicklaus, McCormack realized that players' brands had longevity beyond their playing days. He realized that he could still sell a Golden Bear shirt or a Palmer golf course design long after the players had stopped competing. No-one had thought of licensing, merchandising. IMG did not stop with golf. IMG promoted the Olympics. IMG promoted the Pope's tour of Britain in 1982. IMG, bless them, invented the corporate tent.

Norman's manager, Frank Williams met with Mark McCormack regularly and would swap ideas in brainstorming sessions. 'He was a very hands-on operator,' says Williams. 'In Australia though he left most things to James [Erskine].' Williams can't think of anyone else who did what McCormack did.

> He did have Arnold Palmer, which helped. But he made an art of it. It was a very good business. People think IMG is too powerful. But they are just very good at what they do. On average, they would triple or quadruple an athlete's net worth.

As journalist Clay Latimer wrote in *Investors Business Daily*:

> Over the course of his groundbreaking career, *Golf* magazine called McCormack 'the most powerful man in golf'. *Tennis* magazine said he was 'the most powerful man in tennis'. *Sports Illustrated* cited him as 'the most powerful man in sports'. And the *Times* of London noted he was 'one of the 1,000 people who have most influenced the 20th century'.

Yet McCormack wasn't a brash or outwardly confident man, according to Erskine. If anything, he was socially inept. Erskine explains.

> He was almost awkward. There was a shy part to

him. He wasn't shy doing business but he was not always comfortable in people's company. But it worked for him. He had an amazing memory and was in his way a quietly confident man. But by always letting the other person talk first, if you don't ask the number yourself, someone might offer you double what you think.

Upon McCormack's death in 2003, President of CBS Sports, Sean McManus said that McCormack, like Henry Ford and Bill Gates, 'literally created and fostered and led an entirely new worldwide industry'.

There was no sports marketing industry before Mark McCormack. Every athlete who's ever appeared in a commercial, or every right holder who sold their rights to anyone, owes a huge debt of gratitude to Mark McCormack.

Mark McCormack wasn't just a 'pioneer' of sports marketing. He just about invented it.

**

Little Mac

In 1976 James Erskine was a medical student from Birkdale in the north-west of England. His father ran amateur tournaments and was employed by the R&A to help run Open Championships. Young James was familiar with tournament golf. He grew up 'inside the ropes', part of the scene, friendly with stewards.

At the '76 Open (at Birkdale, won by Johnny Miller by six shots from Seve Ballesteros and Jack Nicklaus), Erskine was helping his father with crowd control when he met IMG boss Mark McCormack. And the pair hit it off. The kid was smart, had an opinion.

McCormack asked Erskine who he'd sign if he could. Erskine promptly said Nick Faldo, Sandy Lyle and Martin Foster. McCormack took him to lunch and offered him a job. Erskine told McCormack that he'd work six months for nothing; after that they could talk money. McCormack said it was a stupid idea, asked what would a young doctor be paid, and paid him that.

And Erskine found he quite liked the sports management business.

'I had two advantages,' says Erskine, today chief executive of Sports and Entertainment Limited (SEL).

> My father ran tournaments so I knew a lot of these players. Nick Faldo in his spare time we'd go fishing for carp, I knew his parents. I knew about golf, knew the people in golf. I knew a guy called Gerard Nicklin, President of the England Golf Union. George Bloomberg, a South African who was very friendly with McCormack, took me under his wing.

Erskine's time with IMG began when he was sent to Jersey to see Tony Jacklin, then the best player in Britain. Jacklin had issues with IMG's management of his affairs and wanted out. Erskine heard him out and talked him out of leving IMG. The pair got on so well that Jacklin asked McCormack to appoint Erskine as his manager.

McCormack sent Erskine to IMG's head office in Cleveland, Ohio, for a meeting with IMG's 'suits'. Erskine sat there listening for an hour to the 'waffle' of business types pontificating, and then said:

> You've got it wrong—all these players want is to play golf while we generate them money. They'll stay with us if we do, and they'll leave us if we don't.

The accountants were taken aback. It couldn't be that simple. Could it be that simple? It was that simple. As Erskine said of the meeting:

> It was common sense. I didn't have a business degree, never been to a business lecture. Never been interested. What I've picked up has been from people, and Mark McCormack.
>
> Me talking out like that, I didn't see it as a risk; it wasn't my 'big chance'. If it didn't work out I could always go back to medicine. I didn't know how good I was going to be at it. But I found out I was pretty good at it, and I enjoyed it. And I had success quickly and was rewarded quickly.

And so, IMG grew. By 1976, there were offices around the world. There was 'competition' not worthy of the name. Nobody had the clout. Nobody had offices in Japan, contacts all around the world. IMG evolved into selling television rights, merchandising, convincing corporations to use sport for the benefit of their brand. There was nobody else in that league.

And IMG signed whomever they liked. As Erskine explains:

> It wasn't like today when there's a pitch to sign a player, where you have to persuade people. I'd sign up anybody I wanted to. I very rarely got a no— in fact I can't remember one. Faldo, Sandy Lyle, Martin Foster. Bernhard Langer, I met him as an amateur in Germany.

Meanwhile there were rumblings Down Under in Australia. Greg Norman had won the 1976 Westlakes Classic at the age of 21 and looked a hot commodity. McCormack sent Erskine to setup an office in Sydney. Kerry Packer wanted IMG within his offices. McCormack liked the sound of that because it would be cheap. Erskine argued that you couldn't do business with the other networks from the office of Packer's network. That was precisely the point for Packer. Erskine set up shop nearby. He was going to stay for two years. He still calls Sydney home today.

✻ ✻ ✻

The Other Masters

In the 1960s and '70s, IMG made the Big Three: Palmer, Player, Nicklaus. And as color TV turned up, their brand awareness among consumers rose. From about 1980, Greg Norman was seen by IMG as the natural progression from those guys. TV loved the man. He was fit, tall and blonde. And he had the golf game of Jack Nicklaus and the gambling instinct of Kerry Packer.

By the time he was 25, Norman knew enough about the possibilities of superstardom. Bjorn Borg had won five Wimbledon Championships in a row. John McEnroe and Jimmy Connors were world-famous and wealthy men. Arnold Palmer was a giant; a man second only in global appeal to Muhammad Ali.

Norman knew enough to know that success relied on a strong media presence. In his first press conference at the 1980 Masters, he talked of shark hunting in Queensland. They started calling him the 'Great White Shark'. It stuck. And he was away. Says James Erskine:

> [IMG] realized very quickly that Greg was a sensational talent. Everyone knew. He had an English manager at the time and wasn't being advised correctly. He was in a bit of a bind with tax based out of Hong Kong. We hatched a plan how

to get Greg Norman which involved solving the tax thing, which we did. And Norman came on board. It was crucial to our business.

Erskine reckons that Norman has had more impact on golf in Australia than any other person.

In the 1980s, television networks wanted golf. And here was this Aussie, number one in the world for over 300 weeks. He looked the part. He mixed with presidents, royalty. And when he walked into a room everybody stopped and listened to him. He had the most amazing persona.

Greg gets criticized for all sorts of things. But for so long he supported Australian golf. Sure he got paid, sure he did deals, sure he was part of the action on all sorts of stuff. But he was very much the pied piper. You could go into Holden or Carlton United Breweries and ask the corporates if they'd like to play with Norman in the Pro-Am. Of course they would. Well, kick in this amount of money and Greg will see you on the tee.

A teacher called David Gair Inglis—who would introduce himself as 'DGI' and tell people it stood for damn good ideas—created the Australian Masters in 1979 as an unashamed copy of the one at Augusta. It would be played at the same course each year—Huntingdale in the Melbourne sandbelt—and winners would receive a yellow jacket.

Gair's experience in running golf tournaments amounted to promoting the local—and extremely modest—Box Hill Open. As he told golf reporter Peter Stone from *The Age*, he'd also written and produced a children's play called *Make Me A Smile*, which was staged at Melbourne's Regent Theatre.

'How long did it last?' asked Stone.

'One day,' said Gair.

But Stone was duly convinced the Australian Masters had sufficient star power — Lee Trevino was coming, Greg Norman was coming, local heroes Ian Stanley and Bob Shearer were on board — and promoted the event in his journal. And thus the famously sports-loving public of Melbourne heard about a brand new golf tournament bearing the oxymoronic slogan, 'A New Tradition'.

Apart from financial stress—Inglis couldn't pay Lee Trevino to attend; the players nearly boycotted when prize-money was reduced, and it took something of a whip-around to come up with $10,000 to ensure the tournament wasn't cancelled altogether—the first Australian Masters tournament got off the ground. And made a $50,000 loss

A successful vacuum cleaner salesman called Frank Williams was approached to bail DGI's Masters out of the financial hole, which Williams did. He'd always loved golf, had played at Sunningdale in England as a boy. So, Williams tipped in the $50,000 on the condition he would own a half share in the venture.

'We did it really well the second year,' says Williams. 'And with my input and expertise we lost a quarter million!'

But Williams and Inglis doubled down. They found money for appearance fees for superstars Nicklaus Palmer, Ballesteros, Langer, Woosnam, Strange. They sold the concept to national TV broadcaster, Channel Seven, who agreed to give them 24 hours of airtime. They sold advertising space to advertisers, recruited sponsors and pitched it hard to the greater Melbourne sports-watching public. And they sold it as a battle between one man, the Great White Shark Greg Norman, and the world's greatest players.

As Williams says of the tournament:

> It was a marketing exercise, the Masters. The
> second year we decided we were going to make it
> a tournament worth coming to see with a lot of
> overseas players. Initially everyone had treated it
> as a bit of joke. So, we spent money on appearance
> fees, which some say is a bad thing, some say is a
> good thing. But if you wanted a decent tournament,
> you've got to have worldwide 'name' players.

Greg Norman bought in. He promoted the event by jumping out an airplane, emerging from a Huntingdale lake in scuba gear. Whatever they asked, the Shark did it. And where the Shark went, people followed. And everyone got paid.

Norman won the Australian Masters six times. Adam Scott won it. Tiger Woods won it. Colin Montgomerie had a rare win outside Europe when he finished 10-under in 2001. The 1961 US Open winner Gene 'The Machine' Littler won the second one in 1980 aged 50. Other winners include Ian Poulter, Justin Rose and Bernhard Langer.

The tournament became so successful that Williams and Inglis visited Augusta to watch the US Masters to see what they could learn from Augusta's green jackets. Their enquiries received short shrift, according to Williams:

> They won't tell you anything, let me tell you! They
> won't tell you how they do it, where they get the
> money from, nothing... and quite rightly so ...
> We tried to pick their brains—it didn't work at
> all. You couldn't see anyone to get a sit-down.

Yet word did reach Augusta National Chairman Clifford Roberts that a pair of Australians were asking questions. Soon enough they were summonsed to Roberts' office. Williams recalls the meeting:

> We had a five-minute meeting with Clifford Roberts in which he told us he'd prefer we didn't use the term 'Masters' and he gave us a list of other names that we could use. We were very polite. We were guests of the tournament. But inwards we thought, you know, 'fuck you'.
>
> So, we left the room feeling a bit patronized. We thought he could've been a little more cordial, made a little more effort, been more forthgiving. But I worked it out later what he was doing was protecting his product.
>
> Even though we told him by copying their Masters it was a form of flattery, he wasn't having it. He said, 'There's only one Masters and this is it. I don't want you to run an Australian Masters. Here's a list of acceptable names.
>
> So he's handed us this sheet of paper with a list of names that he says he and Augusta are okay with as names for our tournament. I can't remember what was on the list. They were pretty bizarre.

So, did Williams keep that piece of paper?

> No, we tore it up pretty quickly! I mean, it was probably flattering for us that Clifford Roberts would take the time to see us, and that he felt that it was important enough that he'd write out a list of 'acceptable' names. But we didn't see it as flattering at the time. [Laughs] We were pretty full

of ourselves!

Basically, Augusta National is a law unto themselves. And the reason that tournament is so successful is that they keep it very exclusive and in-house. Even the television people don't get the co-operation. There's a certain 'look' of it. There's no sponsorship. And I think, for them, it's the right the way to go. I didn't at the time! But thinking about it, if I had a product like that, I'd be protective also.

In 1987 Inglis sold his share to Williams who later sold it to IMG. Williams then joined the company as a 'consultant'. Norman later split with IMG and took Williams with him to form Great White Shark Enterprises. And that became more than a business. It became an empire.

CHAPTER SEVEN

THE SHARK AND OTHER BASTARDS

The Great White Himself

G reg Norman hails from the state of Queensland, Australia—a
massive land famous for many stinging, deadly things, notably box
jellyfish, 20 of the world's top 25 most venomous snakes, and, of course,
the ocean-going, man-eating great white shark. Queensland is so big
you could fit Texas into it twice and still have room for California. You
could slot Spain, France, Italy and Belgium within the state borders of
Queensland. The funny little country of Luxembourg would fit inside
mighty Queensland 700 times. It's a bloody big state, Queensland.

And from it have emerged some bloody big men and women. There
was the crazy, crocodile hunting man, the late Steve Irwin, who never
knew a massive python he couldn't wrestle. Film director George Miller
came from Brisbane to make *Mad Max* and then *Happy Feet* and then
Mad Max again. Then there was Cathy Freeman, Olympic gold medal
winner and the champion golfer, Karrie Webb—to name a few.

Queenslanders call themselves '*Queenslanders*', and tend to thump their chests when doing it.

The state has produced seven major champions: Jason Day, Adam Scott, Wayne Grady, Steve Elkington, Ian Baker-Finch, Karrie Webb and, of course, the great man, the Great White Shark, Greg Norman.

You could say Queensland rubbed off on each person, that the sun-bleached sub-tropics gets into a golfer's very pores. Yet the state seems to have imbued most in Norman. Greg Norman is big.

Big? During the torch relay prior to the Sydney Olympic Games in 2000, Norman passed the Olympic torch to the Mayor of Sydney on the middle of Sydney Harbour Bridge. At the closing ceremony in front 110,000 people, Norman emerged from the fin of a giant shark, touched the brim of his trademark Akubra hat, and whacked plastic golf balls at the crowd.

He was co-pilot in an F-14 fighter plane that landed on the deck of aircraft the USS *Carl Vinson*. He broke the sound barrier in a jet from the US Navy's elite aerobatic squadron, the Blue Angels, passing out under the extreme 8.4 G-forces.

He gave Donald Trump's phone number to the Prime Minister of Australia, Malcolm Turnbull, so that Turnbull could, presumably, explain that Australia is an ally of the United States and not the birthplace of Adolf Hitler—Australia, Mr President, not Austria!

To paraphrase Ron Burgundy in the movie, *Anchorman* (2004), Greg Norman is kind of a big deal. He's massive, Greg Norman.

***

The Madness of Greatness

Before the Shark was 'The Shark' he was a baby, born Gregory John Norman on 10 February 1955 in 'The Isa', short for Mount Isa, a roughn-tumble mining town 1,800 kilometres north-east of the state capital, Brisbane and 2,400 kilometres from Sydney. Up in Gulf Country, closer to the Kakadu National Park in Northern Territory than Canberra, it's the bush, baby, the great Outback—hotter than hell. Lead in the air, zinc in the ground, pubs full of rum-soaked yahoos.

So the family packed up baby Greg and headed due east, a little 10-hour drive away, to the tropical (and aptly-named) town of Townsville, which is effectively the bush by the Great Barrier Reef. And thus Greg grew up hunting things and shooting them with a spear, often underwater. He fished and dived and rode horses bareback along the beach. He rode a skim-board in the shallows and ran with his dog. He was Huck Finn in a footy jumper, with a mop of blond hair—very white-blonde hair, a sun-kissed mix highly coveted in Australian surfing circles.

The bleached hair look was so cool enough that men would wash their hair with any clothes-washing detergent that contained peroxide. And peroxide wasn't used to color men's hair in those times, it would have been considered effete. So, men used the detergent in their hair and pretended they didn't.

When Greg was 14, the family headed south to Brisbane where he played footy in winter and cricket in summer because that's what Australian boys did. He took to surfing and shark-hunting and bombing about in tricked-up billy-karts.

His father Merv was a very handy man and Greg admired that his dad could make things, and improve them. The boy applied the ideal to his own self. Self-improvement became his thing. He strove to be better—with a vengeance.

If young Greg were making a raft, it would be the best raft he could make. It would have an outboard motor and sails and space for a Jacuzzi. When later he owned boats so big they carried boats that carried boats, and helicopters, and executive chefs, and Bill Clinton, if he saw a nick on the timber deck, he'd get down on his knees and sand it off.

> Did I trick up a billy cart? Of course. Every kid tries to trick up a billy cart. I used to make model airplanes to hang from the ceiling. I built model trains. My dad built a sailing boat that we'd sail. I was involved with it. I used to ride my horse bareback all of the time. That was self-discipline, the amount of times you'd fall off that. Snorkelling off Magnetic Island, you're out there on your own, nobody knows you're out there.
>
> Stuff like that where you had to get a sense of confidence, and belief in yourself and no fear. If you get yourself into an interesting predicament, get yourself out of it.

So yes, Norman's is a special kind of madness: the madness of greatness. And then, just before he was 16, Norman found golf. And the kid with a bent for self-improvement found a hobby with no limits. He'd had a crack at stamp collecting, but that was never going to hold him. He had a thing for planes, had a fantasy about wanting to be a fighter pilot (a top gun), had a thing for slashing through the air, 'turn and burn', shooting baddies. Yet he'd decided—while waiting in the recruitment office of the Royal Australian Air Force—that he didn't want to join the Royal Australian Air Force. Standing there with the old man, Merv, thinking about it, he thought, *Nah, not for me.*

But golf, well, how good you could be at golf was dependent on how hard you tried. No limits. Attack. And the more Norman attacked it and strove to improve, the more he improved. He began as a 27-marker and within 18 months he was off scratch. His learning curve was a ski-jump. The kid loved it.

I enjoyed the individual aspect of golf more than I enjoyed team sport. Now, I don't want people to take that the wrong way. What I mean is I always gauged my performance on how I did. So, if I did a tremendous job playing rugby or cricket and my team lost, I'd know the rest of your team did that. Or if my team won but I felt as though I didn't perform I'd question myself and tell yourself not to do that again.

When I found golf, it was a reward-based sport. You go from 27 to 26 to 25 handicap, you feel like you've accomplished something. So, every time you achieve a milestone or there's another milestone to achieve.

He turned pro at the age of 21. A few months later, and just five years after first picking up a club, Norman won his first professional tournament, Adelaide's West Lakes Classic. He won by five shots. Smashed 'em.

A week later he was on the first tee with Jack Nicklaus in the Australian Open. So nervous he cold-topped his tee shot. Nicklaus sat down with him in the dressing shed afterwards, told him he could make it in the States. It was music to his ears. Norman recalls:

We had a good chat together in front of our lockers … and he basically said, 'Look, you have the game, you would play well in America because it was a power game' He was impressed by my driving, he was impressed with the position that I had at the top of my swing. He said 'You have very good control in your game and would be very successful in the United States. If I was you I'd go and play there'.

Norman took it on board but gave himself three years to get better. 'If I was going to go into the lion's den, which the PGA Tour really is, you'd better be ready to fight with the lions.'

He went to Japan, to Europe. He won the Martini International in Scotland. He won the French Open by ten shots. He beat Sandy Lyle in the World Matchplay. By 1981 he was ready.

> I knew I'd like the United States because it's a good culture … very much like Australia. The food, the people, the lifestyle's easy. Same language. I just wanted to make sure I'd be extremely sharp.

Arnold Palmer convinced him to settle in Orlando. He joined Palmer's Bay Hill Country Club. He'd play golf with The King five days a week. They drank beer, played cards, shot the shit as they say. Norman was brought into the King's inner sanctum. And his self-belief grew. And from there he did what he'd always done: tried to get better.

And better he became. So much better that he was better than everyone else in the world for longer than anyone else except Eldrick 'Tiger' Woods. Norman was 331 weeks as number one, six years at the pinnacle, the top golden brick of a pyramid with a perimeter the size of Queensland.

✱✱✱

Saturday Slam

By the end of 1986 Norman was world No. 1 and owned what they'd call a 'Saturday Slam' or 'Norman Slam' after leading every major championship after three rounds. He won the Open Championship at Turnberry by five shots after rounds of 74–63–74–69. Then he didn't win the other three in ever-creative ways.

In the Masters Jack Nicklaus, aged 46, came storming home to shoot

30 on the last nine at Augusta and card 7-under 65. Nobody's holding Jack back; no-one is keeping the great champion at bay.

Although Norman had a crack. He birdied 14, 15, 16 and 17 to square things up at 9-under. And the Augusta crowd thought, *here we go.* Standing the middle of 18, 184 yards out, up hill, Norman needed par to force a play-off. He was in between clubs, a 4-iron or 5-iron. Should he go hard with the 5 or caress the 4? The pin was back right, top tier. His adrenaline was bubbling. He chose the 4-iron. He blocked it right.

When he couldn't get up and down with a bump-n-run, his bogey-five meant Nicklaus had won his sixth green jacket and his 18th major golf championship. Norman later said if he change one thing, it would be that approach on 18. He would swap the 4-iron for a 5-iron and gone at it, hard.

It's how the Shark played. He figured he'd got there by going hard, going at flags; he would bloody well win the same way. Where others (most?) might have hit a 5-iron to the middle of the green before rolling up a couple of putts to get into the play-off, Norman tried to stiff it. He tried to raise the roof. He tried to win.

When it came off, he thrilled us, the great big bomber. Laser-beaming 3-irons at flags, stringing together brilliant runs of four, five, seven birdies in a row. When his putter got hot, he could overpower the field, own the golf course. Except when he couldn't. As he couldn't at Augusta.

In 1986 the US Open was won by 43-year-old husky man, Raymond Floyd who shot a final round 66 and waited two hours while everyone else bombed on in with bogies. Norman was among them. He carded 76; didn't make Top-10.

Norman had told reporters his losses at Augusta to Nicklaus earlier that year and in an 18-hole play-off to Fuzzy Zoeller at Winged Foot in the US Open of '84 had made him smarter. 'I'm street-smarter,' Norman told reporters at a press conference before the '86 US Open. 'The more you play on the American tour, the tougher you get.'

'Boy is Norman getting tough,' observed Rick Reilly in *Sports Illustrated*. The day before Norman had been heckled after a double-bogey on 13. 'You're chokin', Norman,' yelled a man, fortified by beer and the knowledge he was safe on his side of the ropes. Norman hit an 8-iron into 14, strode to the ropes, ducked under and located the fellow. He pointed at the man and commanded: 'You! Come here!'

The man obeyed. And Norman told him: 'If you want to say that, then say it to me afterward. But until then, shut your face!' And said face did indeed remain shut, the heckler giving no indication he fancied continuing the conversation in the car park afterwards.

And so across the Atlantic in July to Turnberry for the 1986 British Open Championship on the outer Firth of Clyde in south-west Scotland.

'The way Turnberry set up that week, I knew it played right up my strengths,' says Norman.

> The fairways were narrow but in practice rounds I was driving the ball well. I was making a lot of power fades in those days, I could aim down the left side of the fairway and I would just use the entire 15 or 18 yards of fairway width. Most people would try to fit the ball into half a fairway. I was using the entire width. I was so confident with my driver that week.
>
> And I told myself—I do remember this very distinctly—'Do not back off your driver. Do not start laying up if you feel you can get in good position. Just keep driving the golf ball'.

And he did. He smoked it down the guts time and again—long. First round in tough conditions he shot 74, four from Ian Woosnam. Second round, boom! 63, and he led by one. His 63 was equal the lowest score in Open Championship history for a round. He might've shot 61 but for an eagle putt on 17 that slid by and three-putting 18. There were times in the round he thought he'd break 59.

Into the last round and Norman led by one from Tsuneyuki 'Tommy' Nakajima of Japan with Gordon Brand (England) and Woosnam (Wales) three back. On the third hole, Norman holed his bunker shot. 'When it went in, it felt like I was never going to miss. It gave me that little extra shot of confidence. I went from a one-shot to a two-shot lead and all of a sudden I was having a three- or four-shot lead very quickly and I just settled to my game.'

He won by five and walked up 18 like he was fighting his way out of a riot. Of that moment, Norman says:

> It was a euphoric feeling, the absorption of how the spectators were so in the moment. I had to punch and get my way through, it was 30–40 people deep. People were slapping me on the back and yelling and screaming—they're happy for you.

It was his first major championship win, at even-par, five strokes ahead of runner-up Gordon J. Brand.

In the PGA Championship of August 1986 at Ohio's Inverness Club, Norman led by four shots over Bob Tway with eight holes to go. His drive on 11 found a divot and he found double-bogey. Tway birdied 13, Norman bogied 14 and they were all square all of a sudden with four holes to go.

It was the first time since the end of round one on the Thursday that Norman hadn't owned sole lead. And there he was, four to play, head-to-head in pseudo match-play action to win the Wannamaker Trophy.

Yet Norman remained confident. His driving, as ever, had been imperious, best practice, the world's most intimidating long-bomber. He found the next three greens and made pars while Tway made miraculous saves on 15 and 17 from terrible greenside rough. And they were square on the tee at 18.

Norman boomed his drive down the middle. Tway found the rough. Tway's approach found a bunker, Norman's the green, before sucking off the front. Advantage Norman.

Tway's bunker shot was on the upslope but he'd short-sided himself, the green running downwards to the flag and beyond. There was maybe six feet between hard green and 3¼ inch hole. So, pretty tough shot.

Which, of course, Tway holed before jumping up and down rather a lot, in unison with hundreds of marshals in long red happy pants. Norman had to chip in to force a play-off but could not. Tway, 27, won his first and only major.

Norman had been unlucky, sure. But he'd also shot 40 on the back nine for 76 to lose a major that he'd led by four with eight holes to go. By the end of '86 he was crowned world's best player for the first time. Yet people wondered, is there some mental weakness? And the press asked him: is there some mental weakness? And he didn't really like it.

And Norman could make a case that, no, there wasn't. Because 1986 was his most successful year as a professional golfer. He won eleven times. He won the Open Championship, Las Vegas Invitational, Kemper Open, European Open, World Matchplay, Dunhill Cup, PGA Grand Slam of Golf and four tournaments in Australia. And people are asking does he choke?

It was like that every year, every major, all through the '80s and '90s. For twenty years, Australians got up early or stayed up late to watch lesser players beat Norman home in major championships. Such were the peaks and troughs of the Shark fan.

In '88 at Augusta, Norman shot 8-under 64 on the final day in a doomed charge at Sandy Lyle. In '89 he shot 67 in the final round but bogied 18 to finish one shot from a play-off with Nick Faldo (65, the winner) and Scott Hoch (69).

In the 1984 US Open, ol' Fuzzy Zoeller watched Norman hit the ball into the grandstand on 18 but hole a 45-footer to make par and share the lead. Zoeller waved a white towel from the fairway in jest then made par to force an 18-hole play-off. They came back the next day for 18 holes. Zoeller won by nine.

In the final round of the 1989 Open Championship at Royal Troon Norman shot a brilliant course record 64 to get into a four-hole play-off with Calcavecchia and fellow Queenslander Wayne Grady.

Norman birdied the first two play-off holes to take a one-stroke lead over the American. On the par-3 17th, he went through the hole, the ball resting on the fringe. He used a chipper that came out hot; the ball hit the flag and bounced away 10 feet. He didn't make the putt. Calcavecchia made par. Grady was as good as gone.

All square on 18, it's here that Norman did what he often did. He attacked. He took a driver because that's just what he did. Even with a steep-faced fairway bunker within his range on the right, the big man launched his mighty persimmon whacking stick because he was the best in the world at launching whacking-sticks, so why not?

Well, because there was a chance, even if slim, Shark, that the ball might run and run on ground packed hard by spectators and sunshine, and that you might send driver into said bunker. And then you'd be left with a sand-wedge that has to come out sideways, and ends up in a fairway bunker the other side of the fairway. And then, desperate, you might go hard at your fourth shot and send it out of bounds.

'I played crap,' Grady told *Inside Sport* much later. '[Norman] played crap. He just out-crapped me.' And that's how Mark Calcavecchia beat Greg Norman to win the Open Championship of 1988.

***

Larry Mize and Other Bastards

Every year, from early 1980s through to the late 1990s—and even once in 2008 at Royal Birkdale when Greg Norman turned back time but not Padraigh Harrington—it seemed like someone would up and mug Norman, occasionally the man himself.

Jack Nicklaus, Ray Floyd, Bob Tway, Tom Watson, Paul Azinger, Corey Pavin, Mark Calcavecchia, Nick Faldo (twice, and we will talk more of him), Larry Mize (ditto, the bastard), Jose Maria Olazabal, Fuzzy Zoeller and that man Harrington all bested Norman in major championships. And how fans keened and sledged Norman in equal measure.

At Augusta in 1987, Larry Mize won his first and only major championship after a chip on the second play-off hole against Norman that hit the flag dead centre and dropped in. And off went Mize on a mad jiggy dash around the green, pumping both fists like a happy, wild man.

Sarah Ballard in *Sports Illustrated* wrote:

> Of the dozens of ways Greg Norman could have lost the 1987 Masters tournament, this had to be the unlikeliest: a 140-foot chip shot that bounced twice up a grassy bank and once on the putting surface before it rolled halfway across the 11th green directly into the hole.
>
> That this miracle shot was hit by 28-year-old Larry Mize, a local boy, no less, who had won only one tournament in his six years on the PGA Tour, and that it beat the luckless Norman, the premier player in the world, on the second hole of a sudden-death playoff, made it downright unbelievable.

Norman was devastated.

> I didn't think Larry would get down in two, and I was right. He got down in one. This is probably the toughest loss I've ever had. The PGA was tough, but this one ... because of the shot ... I think I'm more disappointed now than in any tournament I've played.

Earlier, on the 18th, Norman had sailed the bunker on the left of the fairway and left himself 90 yards up hill to the flag. He hit a sand-wedge to the top tier that sat 20 feet. Birdie would win it. He let the putt go, and thought it was in. 'Don't say a word,' he said to himself ... and watched it trickle along low-side, brushing the left edge of the cup.

Norman couldn't believe it.

> I still don't know how the putt stayed out. When it was about a foot, foot and a half out, I said to myself, 'Don't say a word because it's going in'. I just couldn't believe it missed, nor could my caddie, Pete [Bender]. He was just as taken aback as I was.

Watching on from Jones Cabin was Mize and Ballesteros. The Spaniard turned to the American and said: 'It's okay, Larry, you can breathe now.'

Mize would win twice more on the US tour, both in 1993. He would contend at Augusta a couple of times and won a Champions Tour event in 2010, and still goes around in the Masters where he made the cut and finished 52nd in 2017. And he remains best known as the man who slayed The Shark, and danced a jig on his grave.

Worse would follow.

Car Wreck

Johann Rupert is a South African billionaire who has owned Dunhill and Cartier and many, many things. On the Saturday night of the 1996 US Masters at Augusta, he offered Greg Norman's manager, Frank Williams, $100,000 for a betting stub Williams held that would be worth $140,000 if/when Norman turned his six-shot overnight lead into ultimate victory. Williams response: 'You've got to be joking. It's a six shot lead.'

By Sunday afternoon Rupert was nowhere to be found. Williams has no regrets, however. 'If Greg had ever found out I'd sold the ticket, he'd never forgive me. It was never considered.'

That Sunday, 14 April 1996 marks the Shark's most famous immolation. He led by six strokes going into the final round at Augusta and lost by five to Nick Faldo who fired a sensational, almost completely forgotten, 67.

Because that year at Augusta, it was all Shark. It was peak Shark. He opened his tournament by equalling the course record of 63 (co-held with Nick Price). No-one has shot a lower score in major championship golf. There followed fine rounds of 69 and 71 as most others went south.

And then, after Norman had finished his third round, the (in-part apocryphal) story of how the British journalist, Peter Dobereiner sidled up to Norman 'in the urinal' and uttered the line: 'I don't think even you can fuck it up from here, Greg.'

Norman corrects the story.

> Well, it wasn't a conversation. And we weren't in the bathroom, it was at the bar. I was one of the last few people to get out of the locker rooms and I wanted to have a drink, I was thirsty. I went up to the bar to get a bottle of water and he just walked up to me

and said, 'Not even you could fuck this up'. I turned
to him and I knew who he was and I was kind of
surprised. I said to myself 'Greg, just block that out
as hard as you can'. So I left and I didn't bring it up
until years later. But he's the one and only guy who
has ever come up and said something like that. So
take it for what it is, I guess.

The next day, that Sunday, was a car-wreck, a final round littered with
dropped shots until the great man dropped himself onto the sloping false
front of 15 as a chip for eagle just missed. It was excrutiating to watch.
He would shoot 78.

After they putted out on the final green, Faldo, a man not known for
compassion, displayed empathy that many—and perhaps even Faldo
himself—didn't know he possessed. He hugged Norman and whispered
in his ear: 'Don't let the bastards get you down.'

Coming from a fellow pro, a warrior, a man Norman knew was as single-
minded as himself, it meant plenty. The Shark knew what Faldo meant by
'bastards'—the press, those critical, reptilian man-beasts who would ask the
unflinchingly hard and unfriendly questions the world wanted to know. To
wit: had Norman just perpetrated the greatest choke in the history of the
Masters? Of major championship golf? Of the very game itself?

And so into the tent he went, the Great White Shark, chest out,
shoulders back, to face the beasts. He never flinched. And the journos
didn't hold back, peppering him with allusions to choking. And
men who'd tighten up on the 16th tee in their local club's Wednesday
stableford competition asked the world's number one golfer how he
could have (to coin a phrase) so fucked it up.

Norman did his best to explain it, to break it down. But eventually he
just half-laughed, threw up his hands, actually and metaphorically, and

said, 'I played like shit, okay?'

Post-round Team Norman was terribly dejected. As Williams recalls:

I'll tell you a great thing about Greg. Everybody was very upset. I was with his wife and daughter, who are crying, I'm crying ... and Butch [Harmon, coach] is crying and we all go back to the plane and Greg says, 'I'll be there after I've done the interviews.

So he comes on to the plane and we're all in tears, we're all devastated. He says: 'I don't understand you people. I get paid a lot of money to hit a little while ball from A to B better than anybody else. I've got millions of dollars, I own this plane, I've got an ocean-going boat that is second to none, I've got two helicopters, I've got a home in Florida you'd die for and I've got no education. What are you all crying for?' He said, 'I'll tell you what we're going to do. We're going to stay on this plane until we've drunk it dry'. We used to carry a lot of booze.

We took off, landed at West Palm Beach, taxied into the hangar and sat on the plane for four hours until every drop of booze had gone. He was fantastic! And I know it was probably one of the biggest disappointments of his life but he handled it so well, cheered everybody up.

Yet Augusta had left its mark on the Shark. He continued to go hard at the game, and at life, with his typically half-mad gusto, fixated on improving, achieving, consuming all he could from golf and from life. And he would contend in major championships again, even back at Augusta in '99 when tied with Olazabal, on the final day, before the Spaniard drew away.

Norman turned 45 in 2000 and physically felt he could compete at the top. But his mind was elsewhere—business, family, fishing, whatever. He'd thrown everything at golf and at Augusta. And the course had smashed him.

Norman doesn't see it that way.

> Augusta is a great golf course. It's one of my favorites of all time. I do love the establishment of Augusta. I love the discipline, the principles, the ethic they conduct themselves with. Some people don't, I do, I truly love that.
>
> Do I feel like I've been beaten by Augusta? No, not at all. Do I feel like me that wishes I'd won Augusta? Absolutely! Of course. I'd be telling a big fat lie if I said it doesn't really bother me.

Yet, twelve years after his anguish at Augusta, there he was at Royal Birkdale, in the Open Championship, 53-years-old, leading after three rounds, again. First round he shot even-par 70. Second round he shot even-par 70. Conditions were hellacious; wild wet winds, buffeting gusts, bunker sand soaked into slurry. They'd have called it off anywhere but Scotland, and Iceland, and Lapland.

And yet there was the Great White Shark, thrashing away as he always had, going hard and owning it. He carded a 2-over round of 72 in winds that saw the average score blow out to 76.5. The great man, all class.

And so, again, he stood on the first tee in the last group of a major on a Sunday, leading by two. Six times out of seven previous attempts he hadn't converted a lead into a win. Could the impossible happen? After nine holes of the Championship of 2008, he led by one.

Alas, as Stewart Cink had done to Tom Watson, Padraigh Harrington laid waste to romance. And thus, those who'd taken the 50–1 on Norman and hadn't laid off, watched on in dismay. Harrington smoked a career 3-wood to the par-5 17th hole, make the eagle putt, card a 69 with 32 on the back, and win the Open Championship by four from Ian Poulter (69) with Norman (77) two shots further back T3.

*** *** ***

More Money than God

It's said that Arnold Palmer, on a day off from golf, would play golf. Palmer was still playing golf with his pals well into his 80s. Norman doesn't love golf as much. Doesn't have to. Jack Nicklaus is the same. Norman played because he loved it, was great at it, and he had that thing in him to be the best he could be. He could make a great living from something he loved.

And so here he is, the Great White Shark. A grandfather. A legend. Great White Shark Enterprises isn't a business; it's an empire. Like Kublai Khan had an empire, Greg Norman has an empire. He has presidents on speed dial. He has more money than God.

Is he happy, the Shark? He appears to be, yes. He does of course wish, as many of us wish, that he'd won the bloody Masters at least once in 23 vainglorious attempts. How does Larry bloody Mize and Bob bloody Tway hole out to beat him? Why didn't he take a 5-iron instead of the 4-iron approaching the 18th at Augusta in '86, and make par to force a play-off with Jack Nicklaus? Why couldn't that putt fall on 18 in '87?

So yes, he has regrets, of course he does. Who doesn't?

But that's just the way the Shark went about things, he went for it. And we bayed for him, thrilled at his daring, the audacity of the man, his huge, other-worldly skill. We followed him as devotees do the Pope. You couldn't look away. And mostly it came off. Other times, not so much. But always we were compelled to watch. We had to watch.

But just *two* major championships, Golf Gods? It's not right. He should've had ten. Seven at a pinch. Golfers with more major championships—but perhaps one tenth of the game—include Hale Irwin, Ray Floyd, Willie Anderson, Jim Barnes, Billy Casper and Jimmy Demaret. No disrespect to these gentlemen. But Norman was shit-loads better.

James Erskine, former manager, reckons:

> He'll be in a rocking chair wondering 'how the hell did I only win two majors?'. The answer is probably that he tried to be Jack Nicklaus and Kerry Packer at the same time—the swordsman and the gambler. You can't do both. It's one of those things. Nick Faldo has six majors and Norman has two. Norman had more talent in his right hand than Faldo. But Faldo was lethal between the ears.

Erskine says Norman was 'far brighter than Nick'. But Faldo had steel, a no-nonsense approach, a single-minded focus. 'Faldo knew how to win, and knew how to get over his opponents, Greg Norman included.'

Right or wrong, the mark of a golfer's place in the pantheon is measured by major championships. From the top down it's Nicklaus, Woods, Hagen, Hogan, Player, Watson, Jones, Palmer, Sarazaen, Snead, Vardon. Norman belongs in that company. That he didn't actually win as many majors doesn't make him a lesser golfer.

Norman was world number one for 331 weeks, second only to Tiger Woods. He was runner-up eight times in majors. He was top-5 twenty times in majors. He played golf all over the world; a walking one-man publicity machine. He made tournaments, he made entire tours. He won everywhere—91 times. He was the world's best and most exciting golfer for 20 years.

Hell—he could be bigger than Queensland.

-CHAPTER EIGHT-

OUTLIERS

The Legend of Moe Norman

Moe Norman shot 59 when he was 62.

Moe Norman set 33 course records, made 17 holes-in-one and won 55 professional golf tournaments. In one year, 1957, Moe Norman won 17 of 21 amateur golf tournaments he competed in.

Moe Norman may be the best player that never was.

'Moe Norman?' you ask. According to noted ball-striker Lee Trevino—and just about anyone who saw him strike a golf ball—Moe Norman is the greatest ball-striker who ever lived. Moe Norman is described as 'The Man with the Perfect Swing'.

Moe Norman was born in Kitchener, Ontario in 1930. Aged fifteen he was expelled from school because he was always out hitting golf balls in a field. A socially awkward, sensitive, solitary child, Moe Norman hit so many golf balls that his bloodied palms couldn't grip the club. And by the time he was nineteen he knew he had one singular skill—he could hit a golf ball straight where he wanted it to go, every time.

Moe Norman's swing was aesthetically ugly, at least compared to those of Adam Scott, Ernie Els and Fred Couples, to name a few. He had a wide stance with stiff legs and stood relatively far from the ball. His arms and hands formed a straight line down to the shaft and club-head. He addressed the ball as he would strike it. He had a short backswing and his feet remained planted. The shaft remained on one, immutable plane, and the club head returned square to target every time. And he knocked it out there far enough. And it was *pure*, just about every time.

When Moe Norman hit the ball, it was so pure that the grooves in the middle of his clubs wore flat. Coin-shaped indents formed in the sweet spots of his clubs. His swing was once studied by Titleist, who found that there was zero sidespin imparted on the ball. Titleist has never found another player who produced zero sidespin. Titleist concluded that Moe Norman's ball-striking was indeed, perfect.

Moe Norman's ball flight, according to Tiger Woods, was 'like 'Iron Byron', the mechanical ball-hitting machine. 'The ball doesn't move,' said Tiger. But he was wrong. Iron Byron hits the ball with sidespin.

Moe Norman described his baseball-style grip thus: 'Fingers are fast, fingers are fast. Palms are calm, palms are calm.' He gripped the club tightly, reasoning that it was the best way to ensure the club-face was square at impact.

Moe Norman didn't wear a glove and hit so many balls he'd build up a huge callous on the palm of his left hand. 'It gets so thick that from time to time I take a pair of scissors and cut it off,' he said. 'The edge of the callous gets very sharp, if I dragged it across your face I'd draw blood.'

As a youngster, Moe Norman worked in a bowling alley setting up pins (before there were machines) and caddied at his local club. He bought his first set of clubs by putting 10 cents away per round, and funded golf trips around Canada with meagre income from menial jobs. He slept in his car at tournaments. Before he owned a car, he would hitchhike to tournaments and sleep in the bunkers.

Moe Norman's first victory came aged 20. He'd hitchhiked to a course that he'd never seen before, shot 67, and hitchhiked home without collecting his trophy. He was too shy to stand on stage, to make a speech.

By nature, Moe Norman was insecure, introverted, and really good at mathematics. He could tell you that he'd played 434 golf courses. He could list the yardages for each hole on 375 of those golf courses. He could tell you that in one 11-year period he incurred just one penalty when he hit a ball that went out of bounds by two feet. One day, as Moe Norman could tell you, he hit 2207 balls not including chips and putts.

He had a relentless desire for routine, an incredible mathematical mind and distinctive, repetitive speech patters. Some thought it came from a bump to his head while tobogganing as a five year old. Others thought it might be a form of autism or Asperger syndrome. Moe Norman was never diagnosed either way. He didn't visit a doctor until he was 68.

Moe Norman didn't touch alcohol but did drink 20 cans of Coca-Cola a day. Moe Norman's teeth were not very good.

Moe Norman would shoot 59 three times. The first came in 1957. 'It could've been lower if I hadn't three-putted 10. In fact, I didn't putt that well all day. I just hit it close, is all,' he said.

Moe Norman never lined up putts. He just walked up and stroked it to the hole. He hated putting; felt it was in the way of his true love, repeatedly hitting the ball pure and straight.

Moe Norman saw practice strokes as a waste. On the tee or fairway, he'd approach the ball from side-on rather than behind the ball as most players do. He reasoned that he played the ball from side-on; he didn't want a new view at the crucial moment he setup over it.

Moe Norman played fast. He'd literally walk up to the ball and hit it. He played so fast that tournament organizers asked him to slow down. If

Moe Norman felt his fellow competitors were playing slowly, he would lie down on the fairway. Once, while waiting for a playing partner to putt out, he took off his shoes and went fishing for balls in a pond.

Once on a practice range next to Ben Hogan, Moe Norman heard the legend opine that the ball should always be worked from the left or right to the target, and that any straight shot was an accident. Moe Norman cocked an eyebrow and grinned. With Hogan watching, he hit dozens of perfectly straight golf shots, one after another. As Hogan left he remarked, 'Just keep on hitting those accidents, kid.'

Moe Norman won so many amateur tournaments that he would sell the prizes, often before the tournament had even been played, reasoning that he couldn't watch 10 televisions or wear six watches. Plus, he had to fund his tilt at the next tournament. Because he was selling the prizes, Moe Norman's amateur status was quashed by the Royal Canadian Golf Association. So Moe turned pro.

Moe Norman once played During an exhibition match with Sam Snead, on the 16th hole the players were faced with a stream that cut across the fairway, 250 yards away. Snead laid up and advised Moe Norman to do the same. Moe Norman, instead, took chose his driver. 'You can't clear the stream,' said Snead. 'I'm not trying to,' replied Moe Norman. 'I'm aiming at that bridge that crosses the stream.' Moe Norman took his driver and landed the ball on the bridge where it bounded towards the green.

Moe Norman was invited to play in the US Masters at Augusta in 1956. He teed off while his name was being announced. He set off carrying his own bag before Augusta members found him a caddie. He carded a 75 with six 3-putts. The next day it was the same issues with the putter and a 78. The Masters had no cut then so off to the range (though not the putting green) Moe Norman went. And it was there that Sam Snead—who as John Updike wrote would 'swagger about the range like the sheriff of golf county'—offered Moe Norman some advice: 'You're coming down way too steep on the ball with your long irons,' said Snead. 'The secret to hitting a long iron is to hit them like fairway woods. Don't hit down or try to force it. Hit it like a nice 3-wood. Sweep it.' And so Moe Norman, in his way, practiced Snead's tips until dark, hitting so many golf balls (800) that his hands became bloody and calloused. 'They looked like hamburger,' said Irv Lightstone, a pro and friend from Toronto. 'Moe did things that were totally irrational and off the world.' Barely able to grip the club, Moe Norman withdrew the next day after nine holes. He never took a lesson again.

Moe Norman played only four rounds in major championship golf, all at Augusta, in 1956 and 1957. He would play just 12 tournaments on the PGA Tour in 1959 and 1960. His aversion to slow play—and for Moe Norman 'slow' was anything but walking up to the ball, hitting it immediately and striding quickly onwards—made him noticeably agitated and jittery. He was also sensitive to the jibes and even bullying from fellow players about his unusual swing, manner, diet and dress (he would wear black turtleneck jumpers in the heat and 'a montage of colors that had no relevancy to each other,' according to his friend Irv Lightstone.) Wrote Bruce Selcraig in *Readers Digest*:

> At the Los Angeles Open in 1959, a small group of players cornered Moe in the locker room. Stop goofing off, they told him, demanding that he improve his technique as well as his wardrobe.

Moe Norman sought acceptance from players he so admired. Instead he was shunned. Friends say the episode destroyed his self-confidence. The final straw came with a dressing down from PGA Tour officials who insisted Moe Norman use a caddie, stop hitting balls off big tees, stop lying on the fairway if he thought things were too slow. Just stop being different.

Moe Norman quit the PGA Tour towards the end of 1960. 'Life ate me up,' he told ESPN in 2000. 'Life ate me up. I couldn't do what I wanted to do. That's what hurt me.'

Moe Norman just wanted to be loved. He returned to Canada, among his people, and won 55 professional tournaments.

Moe Norman always carried cash money, thousands of dollars in $100 bills. Once when playing a round with some pals, he dashed into the bush. His friends assumed he was relieving himself. He came back with thousands of dollars in cash. He'd buried it for safe keeping. Moe Norman didn't trust banks.

Moe Norman went through hard times financially in the early '90s. The Canadian tour had lost its sponsor and Moe Norman was back to sleeping in his car. He went to the 1995 PGA Merchandise Show in Orlando, Florida where he was approached by Titleist and Footjoy CEO, Wally Uihlein. 'I see you're still wearing our visor and wear our FootJoy shoes,' said Uihlein. 'You've played our ball for 40 years. Has anyone done anything for you?'

Moe Norman replied that nobody had but nor had he ever asked. Uihlein replied, 'Give me your hand.' The pair shook hands. And Uihlein promised, 'You're going to get $5,000 a month from us for the rest of your life.' And thus Moe Norman, as chronicled in the *Wall Street Journal* was paid '$5,000 a month for life—just for being Moe Norman'. And Moe Norman, aged 65, opened his first ever bank account.

In a 2000 ESPN documentary by Chris Connelly, Moe Norman told viewers why he loves golf.

> Golf is happiness. It's intoxication without the hangover. It's stimulation without the pills. Its price is high yet its rewards are richer. Some say it's a boys' pastime yet it builds men. It cleanses the mind and rejuvenates the body. It's these things and many more for those of us who truly love it. Golf is truly happiness.

Moe Norman was granted entry into the Canadian Golf Hall of Fame in 1995. He entered the Canadian Sports Hall of Fame in 2006. A week before the Canadian Open of 2004, Moe Norman died, aged 75. In his car they found a messy stash of golf balls, clubs, tees, gloves, clothes, books, notepads—and $20,000 cash.

✳ ✳ ✳

The Magnificent Seve

Seve Ballesteros's father, Baldomero Ballesteros Presmanes, worked the land and fished for bream in the sea, and shot himself in the hand so he could fight with General Franco in the Spanish Civil War and not the Republicans whose ideology he disagreed with. Baldomero was given 20 years' jail for treason but escaped and fought with Franco (who won and ruled Spain from 1939 to 1975).

Meanwhile, Seve's mom, Carmen Sota Ocejo just worked cooking, cleaning, washing, and caring for Seve's Uncle Vicente who would bequeath the family his home, and cause a rift in their village of Pedrena in northern Spain.

Seve had four older brothers though one died before Seve was born on 9 April 1957. As the youngest, Seve was the favorite and spoilt so his brothers gave him the worst jobs on the farm. Each morning from the age of five, it was Seve's job to clean out the stables and then run the two kilometres to school. He'd run home for lunch, run back to school, run home again. He became a champion runner. After school he'd milk the cows by hand, muck out the stables and help his father in the fields.

A member of the local Real Club de Golf de Pedrena (now Royal Pedrena) gave Seve and his brother Vicente an 8-iron with which they'd whack around stones or balls they'd found or stolen. While tending to their cows they would practice. Once the cows ran home on their own.

Seve's father was very unhappy.

At the age of six Seve followed his brothers becoming a caddie at Pedrena. They'd find balls and sell them to the members. They would stand on the balls of members they disliked (*Can't find it, sorry!*) and sell them to the members they did. While waiting for someone's bag to carry they practiced.

The boys' Uncle Ramon was the club pro and the premier golfer in Spain. Ramon had run sixth in the 1965 US Masters behind Palmer, Player and Nicklaus and with the prize-money purchased Padrena's third ever automobile. Seve watched Ramon hit balls, and learned. But the club put great restrictions on caddies—Seve was once banned for a week for a practice swing.

He would sneak onto the course to play at dawn or at night if there was a full moon. He would skip school to play. He was expelled from school when he was whipped for a ripped book that he hadn't ripped, and went home to drink too much wine for a 12 year old, returned to school and punched the teacher in the face, a lot.

He would play golf with a kindly local doctor who allowed his caddie to play with him against the wishes of other members. 'I am a member here and I shall play with whomever I like,' said the doctor.

His older brother gave him a 3-iron which Seve would take to the beach—a boy on a big stretch of sand whacking a three-iron, time and again, working it, shaping it, feeling the ball on the club. In the evening, he would steal onto the golf club course, just Seve and his three-iron. And he became really, really good.

Aged 13, he beat his 21-year-old brother Manuel, a European Tour pro. Aged 14 he won the Padrena Caddies competition. All his older brothers turned professional. Seve did too and qualified for the Portuguese Open. He qualified for the Open Championship in 1975 when he was just 19. On seeing links golf courses for the first time, he didn't understand where the greens and fairways were amidst all those dunes. 'They are there,' said his brother Manuel, pointing. Seve was sceptical.

He shot 78–84 in the British PGA at Royal St George's and 70-80 at Carnoustie in the Open.

He went to the United States and was nine holes of par golf from becoming the youngest man to get through Q-School and onto the PGA Tour. Then the thought of being on the PGA Tour and away from his family for months on end dawned on him, and he didn't like it. He shot 40. And headed home, happy.

When he turned up at Royal Birkdale in Southport, England for the 1976 Open Championship, he was no longer under the radar. Touring professional Angel Gallardo, the father figure of the Spanish contingent, urged *Golf Digest* journalist Peter Dobereiner to 'come out and watch Manolo's brother. The kid is fantastic.'

After two rounds of the Open, Ballesteros had shot 69–69 and led by two over Johnny Miller. He added a third round 73 to be 5-under the tournament and still led by two ahead of Miller. Then Miller shot a blistering 66 in the find round to Ballesteros' 74. And Ballesteros sobbed.

He'd sobbed after his first ever professional tournament too, the National Professional Championship of Spain. Expected to win, he'd finished 20th. He hadn't even turned 17. In the Open he hadn't yet turned 20 but he had expected to win.

Within a year people worked out why the expectations were so high for the young man from Spain. He won the Dutch Open in August 1976. He won the French Open in May 1977. He won the Swiss Open the same year as well as the impressively-named, if short-lived, Uniroyal International Championship (in a play-off with another 20-year-old, Nick Faldo). He went to Kenya, won their Open. He went to Japan, won their Open. He went to New Zealand and won the Otago Classic. With Antonio Garrido he retained the World Cup he'd won for Spain in '76.

He hadn't even turned 21.

He won the 1979 Open Championship at Royal Lytham and St Annes by three shots from Ben Crenshaw and Jack Nicklaus. An American hadn't won at Lytham since Bobby Jones in 1926. Dan Jenkins of *Sports Illustrated* described it as a 'strange old links'.

> The gallery at Lytham also had a distinctive personality. Blackpool is a resort catering to the workingman on holiday and he was out on the links in force. There were record crowds, even in the horrid weather—it was wet as well as cold and windy—and they became more mob-like as the tournament progressed. They tore over the crosswalks, spilled out of the grandstands, shouted, cheered and even jeered at players they had not bet on. A pub behind the ninth green was a rowdy place indeed, where the competitors often heard calls of 'Miss it! Miss it!' as they bent over their putts.

It didn't bother Ballesteros, though, who blasted his way around the course, got himself out of scrapes in his inimitable fashion, and wafted in putts with the soft hands of a surgeon.

And thus a man from continental Europe won the Open Championship for the first time since Arnaud Massy in 1906.

Ballesteros won the US Masters at Augusta in 1980 in a procession. After rounds of 66–69–68 he led by seven shots. Gubby Gilbert of Chattanooga and Jack Newton of Cessnock (in the Hunter Valley in Australia) chased him home with 67 and 68 respectively. But the Spaniard's even-par 72 was enough for him to slide on the first of two green jackets that he would collect.

In 1984 the truly sensational moment of his career came when he rolled in a putt on the 18th green of the Old Course, St Andrews.

Everyone who watched remembers (and through the magic of YouTube, those who were not there can see) that moment, Seve Ballesteros on the 18th, pumping his fist like he was feverishly milking one of those cows from days of yore and punching the air to the four corners of St Andrews.

Up to the Road Hole, the par-4 17th that Ballesteros had bogied three rounds thus far. Taking driver from the tee his ball went left out into thick rough, the imperfect place to approach the brilliant, storied 4-banger. The flag was behind the killer pot bunker front; the long skinny green ran almost perpendicular across him.

And so, Ballesteros had a couple of practice swings and then launched his 6-iron with sufficient grace and power to bounce the ball onto the green where it flirted with the sharp drop-off to the road that gives the hole its name, but it held. Under the pump, he'd hit a 193-yard six-iron pin-high. And the people watching knew: it was the shot of a master.

Over to you, five-time champion, Tom Watson, playing in the group behind on that fateful day at St Andrews.

Looking for three on the trot and needing one more title to tie the legend, Harry Vardon as the greatest Open Champion of all time, Watson narrowly missed a birdie putt on 16 and walked to the Road Hole all square with Ballesteros on 11-under.

Watson attacked with driver, cutting the corner of the hotel in the manner of a player seeking reward for risk. And he got it. The ball ended on the very right edge of the fairway, slightly uphill lie but perfect attack angle for the green. Watson took a 3-iron from his bag, lined it up, thought better of it, plucked out a 2-iron. Lined it up, waggled, and went at it ... and flared the ball high and right where it soared across the front quadrant of the green, scooted over the road, hit the wall hard yet didn't bounce back sufficiently to give him any sort of backswing worthy of the name.

Not ideal, Tom Watson. He told *Golf Digest*:

> The shot I tried to play was risky, but it was determined by the lie. The ball was on an upslope, so chasing it in low wasn't an option. I was into a wind, and I had 195 yards to the flag. I tried to hit a 2-iron in the air and have it land softly on the green. I pushed it 30 yards right.

Ballesteros, meanwhile, hit his drive perfectly to left of the middle of the mighty expanse that is 18 leaving a tidy attack angle to the innocuous-looking yet scary 18th green. Doug Sanders in 1970 had called it 'forbidding'. Sanders knew better than most. He missed a knee-trembling two-footer that would have won him the famous jug.

Ballesteros hit down on a three-quarter wedge that bit the ball hard and caused a plume of dusty sand to rise from the ground. The ball pitched and stuck on the green, 15 feet from the hole. Again, in the circumstances, the work of a master.

Watson, meanwhile, needed a 'total miracle to get down in two,' according to the TV man, who was right. He gripped down low on several clubs, tried several experimental variations on the relatively un-practiced 'chop down hard but not too hard yet still exert sufficient force to make the ball whistle hard across a gravel road and up a hard embankment onto the green' shot. There was no chance.

But Watson pulled it off! He chopped down hard on the ball yet with fluency, and saw his ball roll up the bank and to the back lip where it flirted with the death-bunker, but obeyed. Two putts and he'd still be in it, if only just.

As Tom Watson stood over his putt there came a mighty roar from 18. Seve had rolled in an uphill 15-footer that slowed and turned and fell into the hole. Watson knew what the noise meant. Everyone knew. They heard the roar in Edinburgh. Watson had to make a 30-footer or he was gone.

He did not and he was. And Seve, in his natty navy blue jumper with the Slazenger cat on the breast, drank long gulps again from a claret jug.

On the 72nd tee of the 1988 Open Championship at Royal Lytham and St Annes, Ballesteros led Nick Price by one shot. His tee shot flirted with a bunker and some bushes on the right and settled in the rough. His 6-iron from there ended up pin-high in some fluffy rough left. The chip shot had several possible things that could go wrong. None did. He almost sunk it, the ball slowly lipping the right edge. He tapped in. He won.

He'd missed only three fairways. He'd missed only three greens in regulation.

He'd shot 65. On the first hole, he hit a 6-iron to two feet. He birdied 2, 3, 6 and 7 and turned in 30 that would have been 29 if not for a 4-foot miss on 8.

True to form he continued to attack. On 14 he hit a driver into the wheat and a rough looking lie. Instead of chopping out onto the fairway and taking his licks, Ballesteros attacked the pin 240-yards away with 2-iron, advancing the ball only half that distance, the ball ending in a bush, unplayable. He retreated 50 yards. Hit 7-iron, blind, to 15 feet. Nailed the putt for a bogey-5 only Ballesteros could claim.

On 16 he finally put a stake in Nick Price with his 9-iron to three inches. Later Ballesteros described his round as 'one of those that happen every 25 or 50 years'. Asked if it the best he'd ever played, Ballesteros answered 'Yes, so far'.

***

Big A

Annika Sorenstam shot 59. Annika Sorenstam won 93 professional titles including 10 major championships. Annika Sorenstam was so good she played against men, in a PGA Tour event, just so she could see how good she was.

On Thursday, 22 May of 2003 Sorenstam turned up on the 10th tee at Colonial Country Club, the Texas track they call 'Hogan's Alley'. Phil Mickelson was there, Jim Furyk was there, two-time US Open winner Lee Janzen was there. Kenny Perry was there and shot 19-under and won by six. And is remembered for it not at all.

Rather it was the extremely interesting sight of the greatest women's golfer of all time teeing it up in a men's event. It was out there, baby. People went mad for it.

Though not everyone was so enamoured. At the University of Western Australia, a study on the tournament's media coverage found that:

> a close alliance was formed between some golf journalists and some male professional golfers that enunciated stereotypical descriptions of female psychological frailty and male responsibilities for breadwinning, and so framed the event as a novelty that should not be repeated.

As Vijay Singh put it:

> I hope she misses the cut. Why? Because she doesn't belong out there. She's taking a spot from someone else. If I am drawn to play with her, I will pull out. We have our tour for men and they [women] have their tour.

Nick Price derided it as a publicity stunt and Scott Hoch summed it up thus:

> Some people don't believe she should be out here—golfers and men in general. Most guys hope she plays well and that what comes out of this is that she realizes she can't play against men.

In contrast, Tiger Woods, a regular playing partner of Sorenstam's, encouraged her to 'just go out and play'. Mickelson reckoned:

> If there is a female good enough to compete, I think she should. My thought process is apparently in the minority again, but I have a hard time understanding the other side of it.

Speaking from his ranch in Crawford, Texas, about a two-hour drive down the road, the 43rd President of the United States, George W. Bush said: 'I hope she makes the cut. I'm pulling for her, and I hope I'll be watching her on Saturday and Sunday.'

And so it came to pass: Singh did pull out (although he later apologized for words that 'came out the wrong way'). And a few others pulled out, too, for various reasons. And the professional male players—and even some female players—were torn. Is this good or is this bad?

Some made the case that Sorenstam hadn't earned her place; that a start inside the ropes of a PGA Tour event should be earned through skill, grinding and graft. Others countered that Sorenstam *had* done that, on another professional tour, and that she'd so dominated that tour that she deserved a chance to raise the bar and see just how well a woman could play.

Sorenstam herself was a tad taken aback by all the fuss—which had been going on for four months—and said that she wasn't 'putting the guys to the test here, or men against women'.

I would like to emphasize that I don't want to get into any political things. I don't want to put the guys on the defensive. I'm not here to prove anything. I'm here to test myself and face a new challenge.

Whether Price was right and the event was but a 'stunt', is almost moot. Because in terms of publicity, the Bank of America Colonial, a generic enough event in the grinding, weekly machine that is the PGA Tour, went gangbusters.

Sorenstam was all over US television. She was on Jay Leno's *Tonight Show*. There was a profile piece on *60 Minutes*. She threw out a pitch in a Mets game. Her playing partners—a pair of journeymen called Dean Wilson and Aaron Barber who, like Sorenstam, had been chosen at random because they hadn't won an event nor finished top 125 on the money list—were profiled on CBS.

Sorenstam apologized to Wilson and Barber for the circus, but the pair were all good. Wilson wore a 'Go Annika' badge. Barber received more offers of endorsements in the two rounds that he played with Sorenstam than in the eleven years chopping it about on the PGA and Web.com tours.

And people came from everywhere. There were traffic jams to get in. Galleries hung from the trees. Women, little girls, people who'd never cared about golf, flocked to see the amazing Swedish Amazon, a woman locking horns with the men. A girl. One of us? How will she go?

Amid Tiger-like galleries and shouts of 'You, the woman!' Sorenstam shot one-over 71 in the first round. Men who carded a 71 at Colonial across those four days include Luke Donald, Sergio Garcia and Hal Sutton, the winner of the 1983 PGA Championship, who would finish fourth. Lee Janzen shot 71. John Senden shot 71. Carl Petterson shot 71. Billy Andrade shot 71.

Leader Perry said:

I played with Tiger two times last year ... and the media scrutiny was really intense out there. I performed very poorly. And she shoots 71. My hat's off to her. I think she did a great job.

On the Friday Sorenstam made birdie on the second hole and the galleries roared. Even par was the likely cut. And Sorenstam was on the number. But there would be no fairytale. She blocked her drive on five into trees. She chunked a chip on six. She three-putted eight. And ten. And twelve. And boom, she was 5-over. And even-par was still the number.

Sorenstam finished with 71–74 and missed the cut. Her 145 was eight shots better than Las Vegas bookmakers had offered even money for. It was the same score registered by Tim Clark, Heath Slocum and Aaron Oberholser. Fellow cuttees included: Stuart Appleby (2-over), Garcia (3-over) and 2006 US Open winner Geoff Ogilvy who shot 7-over.

'She played amazing,' said Jesper Parnevik. 'I guess we have the Shark, the Tiger and now we have the Superwoman.'

***

Little A

Annika Sorenstam grew up shy. She didn't like to raise her hand in class. She didn't want to win junior golf tournaments because it would mean she had to make a speech on a podium. She'd deliberately miss a putt or fluff a chip to finish second. 'That way I would still get a trophy, but wouldn't have to speak to the crowd,' she reasoned.

Her grandparents worked it out. Told tournament organizers. When she next finished third she was surprised to find the third-placed golfer being asked to make a speech. Which Sorenstam did. And found that it was better than the shame of missing on purpose. And so, she began to win.

She represented Sweden in amateur team events. She represented Stockholm University in a tournament in Tokyo, paired with a girl from University of Arizona. The Arizona coach asked Sorenstam if she'd like to play for University of Arizona. Sorenstam said yes, despite knowing little of Arizona. She arrived to find the heat quite different from Stockholm's weather.

She studied chemical engineering and English. She played golf all year round, also quite different to Stockholm. She became world amateur champion in 1992. She turned professional and missed out on a LPGA tour card by a shot. She went on the European tour, was rookie of the year in '93. She won status for '94. She won the Australian Open. She finished second in the British Open. She was LPGA rookie of the year.

And in 1995 she won the US Open. And boom, she was away. She topped the money list in America and Europe. She won again in Australia. She won the Swedish Open. She won the GHP Heartland Classic in Missouri by 10 shots. She beat Laura Davies in a play-off for the World Championship of Women's Golf. She won the US Open again.

And then she pretty much won everything.

In the five years after that magnificent missed cut among the men at Colonial, Sorenstam won six more major championships. She won in Japan. She won in Dubai. She won in China. She won $22 million, the most by any woman ever.

In the second round of the 2001 Standard Register Ping tournament at the 6,459-yard, par-72 Moon Valley Country Club, Annika Sorenstam's card read: 3, 2, 3, 4, 3, 4, 4, 4, 4 (31); 4, 2, 3, 4, 3, 2, 3, 3, 4 (28). It was a score of 13-under 59 with 13 birdies. The front nine began with four birdies. The back nine began with eight birdies. It was one of the greatest rounds of golf ever played.

And in 2008 she gave it all up.

***

Laura

Laura Davies won four major championships. Her most recent is the 1996 du Maurier Classic, which became the Canada Open when Canada said the deadly products of du Maurier shouldn't be promoted via a golf tournaments, or anywhere, because cigarettes are bad.

But Davies can still claim four majors. It also means she's won the national Open championship of Canada, to go with the Open championships of Spain, Belgium, Italy, Britain, Europe, England, Ireland, Scotland, Wales, Denmark, Norway, Australia, New Zealand, Germany and India.

She won the US Open in 1987, the LPGA in 1994 and '96.

Davies grew up loving golf because it afforded hours of private 'Laura time' on a driving range. There was also the option to play with her pals and her brother Tony, with whom she loved to compete. She got serious about golf at 13 and taught herself by watching pros on television. Always she tried to beat her brother. When she was 16, she did.

Davies turned pro in '85 and won the European Tour money list and rookie of the year. She won the British Ladies Open. And in 1987, aged 23, she went to America. And brained them.

No-one had seen anything like her. She was 5 feet 10 inches tall, broad-shouldered and powerful. She hit the ball 50 yards further than anyone else. She hit a 4- and 5-wood off the tee and still hit it further. And she had soft hands; she could putt. She would bristle at being called solely a long hitter—you needed more strings to the bow to be a player.

She led the LPGA's season-opening major, the Nabisco Dinah Shore invitational at Rancho Mirage in California after a blistering 66. Then the wind picked up to Scottish gale force and it was predicted Davies might thrive. She shot 83.

After four rounds of the '87 US Open, Laura David led with scores of 72–70–72–71 and a 3-under total of 285. It was a number she shared with Ayako Okamoto of Japan and JoAnne Carner of the United States. Given rain delays, the trio would contest the 18-hole play-off on a Tuesday. The British Open began on the Thursday. It would be a close-run thing.

On the 18th hole Davies led by three. She took her driver, 3-wood to the front of the green. Three putt and a par made her the champion, the only woman without an over-par round. And they came from everywhere to praise her.

Said Carner, winner of the US Open in '71 and '76:

> Everything about her is impressive. When Nancy Lopez turned pro and won everything, she was just exceptional. And I think Laura is like that. She is one of those great players now being shown to the world.

Davies accepted the trophy on the dais, thanked everyone and dashed off to catch a plane. She landed in London on the Wednesday. Teed off in the British Open Thursday. Ran second.

'I do not feel I am even on the same plane as her,' said Ayako Okamoto. 'Laura might be the most impressive player I have ever met. She is thrilling to watch.'

Davies was the first woman to be made a member of the R&A. She was knighted by the Queen. She has won 84 tournaments around the world and the Ladies Open championships of Chrysler, Compaq, UNIQA, Hennesy, Valextra and the company that makes cigarettes.

Davies is the only woman—and one of five golfers all up with David Graham, Justin Rose, Hale Irwin and Gary Player—to have won professional golf tournaments on six continents.

Laura Davies is one of the greats.

***

The Problem with Nick

Nick Faldo practiced alone. He played alone. In Pro-Ams he'd walk five yards in front of his amateur partners so they'd have to chase him to have a conversation which would not last long. He had a 'game face' that was resting bitch face and which he adopted pretty much all the time.

His great rival Greg Norman says he and Faldo were never close, have never spoken much.

> He was just a man on his own horse. And you had to let him do what he wanted to do. But I respected that, as I did every one of the top players. All of the top players I played against; I respected their tenacity, their practice, their routine, their desire to beat you.
>
> Nick was probably the toughest guy I've ever played golf against because he could cut your heart out on the first tee and give it to you on the 18th. And that's what you wanted. That's the spirit of the sport I love. We are trying to beat each other. We are trying to go out there and shoot the daylights out.

Faldo set about subjugating golf courses and opponents as if they were his enemies. He played golf like a robot. Like an evil hit-man robot. But the robot could win.

Faldo won six major championships (three Open Championships, three US Masters), placing him second only to Harry Vardon (six Open Championships, one US Open) on the list of Europeans with major championships.

Hard to believe they once called him 'Foldo'.

That was the tabloid headline after he'd blown a lead in the 1983 Open

Championship won by Tom Watson, the great man's fifth. He practiced his buttocks off and celebrated his 30th birthday by shooting even-par 71 on the Saturday at Muirfield in the 1987 Open Championship.

Muirfield suited Faldo that weekend. Thick fog enveloped the course meaning Faldo could walk around in a 'cocoon' of near-silence. Just himself and the ball and the target. Faldo told *Golf* magazine:

> Two steps in front of me was my only focal point. The rest was a blur, partly due to the weather and partly because I was completely engrossed. I knew that one good shot could win it for me and one bad shot could cost me the Open. It's a bit of a knife's edge, isn't it?

In the last round Faldo amassed 18 pars, which does sound robotic. But there was hot action and skill in Faldo's 71. He hit long irons into par-3s. He hit a pure 2-iron that fell short into a bunker, unable to penetrate the pea soup. He got up and down from the wet slurry of greenside bunkers. On the par-5 17th his second and third shots were 5-irons. He had to drain a 5-footer on the 18th to share the lead. Eighteen pars—it was a special round of golf. Faldo said:

> If somebody said you could have 71 before you went out, you'd take it. A par round in the Open used to be pretty significant. We hit long irons in, we hit 2- and 3-irons into the par 3s, we still had 1-irons in our bags. You putted on wet, natural fescue greens that were so undulating, they had bumps within the bumps.
>
> I didn't have a bad putting day, I was just so nervous I couldn't make putts. I also knew that if I parred any hole, I'd pass 90 per cent of the field. My mentality was that par was still good. If anyone

thought making 18 pars at Muirfield was easy, well, good luck to them to do it.

And thus for a decade Faldo was among the game's greats, if not the best. With Norman still in his pomp and Fred Couples winning majors, and Ian Woosnam spending 50 straight weeks as world number one, Faldo was there and thereabouts. He spent 97 weeks as number one, third all time behind Norman (331) and Tiger Woods (683) since rankings began in 1982.

In 1988 he made an 18-hole play-off in the US Open, losing by four shots to Curtis Strange. He won the 1989 US Masters after shooting 65 the last day and going into a play-off with Scott Hoch. On the first play-off hole Hoch missed a two-footer for the win. On the second play-off hole, Faldo jammed in a 25-footer and pulled on a green jacket.

He pulled on another one in 1990 after a play-off with Ray Floyd. Floyd had been leading by four shots with six to play when Faldo started bombing the par-5s. He birdied the 13th with a two-putt. He birdied the 15th after a 230-yard 2-iron over trees. He hit 16 and drained a 15-foot putt. Floyd bogied the 17th and they were all square. And Faldo won on the second play-off hole after Floyd dunked his approach in the drink.

Faldo won the 1990 Open Championship at St Andrews by five shots. In 1992 he led by four shots after three rounds then gave them all back.

American John Cook birdied 16 and led by two. And somehow Faldo fought his way back. He hit a brilliant 5-iron to three feet on 15. He hit a tremendous 4-iron to the par-5 17th and left the 20-foot eagle putt in the jaws. Cook bogied 18. Faldo tapped in and led by one. He hit three-iron into the 18th that shaved the pin. He faced a 25-footer from the back edge. He duly cosied it up to a foot. Just about broke down with relief.

Four years later he won the Masters with a brilliant 67 in the final round while Norman crashed to 78.

Ask Norman if he and Faldo have shared a beer and talked about the round, Norman chuckles: 'No! ... Over our whole career we probably wouldn't have said a thousand words. We were competitors, there was no question about it.'

Robotic, focused, competitive, brilliant and not very talkative—could be the title of a Faldo biography.

* * *

Babe

Mildred Ella 'Babe' Didrikson Zaharias was really good at running, swimming, diving, lacrosse, basketball, bowling and billiards. She could throw a football. She could kick one off either foot. She took up tennis and beat the best players. She could hurl a baseball from the mound; hit homers from the plate. In an exhibition match she pitched an innings for St Louis Cardinals against Philadelphia Athletics. They named her after Babe Ruth. She was better than him.

At the Olympic track and field trials in 1932 Babe competed for the Employers Casualty team for whom she worked as a typist. Other teams entered a competitor per event. Employers Casualty just entered Babe.

Each team was announced over the tannoy and presented to the crowd. Some teams had over 20 athletes. Employers Casualty was announced and out walked Babe, waving, 'a one-woman track team' according to her publicist. That was Babe.

She won five events: long jump, hurdles, javelin, shot-put and how far you could throw a baseball. She amassed 30 points for her team. The next best team scored 22. They had 22 athletes.

She went to Los Angeles for the Olympic Games and was only allowed to compete in three events. She was disappointed. And thus only won gold in the javelin and hurdles, and silver in high jump. Esteemed sports writer Grantland Rice described her athleticism as 'the most flawless section of muscle harmony, of complete mental and physical co-ordination the world of sport has ever known.'

Said Babe:

> That sure is a powerful lot of language to use about a girl from Texas. Maybe they are right about it. All I know is that I can run and I can jump and I can toss things and when they fire a gun or tell me to get busy, I just say to myself, 'Well kid, here's where you've got to win another'. And I usually do.

And then she took up golf and became the greatest golfer of all time. One of them anyway, if you count Annika Sorenstam.

Grantland Rice was covering those LA Olympics and mentioned to fellow famous sports writers Westbrook Pegler and Paul Gallico that Babe could be the greatest woman golfer there's ever been.

> She tells me she's never played golf but would like to try it. How would you like to go out early tomorrow to Brentwood? I'll bring the Babe along and we'll see what she can do.

Babe shot 91, according to Rice, and banged out several 250-yard drives. After one long bomb the club professional, Olin Dutra, champion of the 1932 US PGA and 1934 US Open, and known as 'King Kong', remarked, 'I saw it. But I still don't believe it.'

Babe took to golf with a vengeance. She moved to California and practiced ten hours a day. Practiced until her hands blistered and bled. She putted on the carpet at work. She would take *The Rules of Golf* to read in bed.

She married a wrestler, George Zaharias, who became her full-time manager.

She won the Western Open in 1940. In 1941, nine years after that 91, she shot a course record 64 at Brentwood Country Club. She teamed up with Sam Snead in an alternate shot match and the pair carded 68.

She played with Gene Sarazen, Byron Nelson and Ben Hogan. She played with Clark Gable. She played with Mickey Rooney. She played for laughs with Bing Crosby and Bob Hope. She played with Babe Ruth in a fund-raiser for the war. She called him 'the Big Babe'.

In one year from 1946 to 1947 she won 14 tournaments straight. She'd turn up to golf clubs and bellow, 'The Babe's here! Who is going to finish second?' She riled golf's 'high society' as she dubbed it. She was brash, Texas-tough. She'd toss a cigarette in the air and catch it in her mouth, light the match on her thumbnail. She battled: men, women and the game of golf.

In 1950 she founded the Ladies Professional Golf Association (LPGA).

In 1953 she had an operation to remove cancer. Four months later she won the US Open by 12 shots.

The cancer came back. And she died in 1955.

Noted golfer and US President, Dwight D. 'Ike' Eisenhower said:

> She was a woman who, in her athletic career,
> certainly won the admiration of every person in the
> United States, all sports people all over the world,
> and in her gallant fight against cancer, she put up
> one of the kind of fights that inspire us all.

Imagine if Babe were a man. Imagine if, like Babe, a man had won the Masters, Wimbledon, the Superbowl, World Series and Olympic gold medals. And then founded the PGA Tour. That man wouldn't be called

The King, he would be The King. King of the World. And the world would give him his own island. Like Fiji, say. Or Hawaii. Or Australia as Lex Luthor requested as a gift from General Zod in *Superman II*.

Regardless, Babe Didrickson Zaharias is among the best there's ever been.

***

Choice Joyce

Joyce Wethered grew up watching Harry Vardon, John Taylor and James Braid, and later Bobby Jones when he came to Scotland. She watched how they played and did what they did. She copied them. And she became the greatest player in the world.

In 1930, the year of Jones's 'impregnable quadrilateral' grand slam, he played an exhibition with Wethered at St Andrews and said she was the most naturally talented player he had ever seen. High praise indeed from Bobby Jones.

Walter Hagen played with her too and gushed:

> As I watched her I thought there wasn't a male golfing star in the world who wouldn't envy the strong, firm strokes she played. She hit her shots crisply, like a man expert, but without having any mannish mannerisms to detract from her charm as a gracious young sportswoman.

A woman playing golf in the male-dominated world of golf was always seen through the prism of how she looked and her ability compared to the abilities of male players. She compared favorably. She was better than most of them.

She would out-drive very good players, Walker Cup amateurs. Scottish professional Willie Watson said Wethered 'could hit a ball 240 yards on the fly while standing barefoot on a cake of ice.'

And she did it dressed like she was off to church in her Sunday best.

Wethered was 5 feet 10, fit, supple and strong. She had a long, relaxed and co-ordinated golf swing. Yet her greatest gift was concentration. She could go into a 'cocoon' of concentration. She was six holes down in the final in 1920, made a run of 3s and beat the outstanding player of the day, Cecil Leitch, on the 17th. Asked if a nearby train had disturbed her as she stood over the winning putt, Wethered replied, 'What train?'

Golfer and author Enid Wilson once wrote that Wethered would emerge from

> a quiet house or a secluded part of a hotel, come to the first tee, smile charmingly at her opponent ... at the commencement of their game, and then, almost as though in a trance, become a golfing machine.
>
> She never obtruded her personality, and those who played her had the impression that they, the crowd and the state of the game had ceased to exist in her mind and that her entire faculties were being focused on swinging to perfection and holing the ball in the fewest number of strokes.

Wethered won the Amateur Championships of 1922, 1924, 1925 and 1929, and five English Championships from 1920 to 1924. In 1925 she retired, saying:

> I have simply exercised a woman's prerogative of doing something without the slightest regard for what anybody thinks and because I want to please myself.

She made a comeback and in 1929 won the Amateur Championship at the Old Course, St Andrews against the great American, Glenna Collett. Wethered was five shots down after 18 holes, but won 3-up after 35 holes to mass acclaim from boisterous Scots.

Then Wall Street crashed and her family lost all their money and Wethered had to take a job in the golf department of a store, and thus relinquish her amateur status.

She toured America playing exhibition matches with Bobby Jones and Gene Sarazen.

***

Super Mex

Lee Trevino joined the PGA Tour in 1966. He pre-qualified for the 1967 US Open at Baltusrol and finished 5th. In 1968, at Oak Hill, New Jersey, he won. On the last day, with Jack Nicklaus in pursuit, wearing a red shirt, red hat and high-waisted black pants that exposed red socks, Trevino shot 69 and won by four, tying Nicklaus's US Open record of 275 with four rounds under 70.

Last round he hit the flag on the par-3 15th. He made a 20-foot par save on 17. On the par-4 18th, in thick rough, on a downslope, he stiffed his third shot to four feet. Made the putt, won by four. Dan Jenkins of *Sports Illustrated* described:

> a stumpy little guy, tan as the inside of a tamale, pretty lippy for a nobody, and, yeah, wearing those red socks. [A guy] with a 'spread-out caddie-hustler stance and a short, choppy public-course swing.

And everyone wanted to know about the 'Mexican' from Texas.
Lee Buck Trevino was born in Dallas in 1939. He never knew his dad,

was raised by his mom and grandfather, a gravedigger, in a house without electricity or plumbing. He picked cotton from age five. 'I thought hard work was just how life was,' he said. 'I was 21-years-old before I knew Manual Labour wasn't a Mexican.'

Aged eight he worked at the nearby Glen Lakes Country Club, became a caddie, found balls, sold them. At 14 he quit school to work there, polished clubs, caddied, mowed lawns. And beat hundreds of balls a day.

He created and honed his own golf swing. Strong right hand grip, he faded the ball, never missed on the left. The back of his left hand was aimed at the target on impact. He controlled trajectory. Hit it flat, put big work on short irons. He called the swing 'choke-proof'—he knew what was coming.

Yet the swing still looked 'funny', aesthetically unflattering, and Trevino quickly realized the value in that. He hustled for lunch money; bet men he could beat them with a taped-up Dr Pepper bottle. He played under pressure for $5 a hole with $2 in his pocket.

He joined the US Marines, served four years, based in Okinawa. He played a lot of golf with colonels, quipped that he made sergeant because of it. In 1960 he turned pro, went home, made up to $30 a week working in an El Paso golf shop.

He saw Nicklaus win the US PGA Championship at Dallas Athletic Club. He'd never heard of the guy. He was happy enough beating locals at Tenison Park, where he could shoot 65 as par. But the most he ever won was $100.

Once he was working at a 9-hole municipal club and word had got around that he could play. Some cotton baron types with some coin turned up at his club looking to make a bet with the locals that their guy, 21-year-old Ray Floyd, could beat the 23-year-old Trevino.

Floyd met Trevino in the locker room, asked him what he did. Trevino said a lot of things—clean shoes, clean lockers, open and shut the place.

Floyd asked whom he was playing against. Trevino said it was himself. Floyd was asked if he'd like to check out the course. Floyd replied: 'No, I'm playing the locker room guy.' Trevino shot 65, beat him. Floyd wanted to go another 9 holes. Trevino said, 'Mr Floyd I can't. I have to put the carts away.'

'Oh great,' replied Floyd. 'Now I'm playing the cart man too.'

Trevino beat him the next day too. Floyd said he'd had easier games on the PGA Tour. For Trevino, it was another $100.

Trevino told *Golf Digest*:

> It was success to me, but it made me like Dracula. Once I tasted a little bit of blood, I wanted more. I guess I was smart enough to understand that if I was going to get more, I was going to have to give more. Getting out there and doing it. Mastering it. Figuring it out on your own. And the more I practiced, the more I could see the improvement. In leaps and bounds.

He won the Texas Open twice, the New Mexico Open. He was still a small fish, even after running 5th at Baltusrol in '67. When he turned up at Oak Hill in '68 they thought he was with the greens staff. He shot 69 in the first round, drank beer in a cart, no-one approached him. He shot 68 in the second round, drank beer in a cart, same thing. But after 68 in the third round, the game was up.

In the final round Trevino was followed by a bunch of guys calling themselves 'Lee's Fleas', a version of 'Arnie's Army' except made up of Mexican-American dudes, some of them club pros like Trevino, who urged him to 'Whip the Gringos'.

After his fourth round at Augusta in 1969, Trevino said:

> Don't talk to me about the Masters. I'm never going

to play there again. They can invite me all they want, but I'm not going back. It's just not my type of course.

Trevino felt the course didn't suit his prevailing shot shape—the lower trajectory hard fade with bite, and he could make a case given Alister Mackenzie had designed the course for Bobby Jones's high draw.

He also didn't feel comfortable in the posh 'country club' atmosphere of Augusta National. He put his golf shoes on in the car park. He rarely went into the clubhouse. He boycotted '70 and '71. Was talked into playing again by Nicklaus '72 and '73. Boycotted '74. Was talked around again. He made the cut in his last Masters in '91. His best finishes were T10 in '75 and '85. In 1989, battling strong winds and a bad back he shot 5-under 67 to lead by one. In 2009 Trevino said:

> The tournament is the eighth wonder of the world. I watch it every year, but it's not a great golf course. Never was a great golf course. It's a great venue, it's got a tremendous amount of history, but as far as a great golf course, it is not.

Even without playing Augusta, Trevino led the money list in 1970. In February of '71 Nicklaus said to him, as a half-joking aside:

'You know Lee, I hope you never find out how good you really are.'

'For the best player in the world to tell me that,' Trevino responded, 'just filled me up with confidence.'

He won six times in '71 including the US Open, British Open, Canadian Open. Nobody had ever done it. He won four times in '72, defended the Open Championship. Only Gary Player and Arnold Palmer could claim a comparable head-to-head record against Nicklaus.

On the 72nd hole of the 1971 US Open, Trevino was disturbed when a kid fell off a chair and made a commotion. Trevino backed away, returned, missed a 7-foot putt. Nicklaus missed a longer one for the win and the pair came back for 18 holes, the two premier players in golf.

Before they teed off Trevino produced a rubber snake and had the galleries roaring when he teased Nicklaus with it. Nicklaus took it in good spirit. Trevino shot 69, won by three.

In the third round of the 1972 Open Championship at Royal Birkdale, Trevino birdied 14 and 15 and hit his tee-shot on the par-3 16th into a bunker. His shot from a downhill lie without much backswing, shot out thin and hard and would've ended up halfway up the 17th fairway had the ball not taken one hot bounce and leapt into the hole.

He birdied the par-5 17th with a regulation two-putt. Trevino loved Birkdale. There were five par-5s and Trevino could reach them all in two then made a 'regulation' chip-in from rough off the 18th green. Five birdies to finish and a 66.

As Trevino said:

> I think things like that happen to a man sometimes
> when he's trying. I was trying. I was aiming at the
> cup. I didn't come to Scotland to help Nicklaus win
> any Grand Slam. If I played golf with my wife, I'd try
> to beat the daylights out of her.

Watching the golf up close was Tony Jacklin, who would play well enough himself to watch it again the next day. Jacklin thought lightning couldn't strike twice and that, with patience, he could match Trevino and beat him. And that's how it largely played out for almost 17 holes.

On the 17th tee Trevino hooked his drive into a bunker. He chipped out sideways. He hooked again into rough. Trevino never hooked, his 'choke-proof' fade swing was going bad under pressure. His body language was shot. He airmailed the green, was faced with a downhill chip from a fluffy lie. He looked as if he'd given up. He admitted as much later. And then he chipped the ball in for par.

Jacklin's birdie putt for a one-shot lead slid two feet by. His putt coming back was pulled hard left and didn't touch the sides. Trevino went to the 18th tee on up and smoked his drive right down the pipe. And Trevino won by one from Jack Nicklaus. Jacklin never again competed for one of golf's four biggest prizes.

Trevino beat Nicklaus again at the 1974 PGA Championship.

Then he almost went bankrupt. Then he was struck by lightning. And he was never the same. There was back surgery, twice. He couldn't hit confidently from downhill lies. He was often in pain. He had to 'manage' his golf swing rather than freely do what he'd always done. Pros had warned Trevino his swing wouldn't hold up. Eventually, they were right. After he'd won seven majors.

At 45, his back so bad that he couldn't practice, Trevino won the last of them, the 1984 PGA Championship. When he rolled in a 15-footer on the last he kissed his putter and became the first player to shoot four rounds under 70 since the PGA Championship became a stroke event in 1958. That putter was a bit of kit he'd bought for $50 in a shop in Rosendaelsche in Holland prior to the Dutch Open.

Great outcome for fifty bucks. Took a great player to make it sing.

CHAPTER NINE

TIGER ECONOMY

Crazy people, voodoo people

In June of 1997 Tiger Woods was contesting the Buick Open at Westchester County Club in upstate New York. Coming a scant few months since he'd so destroyed the field in the Masters at Augusta National, 'Tiger Mania' was at fever pitch. Fans were like happy clappers in rapture.

I was one of four Aussies in short footy shorts following the Tiger along with nigh-on everyone else on the course. There might've been 8,000 people in the gallery, half of whom were just trying to catch Tiger's eye.

'Yo! Tiger!' they would yell, and wave as he walked the fairway. 'Tiger! My man!' And if he did glance their way, they'd wave and say, 'He looked! He looked!' And they would continue with the 'Yo Tiger!' gibber-jabber which was all a bit much.

Especially given that the highlight was Tiger taking driver to smack it towards a 'drive-able' par-4, and people saying 'Yee-haa!' and variations thereof as Tiger sprayed it so far away right he had to take a drop off another green. Then he airmailed the correct green, the ball coming to rest halfway up a hill so steep that his caddie with the white walrus moustache almost fell down the hill.

Tiger made bogey and still they called, 'Woo-hoo!', the crazy people, voodoo people who loved Tiger no matter what. All a bit much.

So with my three Aussie mates, we followed Ernie Els and Frank Nobilo (we had money on him that we'll never see again) and effectively had these players to ourselves. Because everyone else was following Tiger Woods and Clumsy Fluff, and watching him chop his way to 72, as golfers do occasionally, the game a fickle mistress.

Tiger had a mistress or two in one period of his life. Now, I don't care what Tiger or anyone else I don't know gets up to in their own time, for mine it's his business and not anyone else's. And it happens quite a bit to other people I don't know, pass the beer nuts.

And for a time, the popular presses 'respected' that about Tiger and his tooling about, even though it was something of an open secret.

Yet when his wife took a dim view to certain text messages on his phone and Tiger's car ran into a fire hydrant, the story was set free. And Tiger—and stocks in Tiger Inc.—took a massive hit.

And thus we learned that Tiger wasn't that cool around girls. Why would he be? He'd spent his entire childhood and teenage years playing golf, and knocking about on golf courses. There weren't a lot of girls at golf courses and that's where Tiger was just about all the time.

When he became a famous dude and started knocking around with other famous dudes like Michael Jordan, Tiger had to ask for advice on how to approach girls.

'Just tell 'em you're Tiger Woods,' advised Jordan. And so Tiger did, many times. And that was cool. Until he was married when it wasn't cool. And sponsors dropped him like a steel prong heated to molten redness in a blacksmith's forge.

And so Tiger apologized in a funny, contrived press conference of sorts that didn't have any press and wasn't much of a conference; it being just Tiger at a lectern reading a statement and appearing very, very contrite.

And he hugged his mother, Kutilda, and asked forgiveness and understanding from America, and other places, and it was all a bit weird.

And there followed many injuries and operations. His last major championship was the 2008 US Open, after that incredible putt on 18 to tie with Rocco Mediate and force an 18-hole play-off. And that (if you're reading this book hot off the presses) was about nine years ago.

In October of 2016 we saw him creep back on tour to contest the Safeways Open. Then he pulled out saying his game was too 'vulnerable'. As one PGA Tour pro called it:

> It means he's mentally gone. 'Vulnerable' means he didn't want to embarrass himself. And if his game is so bad he's worried about being embarrassed, then that's it, he's fucked. He won't win again.

Now, maybe this is fairyland and who am I to disagree with a 10-year tour pro. But I disagree. It's only physical fitness holding him back. It's just about keeping his body together. It's about swinging the club so that the spongy stuff between the vertebrae in his spine doesn't turn into so many crusty demons of dirt. The finest surgeons and experts have been consulted.

Granted, there are many 'ifs' and 'buts'. And there's plenty who will line up to tell you why Tiger won't win again, not anywhere, much less a major championship. The kids are all so hot, his flame has extinguished, no man can recapture the ebullience of a gilded youth. And once you've had a back injury you'll always have a back injury, is what they say.

Be great to have him back though.

The Human Highlights Reel

Tiger Woods was so powerful at his peak that he wore a t-shirt in a PGA Tour event and no-one in the golf's Established Order called him out. They may have been thinking something akin to: *Ooh-ooh, Tiger's wearing a t-shirt. We can't tell him to put a collared shirt on, he may pull out, and we will lose millions.*

So Tiger wore a t-shirt. Too bad he didn't go with shorts, thought John Daly, a noted exposed legs advocate.

And so Tiger played PGA Tour golf in a t-shirt. You think Daly or Duffy Waldorf or Boo Weekely could get away with a t-shirt? They'd be put in jail. But Tiger—and the Tiger Economy that bubbled about him like the frenetic Wall Street scenes in *Trading Places* (Sell, Winthorpe! Sell!)—was too big to fail.

Inaugural Augusta National chairman Clifford Roberts would've called Tiger on the t-shirt, among other things, because Clifford Roberts believed black men should only be caddies and that white men should care for them as one would pets. But the old fellow died in 1977 when he shot himself in the head by a fishing pond he'd built for President Eisenhower.

And here we are. Adding to the billions of electronic digits that have been pumped into keyboards about Eldrick Tont 'Tiger' Woods, the wunderkind who ruled the world. The man's a human highlights reel.

When Jesper Parnevik finished 19 shots back from Tiger in 1997 at the Augusta National he said: 'Unless they build Tiger tees about 50 yards back, he's going to win the next 20 of these.' And the concept of 'Tiger tees' was born.

'When Nicklaus said last year that Woods would win 10 green jackets, everybody figured he was way off,' wrote Rick Reilly after Tiger's Masters master class in '97. 'We just never thought his number was low.

There was the shot on 16 at Augusta, the chip-in and the ball rolling inexorably to the hole, pausing at the Nike swoosh and toppling in. How about that? 'In your life!' exclaimed Jim Nantz. 'Have you ever seen anything like that.'

No, Jim. We had not.

When Tiger was two years old, he met Bob Hope on TV.

Before Tiger was 'Tiger', reporters asked Scot Sandy Lyle, the Scottish born golfer, what he thought of Tiger Woods. 'Tiger Woods?' replied Lyle. 'I never played it.' Orlando Sentinel columnist Leslie Doolittle thought Tiger Woods was 'some kind of woodsy musk oil for men'.

There's that probably apocryphal yarn that during the 1996 Quad-City Classic (now the John Deere Classic), Tiger was playing black jack on the Lucky Lady Riverboat Casino in Iowa (true). At 20 years old, he was underage using either a false ID or one someone had not checked (also true). When Tiger tried to enter an adjoining nightclub, the conversation is probably too good to be true.

'ID, please,' says the bouncer.

'I'm Tiger Woods,' says Tiger Woods.

'I don't care if you're the Lion King,' says the bouncer. 'Show me some ID.'

A mate of mine, from Ireland—same age as Tiger—was so good at golf as a boy he was invited to Stanford to play the same time Tiger was. My man turned it down because he'd heard you couldn't drink in America until you were 21. He works for a bank now in Sydney. Tiger, meanwhile, is worth somewhere around half a billion dollars and lives in a mansion on an island.

Tiger was fastidious about the weight of his putters. He worked with Scotty Cameron who drilled out three little holes to give his putter better balance. Cameron painted them Tiger's Sunday color of red, and that's why Scotty Cameron's putters sport little red circular holes.

Tiger won the Open Championship St Andrews in 2000 and 2005.

At Holyake in 2006 he put on a master class of stinging 2-irons. He didn't hit a bunker in 72 holes. He hit a driver once and shouldn't have.

He beat Sergio 'El Nino' Garcia in a crackerjack US PGA Championship at funky old Medinah in 1999, the highlight of which was Garcia cutting a ball around a tree and chasing after it and ripping off a little leap in the middle of the fairway to see what happened. Good times.

Bad times: When Woods beat the all-yellow-clothed Garcia at Holyake in '06 he texted friends: 'I just killed Tweetie Bird'.

Tiger won the 2000 US Open at Pebble Beach by 15 shots. Repeat— by 15 shots. He slaughtered them. He shot 19-under at the 2000 Open Championship at St Andrews and won by eight shots. He was 24-years-old. He won the PGA Championship too but his fifth place in the Masters precluded a grand slam.

So he won the next Masters and they called it the 'Tiger Slam' and Jim Nantz declared it as 'grand as it gets'. And who could argue?

He won the Masters the next year too. And in 2005. Not since. But a few things happened, including two more Open Championships, two more US PGA Championships and the 2008 US Open that he won in a play-off over Rocco Mediate after draining a putt on the 72nd hole that made the Torrey Pines golf course shake as though the San Fernando Fault had finally given way.

When Tiger is playing in a PGA Tour event, ratings are up 50 per cent, according to CBS analyst, Ian Baker-Finch. 'And that was the case pretty much through the 2000s. And the Major numbers, when it was Tiger in contention, the numbers were astronomical.'

People who didn't watch golf watched Tiger Woods playing golf. The regular Golf Channel audience, they'll watch golf every week. But when Tiger's playing, everyone wants to see him.

Baker-Finch again:

Look at the 2015 Wyndham Championship.

Compared to other PGA Tour events it's not a big one, it gets relatively low ratings. When Tiger was in contention at that Wyndham, ratings were 40% bigger than any other tournament in 2015 outside the majors. That tells the story right there.

Broadcaster Scott van Pelt was recruited by *ESPN* from the Golf Channel in part because of his working relationship with Woods. Van Pelt says Tiger 'changed everything'.

There's no other way to say it, and it's not an original thought. It's just the truth. In '97 Tiger came along, and clearly that's when every single thing about the way golf was covered and talked about changed. Everything. And the Golf Channel, where I was at that point in time, was just a baby, it was two years old. How we covered golf was a byproduct of this enormous tidal wave that Tiger created.

When Jack Nicklaus won his Masters in 1986, the story goes that *Sports Illustrated* writer Rick Reilly was walking around the media tent muttering, 'It's too big, it's too big', meaning he was worried he couldn't find adequate words to cover its scale. Van Pelt says it was similar in '97 when Woods won at Augusta.

There was nothing to compare it to. In Jack's case there was no historical context [for a 46-year-old to win the Masters]. In Tiger's case there was no historical context for a 21-year-old to win. And not just that but a 21-year-old to win and shoot the lowest score. And not just that but a 21-year-old to shoot the lowest score and win by the largest margin. And not just that but at Augusta National for someone who's dad was a black man … I mean, you don't try to find context because none exists. You just put it out there and say 'well here's what happened and boy, well, this was something"

And only now, 20 years later, do you look back on it and really understand. That's why it was seismic and it was game changing and it was the most significant event to happen in the sport in recent history, because all of those things are true.

Tiger Woods has won 14 majors. But you know that.

-CHAPTER *TEN*-

ONCERS AND THE BOULVEARD OF BROKEN DREAMS

The Dark Shark

Ian Baker-Finch won the Open Championship at Royal Birkdale in 1991 and was so good they called him 'The Dark Shark' in homage to the Great White Shark, Greg Norman. They also called him 'Finchy', 'Sparrow', 'IBF', 'The Boy from Beerwah', 'a top bloke' and, rarely just 'Ian'.

In 1992 he was ranked tenth in the world. He had three Top-10s at Augusta. He was one of 'them', a top man, a contender.

He had the hands of Mozart. Super touch, a flawless short game. His swing was *svelte*. He looked good; a tall and handsome man, open smile and sparkling eyes. Woman liked him. Men liked him so much they could cop his pink shirt.

And then, roughly the time John Daly won the PGA Championship, Baker-Finch figured (because so many people told him so) that he needed to 'compete' with the New Wave of Long Bombers. And he tried to fashion a long game to go with his short one. And he couldn't hit a fairway wider than the Straits of Hormuz.

In 1984 Baker-Finch led the Open Championship at St Andrews after three rounds with scores of 68–66–71. He was 23 years old, it was his first Open Championship, and paired in the final group with five-time winner Tom Watson chasing six and a third on the trot. Seve Ballesteros and Bernhard Langer were in the group behind, two shots back.

Before tee-off, another five-time Open-winner and fellow Australian Peter Thomson (who'd accompanied Baker-Finch in practice rounds) advised him to forget about the pin on the first green but rather to knock the ball onto the back, make two putts and move on.

Said Thomson to historian Andrew Crockett in *Inside Golf.*

> He had a friend caddying for him and I don't know how they figured out what club it was, but he had a go at the flag and he actually pitched right by the pin. It had rained quite a lot and the ball spun back into the burn and he made a six. That was the end of him, he shot 79.

As Baker-Finch tells it:

> I was obviously apprehensive because of the way I played. But I didn't feel like I was nervous. I didn't feel like I wasn't going to win or I didn't have a chance of winning. I just thought I was going to go out there and play the way I had been.
>
> Started out poorly. Hit the second shot out on the green and come back into the burn. I think it was the first time anyone had seen a ball spin in the water there, but mine did. Nine-over the

first 15 holes. Birdied 16 and 18. Tom would have
liked my finish.

That he would. Baker-Finch had a ringside seat as Watson airmailed
the 17th and Ballesteros birdied 18.
It was a memorable Open for me, but also in a lot of
other ways. Tom going for his sixth Open. And Seve
winning so famously with a great putt at the last.
It was a great experience, even though I played
so poorly early. I started to realize that I was
probably playing at Tom's pace. I got a bit quick, a
bit uncomfortable. But hey, that's what happens to
a 23-year-old. You don't think it at the time but not
often does a young bloke go on and win.

Baker-Finch took away belief. It made him think he was world class,
that he could compete with the best. 'It changed my life,' he says. 'I reset
my goals and I changed my attitude and made a plan to win the Open
Championship.'
There came an invitation from Augusta National. It wasn't because he
was Top-50 in the world or anything. Augusta didn't give a reason—
didn't have to—they just invited whom they liked. Baker-Finch was Top-
25 in 1986 through to '88, didn't get a guernsey.
Baker-Finch remembers his luggage not arriving (though his clubs
did) so he bought all the clothes he wore that week at Augusta's pro shop.
Augusta hat, Augusta shirt. The logo on everything. He also remembers
the greens.
I'd never putted on greens that fast in my life. I was
shocked how fast they were. I'd have a three-foot
putt and hit it ten feet by. I nearly holed out on the

sixth in the first round. I had a two-footer with a bit
of break that I thought I'd just ram in. I hit it thirty
feet past, down the bottom of the hill.

He returned home to Australia, went to Royal Melbourne and
Kingston Heath, the jewels of Melbourne's sandbelt, and learned to putt
on fast greens. In 1990 he was in the last group at St Andrews again, this
time with Nick Faldo who led by five, won by five. He went to Augusta,
finished T7, had a chance to win but didn't putt well.

As Baker-Finch recalls:

> I had a chance a couple of times at Augusta but
> just couldn't get it done. But so be it. Finishing
> top ten gave me the confidence when I did get to
> the British Open that I belonged there. The main
> thing was that British Open in 1990, seeing how
> Nick Faldo went on to win, it really gave me a lot of
> confidence, that intangible knowledge of how to go
> on and win the next time I had the chance.

When he got to Royal Birkdale in '91, Baker-Finch's game was prime.
He was a thirty-year-old world top-10 player at the peak of his game. He'd
won in Europe, he'd won on the PGA Tour. His previous tournament
he'd lost in a play-off. His short game was piping hot.

He'd seen his mates win majors. His great friend Payne Stewart had
won the '91 US Open. Contemporary Wayne Grady won the '90 US
PGA. He felt he was as good as anyone out there. If you can make pars
in a major, particularly in the weather of the UK, when everyone else is
battling, that can be good enough.

Baker-Finch made birdies. Many birdies. After two rounds he tore
Birkdale apart. Shot 64 in the third round. Owned it.

He went into Sunday in the last group equal leader with Mike Harwood and Mark O'Meara, both mates. He'd played with Harwood on the Queensland Troppo Tour. O'Meara was like a big gentle bear. Seve Ballesteros was thereabouts but couldn't conjure more than one-over 71. Freddie Couples shot 64 but started too far back to be frightening. Greg Norman's 74 in round one had scotched his title hopes early.

And the Dark Shark in the pink shirt burned them all. He shot five birdies in his outward 29 and 66 in all, and won the claret jug. And the boy from Beerwah in Queensland who'd left school at 16 to pursue a crazy dream became Open champion.

And Aussies came from everywhere to help him celebrate. There was Penfold's Grange, his wife Jenny's spaghetti bol, and good times on the 18th green with the claret jug. He still drinks out of the replica today.

> I get the jug down and give it a wash out and fill it
> up with some good red. I've got some great photos
> from lots of celebrations with it.

And then everything went to shit.

No, it didn't. That's 'the story'. And it annoys the Sparrow that the timeline in people's minds is that he fell off a cliff after Birkdale in '91.

> The problem I have with all of the stories from '91–
> '97, when I quit, is everyone makes it sound like the
> day after the British Open I couldn't bust a break.
> That always annoys me because I kept playing and I
> kept winning. I was top ten in the world.

He won in Australia, the '92 Vines Classic, the '93 Australian PGA. He ran sixth at the '92 Masters, was second in the '92 Players Championship. He shot 71–71–72–68 in the '93 Open Championship at Muirfield. Ran T19. Hardly the work of a hacker.

And then he tried to hit the ball further. Lost confidence. Tried harder again. Lost more confidence. Tried harder again. Again, lost yet even more confidence.

And repeat.

> I missed 15 cuts in a row in 1995. I started out in '96 and the British Open was the 11th tournament I played on the tour and I missed all 11 cuts, so I missed 22 cuts in a row. Basically, I quit then.

Baker-Finch says if he could look back today with a '50-year-old head' he'd realize his problems were 100 per cent mental.

> I needed to see one coach, get myself fit, stop concerning myself with why and just go and do what I did. Get back to being me again. And I think I could have turned it around.

Instead he asked, and listened to, just about everyone.

The next major championship after the '91 Open was the US PGA, won in sensational style by Long John Daly, who'd driven through the night and a fog of Jim Beam to blast his way around Crooked Stick and won by three.

Daly seemed to be golf's 'new' normal—massively, stupid long. Daly was a wild man who emasculated the golf course, went at it like the Tasmanian Devil. Dog legs on a fairway? Pff! More room in the air.

And well-meaning types lined up to tell Baker-Finch he needed an extra 20 yards to keep up. And Baker-Finch, nice man that he is, nodded along. He thought, *You know what? You're right.* And he began to hit the ball harder and all over the shop.

Yet rather than going back to what had won him the Open Championship—finesse, touch, accuracy, classy up-and-downs, and just playing the bloody game—Baker-Finch tried to compete with Long John and the bombers. And things went worse again.

And as they did, he tried to fix them. That duck hook? 'Compensate thus,' they said. That blocked drive? 'Compensate with this,' they said. 'That shank, Sparra? Mate, loosen up! Be the ball!'

And even though Corey Pavin won the 1995 US Open at Shinnecock Hills despite being the shortest hitter on tour—and still making more birdies on par-5s than most—Baker-Finch lined up and sprayed it ever further. And no-one was safe.

He could stripe it on the range, shoot 67 in the Pro Am and take money off his pals. But with the lights of competition on, he was a goose. In 1995 he entered 18 PGA Tour tournaments and was cut in 14 of them, withdrew from three and disqualified in one.

In the Open at St Andrews he was paired with Arnold Palmer (in the great man's final Open) and snap hooked it out-of-bounds off the first tee. And if you've ever stood on that famous tee-box, you'll wonder how that's possible. It'd be like missing your mouth with your fork.

Baker-Finch told Rick Reilly in *Sports Illustrated*:

> I dreamed of doing it. Before it ever happened, I dreamed I hit it out-of-bounds with Arnie watching at St Andrews on the first hole at the British Open. That's when it got scary, when my nightmares started playing out right in front of me.

He couldn't even visualize hitting a fairway off the tee. He could go home and shoot 66 on the Monday, do the same in the Pro Am. Come out Thursday and shoot 82.

> I got to the point where I didn't even want to be out on the golf course because I was playing so poorly. I would try my hardest but when I came out to play,

I managed to find a way to miss the cut time and time again. It became a habit.

In the '96 Open Championship he shot 78–84. His game was shot. The end analysis now is that doesn't bother me anymore. But at the time, in '95–'96 it really did bother me. I loved the game and I couldn't figure it out. I wore myself out mentally and physically. I would hit 100 drivers a day, every day for the year in 1995 and I'd go to the first tee and snap it out of bounds.

So that's not a swing issue, that's a mental issue. But all of the swing coaches would look at my swing that I hit out of bounds, and try to 'fix' that. But that wasn't really my swing. It was a mental issue, a fear, a fast transition, whatever you want to call it.

He still fronted up in '97, though, at Royal Troon. He double-bogied six after a hook. Double-bogied the postage stamp 8th out of the bunker. He signed off on a 21-over 92. A big 'W/D' went up on the scoreboard. Withdrawn. He retreated to Troon's thankfully empty Champions Room, lay on the ground with his wife and wept.

And he didn't play again. The game of golf had smashed him.

Through the course of time, though, the man grew. And it surprised few who knew him that he could find positives in his journey. He even joked that he was the PGA Tour's Father of the Year—he was always home on weekends.

Having two years without earning any money on the course, I thought to myself, 'Shit, I'm young, I've got Jenny and two young girls at home, I think

I can go do something else, and feel good about myself and do better at that', which I've proven and done well in another side of my career.

So in some ways I could look back on it and think, 'Yes I'm disappointed that I didn't go on and continue to win, and win more majors. But I've had 20 years in the business of TV and off course in the golfing world and I've done pretty well with that.

Baker-Finch's friend and fellow broadcaster Luke Elvy has shared the odd drink from the replica claret jug, and has heard Baker-Finch's tales of Birkdale and the Old Course, and snap-hooks with the King.

Says Elvy:

The game humbled him. He'll tell you, he can't walk around thinking he's anything special. Not that he ever did. But he'll say, 'The game brought me to my knees. It ruined me. It changed me as a person.' Thing is he's probably become a better person. A champion player to a champion bloke.

Baker-Finch's report card—a top bloke, could have done better, still a top bloke. Oh, and the Open champion golfer of the year in 1991.

***

Dapper Doug

Doug Sanders is best known for missing a two-and-a-half foot putt on the 18th green at the Old Course, St Andrews, that would have won the 1970 Open Championship. He's also known as 'The Peacock of the

Fairways' given his very colorful clothes. But mainly for that putt, that tiddly, 30-inch putt.

Sanders was leading the Open by one from Jack Nicklaus when his approach shot on 17 found the Road Hole Bunker. And there he faced one of the hardest examinations in golf. A riveted, steep-faced and aptly-named 'trap', Sanders had to extricate his ball high and soft over a ridge and down a slope to a short-sided flag. There are easier up-and-downs from ball-washing machines.

But our man Doug Sanders pulled it off, lofting the ball out softly and stopping it close. The big gallery was thick with appreciation. What a shot! Nicklaus called it one of the greatest bunker shots he'd ever seen. Sanders acknowledged the applause and there seemed to be just the barest hint of strut in his stride. He put an arm around his buddy Lee Trevino's neck and shared a laugh that belied his nerves.

And so Sanders dressed in purple cardigan, turtle-neck skivvie and shoes with light-mauve pants (Sanders was described by the commentator as a 'genial, gay fellow') went to the 18th tee with a one shot lead over the game's best player needing par to win.

The 18th, named 'Old Tom Morris' after its creator, is a short, straight, wide and ostensibly 'easy' par-4. There's out of bounds right in the town but there's so much room left you can hook it across two fairways and still be in play. It looks like there's nothing to it. And therein lies part of its genius.

Sanders was playing in the group with Lee Trevino. Sanders had been one of the 'first players to embrace me, to play practice rounds with me, take me to dinner,' Trevino told Matt Adams on the Golf Channel. 'He could see I was kind of a lost guy and we became close.'

So close that Trevino, who'd begun the day leading by two shots and would finish two back, offered Sanders this advice: 'Don't drive this ball straight to the green.'

The 18th fairway at the Old Course shares the same giant green swathe of fairway as the first. A drive at the flag on 18, as on so many Old Course holes, is not necessarily the best angle for the approach. Such is the genius of Old Tom Morris's famous links.

The angle from the first fairway, however, opened up the green a bit and didn't leave the player with a nervy half-wedge from a very tight lie over the 'Valley of Sin'. Golfers could consider hitting a 3-iron off the tee, leave themselves a full wedge in.

Sanders took a driver. And hit it straight down the middle of 18.

With a howling wind behind him and Nicklaus one shot back, the implications of what he was so close to achieving—joining Bobby Jones, Sam Snead, Peter Thomson and Bobby Locke as a winner of the Open at St Andrews—added to the pressure.

Sanders was faced with 74 yards to a flag just over a ridge that sat bulbous above said sin-filled valley. The fairway was 'hard as concrete', according to Trevino who reckoned 8- or 9-iron bump-n-run would be the best option. Sanders chose a three-quarter sand wedge, knocked it 40 feet past, the wind carrying the ball to the back. The ground was rock hard and the elevation was nearly impossible. 'He played the hole completely wrong,' said Trevino.

As Sanders surveyed the putt, commentator Henry Longhurst noted with more prescience than he could know: 'You can see yourself going down in the history books as the man who had two putts to win the Open Championship, and took three and lost in the play-off.'

Sanders stood over the putt. Two putts and he'd win the Open Championship at St Andrews. He lined up. A photographer's shutter clicked, and he backed off. He set himself again and set his downhill putt from downtown free. And it looked a good one, though lagged and left him a knee-trembler to finish. 'Oh Lord,' remarked Longhurst. 'That's not one I would like to have.' Downhill. Left-to-right. To win the Open.

Sanders looked at the thing from everywhere. He stalked it. He bent down on one knee and surveyed it. Then he got himself over it, looked at the ball, looked at the hole and stood very still ... and noticed a little pebble or a bit of sand or something in his path. He bent down to pick it up. 'Oh God,' murmured Longhurst. The crowd gasped softly. Trevino waved to settle them. And Doug Sanders got himself over the ball again with his feet slightly more open to the target.

'Back away, Sanders! Back away!' roared Ben Hogan watching on television in Forth Worth.

Hogan knew the value of restarting the process and clearing the mind. Sanders, though, wanted to get it done. He didn't back off.

He set himself again over the ball for what seemed an age, his feet facing left, a hunched purple statue. And then he let rip. And stabbed it by the right edge. His upper body fell right; his entire being willed it in but no cigar. And a brilliant golfer, a Ryder Cup player, was reduced to the level of club hacker choking up over the C-grade medal.

And back for the Open's first 18-hole championship they went.

Things were differently for Sanders on 18 the next time when he drained a 3-footer for birdie. Unfortunately for him, Nicklaus, faced with a six-foot left-to-right downhill putt for the win—the line almost identical to that which Sanders faced the day before—had already curled it in for the win (then leapt with excitement and tossed his putter into the air before it nearly came down to brain his playing partner, Sanders, dressed in golden cardigan with yellow trim and white skivvie).

George Douglas Sanders was born in Cedartown, Georgia, in 1933 at the height of the Great Depression. He was called 'Doug' because a family friend wanted him named after swashbuckling actor Douglas Fairbanks. As Sanders told Guy Yocom in *Golf Digest* about his childhood.

We were too poor to make it. My dad walked five

miles to work in Cedartown, Ga., for 50 cents a day. There wasn't enough to eat. No doctors. Lice in our hair. Ratty hand-me-down clothes. So many people in the Depression had it like that. The strange thing is, nobody complained. Everybody just floated through it, waiting for the nightmare to end.

He picked cotton at the age of seven. He made moonshine the color of gasoline and more potent. He caddied at a local course. The local professional could see he wanted to play, allowed him to hit balls out of view. Sanders would hit one then put the next ball behind the divot. 'I'd do this over and over until I'd made one long, 20-yard divot. I'd fix them, then start a new strip.

Sanders recalls those times:

> I chipped and putted for nickels and dimes against older guys, grown men. I never won. They chided me. 'Come on, sucker,' they'd say. They'd clean me out and I'd walk home in the dark, depressed and discouraged. The lightning bugs flashed around me; they looked like ghosts. I had to quit playing. But I'd show up at the course before the sun came up and practice. I'd practice more at night. Regardless of the weather, Sanders was there. After three months of practice and no gambling, I showed up with $5 and said, 'Let's go.' We chipped and putted, and I took all of their money. I walked home that night with $20 in my pocket, the most money I'd ever had. The lightning bugs didn't look like ghosts anymore. They looked like stars.

Soon enough the stars were his friends. Frank Sinatra, Dean Martin, the famous stuntman Evel Kneival. He played golf with US Presidents. He was a 'playboy', a pants man. He didn't own a pair of shoes as a child. By 1970 he owned 271 pairs.

Sanders won 20 PGA Tour events, the same number as Greg Norman, one more than Ernie Els and Ben Crenshaw. As an amateur he won the Canadian Open and the Colombian Open. He turned pro in '57 and won the Kemper Open. He was T2 in the 1959 PGA. He ran second in the 1961 US Open (to Gene 'The Machine' Littler), was third on that year's PGA Tour money list (behind Arnold Palmer and Gary Player) and second in the Open Championship of 1966 (behind, of course, Jack Nicklaus). He finished in the top 10 of every major championship of 1966.

So yes, Doug Sanders could play. But it's two other tales that highlight why the Doug Sanders story shouldn't begin and end with that missed putt at St Andrews.

The first one sees him as a teenager playing a big money golf match at Cedartown. He watched a man called Dallas Weaver hit his ball behind a tree. Sanders and his fellow players assumed Weaver was gone. And then along came a train.

Says Sanders:

> There were tracks running by our course, and just then a freight train came through. Dallas Weaver turned sideways, took some kind of low iron and banked a ball off the side of a freight car and almost onto the green. That was 50 years ago, and I've never seen anyone top that shot.

The second yarn sees Sanders being diagnosed with a rare condition called Tortocollis. It was like having a never-ending cramp in his neck that was so painful he wished he were dead.

The doctor said he could operate for eight hours
and probably straighten my head, but the chances
of curing the pain were only 50–50. I didn't want to
live anymore. I started looking for a possible way out.

So Sanders made a phone call to a man who hung with the Rat Pack.
He had 'connections'. Couple weeks later 'Tony' turned up at his door.
The pair sat down to discuss how things would pan out. Sanders was
ordering a hit on himself. Sanders wanted it to look like a robbery to
avoid the stigma of suicide. The man gave his price. Sanders said it was
too low and upped it to $40,000. 'For that kind of dough,' said Sanders,
'I knew I could count on him to do the job right.'

But first the operation. It was a success!

I called the man in charge and told him I wouldn't
be needing Tony. He said congratulations, good
luck, and if I needed him I knew where to find him.

In July of 2015, 83-year-old Doug Sanders was attending the Open
Championship at St Andrews. He was asked, of course, about the putt.
But plenty more. All those yarns. All that living.

It's hard to believe when I sit down and tell stories
about my life. To be a poor kid from Georgia, my
mother working in a cotton mill, there are just not
the adjectives to express the life I have been able
to live. It was better than I ever thought it could
possibly be.

Sanders remained friends with Nicklaus who never once mentioned
that putt.

***

Jean Clod

In 1999 Jean-Claude Van De Velde stood on Carnoustie's 18th tee needing a double-bogey to win the Open Championship. Instead of taking on the 480-yard par-4 with a 5-iron, 5-iron, wedge and two or three putts, Van De Velde took a driver a smashed the ball a long way away.

His second shot was 240 yards and the odd water crossing away. Two 120-yard wedges and three putts, and he would be champion golfer of 1999. Van de Velde decided upon a 2-iron and flogged it. The ball ricocheted off a grandstand and bounced into grass so long he could barely see it. He chopped the ball out, straight into a burn.

So there he was, lying three shots, the top of the ball just visible in the water. He took off his shoes, rolled up his pants and stood mid-burn contemplating how to extricate himself. He took a drop. Then chunked his fifth shot into a greenside bunker. He splashed out and needed a six-footer to force a play-off with Paul Lawrie and Justin Leonard who had both finished 6-over. Van de Velde made the putt. Double-bogied the first of four play-off holes. And watched Lawrie lift the claret jug, a man who had begun the round 10 shots back.

***

David Duval: Unrivalled, Unravelled

David Duval shot 59 in the final round of the 1999 Bob Hope Classic at the PGA West Palmer Private course at La Quinta, California. Start of the day, he was seven shots back. He birdied the first three holes. He birdied the fifth hole. He birdied 9, 10, 11 and 12. He led the tournament.

On the 14th his driver found the fairway bunker. He nipped a 5-iron out, knocked a sand-wedge to 10 feet and made the birdie putt. On the

15th he stiffed an 8-iron to 18-inches. On the 16th he hit a two-iron off the tee and sand-wedge to six inches. He had a 5-footer for par on 17 that he said was his day's most nervous putt. He wanted to break 60. Winning the tournament was almost inconsequential.

David Duval walked onto the tee of the 543-yard par-5 18th needing eagle for 13-under 59. He smoked his driver. Hit a beautiful, pure 5-iron to the back third of the green, the ball running up to the top tier leaving 8-foot putt for eagle and history.

With his long-sleeved cream-yellow shirt slightly untucked out of bone-ivory baggy pants, with his sunglasses wrapped tight under a bone-ivory Titleist cap with blue trim—a look copied by no-one ever since—David Duval lined up the putt, stood over the ball, and stroked it into the cup.

Fifty-nine. The stratosphere.

Funny thing was, while it was considered extraordinary and people sat up and remarked 'wow', if anyone was going to do it in 1999 it was going to be Tiger Woods. But David Duval was the 'other one'. David Duval was so hot he was a river of molten lava.

He was the world's number one player in a time of Peak Tiger. He was the PGA Tour's leading money-winner in 1998 with $2.6 million, a record. He was that year's PGA Tour lowest average score. *Sports Illustrated* put him on the cover with the heading: 'David Duval is on fire'.

Two weeks before he won the Bob Hope by one shot from Steve Pate who shot 66 and had a 20-footer for birdie on 18 that lipped out, he'd won the Mercedes Championship by nine shots. Then he went skiing. Then he won the Players Championship at TPC Sawgrass. In an 18-month period, end of '97 to start of '99, David Duval won 11 of 34 tournaments.

David Duval has won $19 million in prize money on the PGA Tour. He could've won the US Masters four times. His Augusta record from

'98 through to 2001 reads T2, T6, T3, 2nd. His US Open record in the same period is T7, T7, T8, T16. He won the 2001 Open Championship at Royal Lytham & St Annes, shooting 69–73–65–67 for a 10-under 274 and won by three shots.

And then, as he entered his thirties, the decade that for most golfers represent the prime salad years, when a man's golf smarts and experience mesh with a still-fit frame, David Duval couldn't play anymore. Nothing like he had been, anyway.

He hurt his wrist and his back and his neck and his shoulder. He was diagnosed with vertigo. He split with his childhood sweetheart. He got married. Pretty soon he had five kids. His marriage broke up.

Somehow, amidst all the missed cuts and drudgery, like a last gusset of lava shooting out a volcano believed extinct, David Duval was runner-up at the US Open of 2009 behind Lucas Glover.

In 2010 he finished T2 in the Pebble Beach Pro-Am and T6 in Frys. com Open. Made nine hundred grand. Finished outside the top 125. And that was about it. There was no encore (unless you count a 2016 father and son challenge, and people don't, not really).

Duval is still playing on the PGA Tour. He knocked out scores of 70 and 73 in the Sandersons Farms Championship, the first event of the 2017 tour (in October of 2016). And was cut.

David Duval today talks—very well—on the television about golf.

CHAPTER ELEVEN

CREATORS

The Good Doctor Mackenzie

Old Tom Morris carved golf courses from the raw building blocks of duneside links land. When designing the routing of a golf course, there were no trees to skirt around, no lakes. There was the odd 'wee burn'. But mainly it was just a chunk of land where he'd put a tee and a green and devise a fun way to commute between the two that was nice to look at.

Donald Ross was apprenticed to Old Tom Morris and created Pinehurst No. 2 when he was 29. It remains his masterpiece. Ross had a hand in 400 other courses but is most famous for Pinehurst and its 'turtleback' greens: upside down bowls from which approach shots are repelled into low basins.

Ross is also known for creating a mound called Maniac Hill upon which golfers could take lessons and practice hitting balls. Before Maniac Hill the norm for practice was to do it on the course. Donald Ross may have invented the driving range.

Albert Warren 'AW' Tillinghast was another disciple of Old Tom Morris and had a hand in Winged Foot, Baltusrol and—in concert with Joseph Burbeck—the beast that is Bethpage Black. AW Tillinghast had all sorts of funky stuff going on: roller coaster greens; double dog-leg fairways and deep, amoeba-shaped bunkers. He was part artist, part architect, part warlock.

Study their work and you'll find these old boys of architecture weren't necessarily (or even at all) concerned with 'fair'. They wanted all standards of golfer to enjoy the game and believed that 'fair' was a relative, even moot concept. Part of golf was how you dealt with adversity. *Man up, man!* This influence remains today.

Yet it was Dr Alister Mackenzie who revolutionized golf. He literally wrote the book on golf architecture, in 1920 publishing *Golf Architecture: Economy in Course Construction and Greenkeeping*, the first tome to explain just what the hell was going on.

Some designers look to punish bad shots by bad players. There are bunkers running the length of fairways, waist-high grass miles from the hole. Courses could be penal, and harsh, and no fun at all. Strategy can amount to little more than 'hit the ball straight'.

This was anathema to Mackenzie. His muse was the Old Course at St Andrews, which has super-wide fairways, bunkers in the middle of fairways, a course that required lots of strategy. He detested long rough, and the time spent looking for balls. He didn't want to beat up average players. He didn't want to make the game more difficult. He saw it as a sport; as a sporting game. Mackenzie wanted to make the game fun. He wanted golf courses to be playable.

Not to say he never created a shot the average player couldn't play. But he gave them a way around it. Of Augusta, he said:

> There should be a sufficient number of heroic carries
> from the tee, but the course should be arranged so

that the weaker player with the loss of a stroke or portion of a stroke shall always have an alternative route open to him.

Mackenzie wanted constructions looking natural, beautiful and 'indistinguishable from nature.' He'd served in British Forces in the Boer War, was interested in camouflage, how to make the hidden look natural.

Mackenzie loved to watch Bobby Jones play golf, and designed Augusta to suit the great man's high draw. Look at the 13th that follows the curve in Rae's Creek. Phil Mickelson hit the greatest six-iron you've ever seen from the trees. Two-time Masters champion Bubba Watson—a self-taught man with a wild, slash-and-burn style that would have appealed greatly to Dr McKenzie—often cuts the corner on 13 and drives the ball over everything, leaves himself a wedge in lying one.

Augusta was made for adventurers. Seve Ballesteros won there. Jack Nicklaus won there. The great swashbuckling Great White Shark, Greg Norman should have won there half-a-dozen times. Yes, the robotic Nick Faldo won there three times but he had magnificent skill: he could hit greens like 16-time world champion darts player, Phil 'The Power' Taylor hitting the pizza-shaped wedge bottom of a dartboard.

Lee Trevino played there in 1969, declared that wouldn't be back. The course didn't suit his flatter trajectory, his hard little fades.

Mackenzie believed that 'the ideal hole is surely one that affords the greatest pleasure to the greatest number.' Look at that 13th at Augusta and ask yourself if an 18-marker would enjoy hitting the fairway a couple of times and knocking a 9-iron on.

Look also at the downhill 10th hole where Adam Scott rolled in a winner in the 2013 play-off. Same hole, Bubba Watson hooked an 8-iron out of a little forest, won the Masters on the second hole of a play-off with the indefatigable gap-toothed South African Louis Oosthuizen.

Mackenzie would've been fond of Big Bubba. He'd loved watching Walter Hagen; loved how he played. Hagen could be erratic but he played with flair. He had a crack. And big Bubba's work from the pine straw, to hit an 8-iron high and drawing up through a gap the tree tops, to a green he couldn't see, well.

Ballesteros was the same. Renowned course designer, Mike Clayton reckons that:

> Ballesteros was the style of player that Mackenzie was encouraging ... Mackenzie didn't want people to play golf like Hale Irwin. Hale Irwin—one of the greats—his playing style was to hit it down the middle, then hit it on the green, make two putts, and move on. And he'd do it 72 times and he'd win the US Open. Great player. Won the US Open three times. But his style was robotic. Which I think would've been anathema to Mackenzie.
>
> For that reason I think Mackenzie would've hated the US Open, the way they always set the course up. The 'strategy' is to hit a fairway thirty yards wide, then hit the green.

Consider the 18th hole at Cherry Hills in the 1978 US Open. Andy North had led by four shots with five holes to play but bogied 14 and double-bogied 15 to give Dave Stockton and JC Snead a sniff. North composed himself enough to make pars on 16 and 17, and walked onto the 18th tee with a 2-shot lead. Bogey the last and he was (probably) US Open champion.

But the 18th was a beast. A monster. There was a 15-yard landing area protected by long rough and out-of-bounds to the right, watery death to the left. *Sports Illustrated* scribe Dan Jenkins wrote that it 'combines such length and danger it should have been the place where all of those movie companies went looking for King Kong.'

After finding the 15-yard landing zone—it didn't matter if you hit 4-iron or driver, that was your target—the second shot was a long one up a hill to a hard green surrounded by yawning bunkers. There'd been three-putts all day. The 18th had been played 432 times that tournament and given up just 11 birdies.

Andy North had two of them. But this was a bit different.

His drive went right into the thick rough. He couldn't hit the green so he hacked it out far as he could, which was just below the left-hand bunker. The green and flag were above him.

Snead and Stockton couldn't reel in any more of North's lead so the 28 year old from Florida, who'd won just once before on the PGA Tour, knew that he needed a chip and two putts to win the US Open. And thus he promptly, daintily, chunked his wedge straight into the pot.

And so he stood over his ball in the bunker, with the memory of leaving two in the sand on 15 relatively raw, and hit perhaps his best shot of the week. The ball flopped out and released, rolled to four feet. But he certainly wasn't done. The wind was strong. He stood over his putt and backed away. He stood over his putt and backed away again. He stood over his putt, lemon yellow bell-bottoms flapping in the breeze, and stroked the ball into the cup.

'Making a four-foot putt to win the Open is something you usually only pretend to do in practice rounds,' said North, who finished 1-over for the championship. In 1983 he had a one-foot tap-in to win the 1983 US Open. He won three times on the PGA Tour.

Before his second round of the 1980 US Open at Baltusrol, Seve Ballesteros was stuck in traffic getting to the course and arrived five minutes late for his tee-time. He was disqualified. Ballesteros spoke to the press afterwards, the same scribes who had written him off. 'It doesn't matter,' he said sarcastically. 'I couldn't win here anyway. The rough is too severe.'

Yet the scribes could make a case. Ballesteros shot 75 in round one. Jack Nicklaus (who would win) and Tom Weiskopf had 63.

The US Golf Association unapologetically setup the national title of the United States to be tough. They want par to be the lowest achievable score; for the greatest players of the day to achieve parity. Yet the old boys—Old Tom Morris, Mackenzie, Ross, Tillinghast, Bobby Jones— wanted golf played as it is at St Andrews. Mackenzie designed Augusta National (and Royal Melbourne) with space, options, beauty and diverse routes to the green. If you hit a crooked shot, you weren't automatically dead, you just had a more difficult next shot.

It's instructive that the great Ballesteros is the only man to win at St Andrews, Augusta and Royal Melbourne. All three courses are quite different. All three give the golfer a look at the green from most places, even if there are routes only the very special can see. Ballesteros could hit the ball in the wrong place but recover with genius. He could see in his mind in technicolor that which others could not. And he could pull off shots, under pressure, and the people roared for him—how did he do that? The man's Mandrake!

And that's why Seve is a legend, and Hale Irwin is appreciated like a human version of Iron Byron the mechanical ball-whacking machine.

Of course, this is not entirely, or even at all, true. And granted it's a bit facetious, and with great apologies and respect to Hale Irwin who won on six continents and is one of the greats. All hail, Hale Irwin.

But, you know, Seve, well, Seve was Houdini in golf pants.

Mackenzie built beautiful courses. Beautiful greens, beautiful bunkering—the 'fingers' of green jutting into bunkers, a Mackenzie thing. He eschewed the traditional 'pot' bunkers for grander, more amoeba-like designs. His greens angled away from fairways, placing a premium on strategic placement.

He teamed up with a lawyer called Harry Colt, a golf architect and one-time captain of the Cambridge Golf team. Colt always said trees should be part of the scenery not part of the stage. Mackenzie ate that stuff up.

Part of Mackenzie's genius was that he could find people to build his courses. He came to Australia in 1926 and found Royal Melbourne members Hugh Ross and Alec Russel (winner of the 1924 Australian Open), and greenkeeper Mick Morcom, a master craftsman. Mackenzie laid out his ideas, told them what to do and left. And the locals pulled it off. Mackenzie conceived the thing, the locals made it happen. Mackenzie did the same with Cypress Point.

On the same trip in 1926, Mackenzie said that the Royal Adelaide course, with the possible exception of the old course at St Andrews, could be made to be superior to anything in Great Britain. With that he laid out a master plan, told them what to do and left. And the club implemented just about none of it.

'Some of the golfers of Adelaide found it a little difficult to analyse the statement of Dr Mackenzie, which seems to them somewhat ambiguous,' reported *The Adelaide Advertiser*. Wrote a Mr 'Eagle':

> Dr Mackenzie would not or could not justify his [tee] placings [and] when his attention was drawn to the proximity each to the other of some parallel fairways and the bad position of the tees he merely responded (I am authoritatively told) with the puerile remark that 'You will find the same thing at St. Andrews, and no undue trouble caused,' or words to that effect. What in the name of all that is sane has the confined nature of St Andrews course got to do with [Royal Adelaide]?

The more things change …

Overall, Mackenzie's views were highly regarded and recorded in major newspapers. And his work on Royal Melbourne; they're still talking about it today.

Says Mike Clayton:

> They talk about Royal Melbourne as the Augusta of Australia, but I disagree. Augusta is the Royal Melbourne of America. And Royal Melbourne is better.

As with the old course at St Andrews, Mackenzie's layouts are best learned backwards, green to tee. Then you can see where the trouble is and steer away from it. You can find the best part of the fairway to approach the flag. Perhaps counter-intuitively, the middle of the fairway is rarely the ideal route to the hole. Clayton points again to Augusta and St Andrews.

> The 13th at Augusta might be the best hole in America. If you can draw it down close to the creek there then you've got a great angle into the green. But you put it in the middle of the fairway and the ball's above your feet. Go right from there and you're done. It's a ballsy drive to hug the creek, hit if 5 yards left you're in the water. But get it there, it's a flat surface and the best way to approach the pin.
>
> Same at the Road Hole, probably the greatest strategic hole in Britain. If you hug the right side of the fairway, you'll get the best approach into the green. Go too far right and you're in the hotel, out of bounds. Too far left you're alive but hitting the green is very hard.

Where there is risk there is reward. It could be the title of a Ballesteros book. The beauty of Royal Melbourne and St Andrews, according to Clayton:

the questions are not that complicated but the answers are ... On a bad course, the questions are complicated. What the hell are you asking me to do, I don't get it. Is this asking me to do anything but hit straight shots? The best courses ask simple questions but the answers are complicated.

Simple really.

∗∗

Post-War Pete

Mackenzie died and Donald Ross died and Charles B. MacDonald, founder of Chicago Golf Club, creator of the National Golf Links of America, co-founder of the United States Golf Association, died. Stanley Thompson (Banff Springs Hotel golf course and co-founder with Donald Ross of the American Society of Golf Course Architects) died, as did Harry Colt, Mackenzie's mentor and collaborator. And with these men the 'Golden Age' of golf course architecture died too.

In the boom after World War II Robert Trent Jones made golf courses that looked like, as Peter Thomson described them, Cadillacs with wings: flashy, sort of attractive, not good for very much.

This is not absolutely true. Many fine courses were created. But in the USA, in golf architecture, there was a 'cookie-cutter' thing going on which lasted several decades. You could buy a burger at McDonald's, Wendy's, Jack in The Box. Like greed in the '80s, copying was good.

During World War II a young Pete Dye was stationed at Fort Bragg, about an hour's drive from Pinehurst No 2. Dye told Lee Pace, a

Pinehurst historian:

> The lieutenant colonel was an avid golfer and had a car. It was a lot easier to come over here and play golf for three bucks than stay on the base and do KP duty.
>
> I had the greatest time coming over here. I've played that golf course more than the law should allow. I've looked at that thing 'till I'm blind.

Dye was playing Pinehurst No. 2 in a practice round of the North and South Amateur, when he noticed a couple of older gentlemen walking the course and talking to players. He discovered that one was James Cash 'JC' Penney, the supermarket mogul and the other was Donald Ross, famous golf architect and the creator of Pinehurst No. 2.

Dye met Donald Ross in the bar afterwards and couldn't believe what he was seeing. 'Everyone else was excited about having met J.C. Penney,' said Dye. 'I can't remember a single person thinking it was special he'd met Donald Ross. That's hard to believe looking back.'

Pete Dye married Alice O'Neal (also a golf architect and noted player who would win the Women's North South Amateur in 1968) in 1950. They remained avid golfers and wannabe architects.

In 1963, on the advice of Richard Tufts, president of Pinehurst, Pete Dye entered the British Amateur Championship and travelled to Scotland to learn about links golf.

There he and Alice saw Old Tom Morris's masterpieces St Andrews old course and Carnoustie, and Donald Ross's Royal Dornoch. They saw pot bunkers and Alister Mackenzie designs. They saw Prestwick where the first Open Championship was played in 1860. And they returned home to create many courses: TPC at Sawgrass, Harbour Town Golf

Links, Whistling Straits, and Crooked Stick in Indiana where John Daly won the 1991 US PGA. Pete Dye's autobiography is called *Bury Me in a Pot Bunker*.

And so came the era of Pete Wilson who made Bay Hill and the TPC Blue Monster at Doral, Florida. Arnold Palmer made courses, Jack Nicklaus made courses, Gary Player made golf courses. Bill Coore and Ben Crenshaw teamed up to give golf Barnbougle Lost Farm in Tasmania, Kapalua Plantation Course in Maui and two of the six golf courses at the bucket-listed Bandon Dunes in Oregon.

And while it's a subjective, and never-ending, argument among golf architecture nerds the world over, the greater consensus among those who know about these things is that the output from the pre-Depression era is better. Golf courses were better before the Depression than those which were constructed after World War II.

Well, at least until Tom Doak came along to create the world's best golf courses.

⁕ ⁕ ⁕

Bouncing About at Chambers Bay

Today when you watch the PGA Tour on the television, you're taken by the 'sameness' of the courses. Yes, TPC Sawgrass has an island green and Jack Nicklaus made a 'Bear Trap' at PGA National and Pebble Beach is Pebble Beach. There's Dove Mountain in Arizona that looks like the set of Road Runner's never-ending dice with Wile E. Coyote.

The European Tour, meanwhile, has tournaments in Scotland, Belgium, Turkey, Singapore, Dubai and the far-flung European principality of Perth in Western Australia. And the 'look' of it is diverse. And the golf is too. There's links golf in the Dunhill Cup, oasis-in-a-desert golf on a Race to Dubai. There's kangaroos, crocodiles and the dangerous monkeys of Macau.

And on the PGA Tour, there are rather a lot of things that are green; jackets, fairways, trees and greens. On some courses, the sand to fill your divot is colored green.

Yet the PGA Tour—ubiquitous leviathan of ridiculous money that it is—is not American golf. Courses that don't host televised PGA Tour tournaments include: Chicago Golf Club, Sand Hills, Bandon Dunes and Shoreacres. If you're watching the PGA Tour, you're watching what members of the Professional Golfers Association of America want in a golf course: conformity, uniformity, fairness. PGA Tourists want everyone to be punished equally should they go off target. They want courses cut, modelled and manicured from the same choc-chip cookie mould.

Same speeds on the stimp, same cuts of rough, same sugary sand in bunkers raked into artistic concentric circles. They want bunkers to be less 'traps', more launching pad for an up-and-down.

And they get it, for their lobby group is powerful, and money speaks. And thus, there is—looking at it on television—a sameness about the tour. The fairways are uniformly wide. There's a first, second, third 'cut' of rough. There's rough around the fringes of the greens—more decorative than punishment. Bunker sand is uniformly like sugar. If it gets too rainy or windy, they stop play.

You could argue it's a bit like America itself. Go to a Holiday Inn or rent an Avis rent-a-car or look into the calculating eyes of a woman in a white singlet in a Hooters bar, and you know what you're going to get. Miss a green on the PGA Tour, pull your lob-wedge out and flop it on, thereabouts.

A generalisation? Yes, it is. Pete Dye's and Jack Nicklaus's Harbour Town in South Carolina; Pete Dye's Whistling Straits in Wisconsin, there is funky, 'linksy' action there. Pinehurst No. 2, Cypress Point and Augusta—that is golf heaven.

But the pros want golf to be fair. Tour golfers are mostly grinders, accumulators, 72-hole marathon men. In the main they have more in common with Ben Hogan, Hale Irwin and Iron Byron than Walter Hagen and Sam Snead and Seve Ballesteros. They are professionals: the course is where they 'work'. And they want equity of punishment and of reward. They want fairness. Which is understandable. Lose a million dollars because of an unfair bounce? You would be upset.

Yet this is not golf as Mackenzie and Old Tom Morris, and other purists and idealists and hopeless romantics, idealized the game. Golf was never meant to be fair. A big part of the game is how golfers deal with the unfair.

As Stuart Cink said after shooting 69 on the final day at Turnberry to beat Tom Watson:

> [Links golf] requires patience. You hit good shots
> that don't end up good. Or bad shots that end up
> really bad. You have to be prepared for that.

Jordan Spieth notched his second major championship when he won the US Open at Robert Trent Jones Jnr interesting, rolling, 'linksy' creation, Chambers Bay, which sits on Puget Sound in Washington State and is just about universally hated by pros. Spieth's first win was at Augusta two months earlier.

Pros, you see, by dint of being professionals who see golf as work and expect to be commensurately rewarded for 'good' work, expect that golf shots struck centre fairway should not roll into great chasms of angst and death.

Tiger Woods shot 80 and 76 and was 16-over after two rounds at Chambers Bay. Gary Player said of the course: 'the man who designed this golf course had to have one leg shorter than the other.'

After Spieth double-bogied 18 in the second round at Chambers Bay he said: 'All in all, I thought it was a dumb hole today, but I think we're going to play it from there again, so I've got to get over that.'

All part of the long journey to Zen.

In fairness, though, most pros didn't knock the layout so much as the surface of the greens which 'were like putting on broccoli' according to Henrik Stenson. Justin Rose compared putting to 'outdoor bingo'. Ian Poulter said the greens were 'simply the worst, most disgraceful surface I have ever seen on any tour in all the years I have played.' And they could make a case. The greens were a mite lumpy.

But Dustin Johnson liked them well enough, even with a three-putt on 18 that gift-wrapped the title for Heir Jordan who was also mostly complimentary about the track, though he told his caddie that the 18th hole—which at 514 yards can be played as a par-4 or a par-5—is 'the dumbest hole I've ever played in my life'.

After three rounds Spieth (−4) shared the lead with Jason Day, Branden Grace and Johnson. Grace was co-leader but bombed one out of bounds on 16. Louis Oosthuizen came from the clouds to birdie six of his last 7 and post 67, and tie the lead. But Spieth hit the last green in two, two-putted, and watched Johnson three-putt, and that was all she wrote.

CHAPTER TWELVE

KIDS AND TIGER KILLERS

The Greatest Hybrid Ever

Yang Yong-eun, known as 'Y.E. Yang', of South Korea won the 2009 PGA Championship at Hazeltine with the greatest hybrid ever seen in professional golf.

From an uphill lie on 18, in the fluffy, dense first cut of rough, 210 yards from the flag, into the wind, with his playing partner, Tiger Woods, the winner of 14 major championships sitting pretty right side of the fairway, Yang unleashed a hybrid from heaven. Purely struck, it soared into the sky, cleared a mighty oak, continued upwards, reached the zenith of its parabola, descended over a greenside bunker, and landed like a butterfly in a strip of green no bigger than a billiard table right next to the flag. He almost slam-dunked it, the ball rolled 10 feet by.

And it was over to you, Mr Woods.

When the round began Yang was two shots back and thought himself a 70–1 chance given Woods' 70 titles and Yang's one. Yet on the sixth hole,

Yang showed that he wouldn't be overawed playing with Woods when a rules official chided the pair for slow play. Yang pointed immediately at Woods and said: 'Not me, him.' Woods didn't blink. Not outwardly.

The pair was tied when Yang hit his approach on 13 into a bunker and Woods stiffed a beautiful 3-iron to eight feet. Yang got out of the pot and made a 12-foot par save. Tiger took two putts for his par. Yang moved to 14 with confidence high. And Woods' eyes widened just a tad.

On the short par-4 14th Yang almost drove the green. Woods hit his driver into a greenside bunker, and flopped out to seven feet. Woods largely didn't see what happened next because he'd turned his back on Yang. Yang took out his 52-degree wedge, gripped down on it, and set the ball free. It rolled and rolled and rolled centre cup. An eagle two. And Yang punched the air like, well, like Tiger Woods. Woods made his birdie. But he trailed by one, for the first time that tournament.

Both men laid up with hybrids on the par-5 15th. Woods's shot popped slightly into the air. 'Tiger is nervous,' noted Yang to his caddie, A.J. Montecinos 'You bet your butt he is,' replied Montecinos. Both players made par. Parred 16, bogied 17.

On 18 Yang's drive was left and relatively short. Not dead, but certainly not ideal. Woods responded by peeling off a terrific drive that rolled to the far right side of the fairway. But then he watched the apparently nerve-less Korean stiff the greatest hybrid in history and knew he had to get close.

As we've seen him do many times (such has been the coverage of the man, we know his little mannerisms) Woods plucked some grass and let it float from his fingers. He lined up and waggled, and let rip with a beautiful 5-iron, straight at the pin. But the ball turned over in the air just a tad and drew down into the second cut of rough, pin-high left.

Woods now had to go hard to sink it. He knew immediately he had missed. Yang had two putts to win. Needed only one. And a man from

Asia won a major championship for the first time. It was the first time a man from anywhere had run down Tiger Woods after he'd led after three rounds in a major.

And there followed a scramble to find out things about Y.E. Yang. And we learned.

Yang liked body-building and considered a career in the industry. He didn't touch a golf club until he was 19 years old. Yang did two years of military service. His father was a farmer and thought golf was a game for the idle rich. Yang taught himself to play by watching instructional videos by Nick Faldo and Jack Nicklaus. He spent many hours hitting balls at a range with a baseball grip. He moved to New Zealand and turned professional when he was 24. Ten years later he won the Korea Open and the HSBC Champions Tournament.

By the end of 2008 had made it through PGA Tour Q-School by one shot. By March of 2009 he won the Honda Classic. By the end of 2009 he'd made 19 cuts in 23 starts, run T25 or better 12 times, and won $3,489,516. And he didn't win on the PGA Tour again.

He did win the 2010 China Open and Korea Open (again). In the 2010 Masters (won by Phil Mickelson) Yang, carrying four hybrids, shot 67 in the first round and finished T8. He shot 67 again first round of the 2011 Masters (Charl Schwartzel) and finished T20. And in the 2011 US Open he finished T3 behind Rory McIlroy who won in a canter.

Asked after his major victory about the 'pressure' of playing against Woods, whom Yang had bested in China in the 2006 HSBC Champions Tournament, Yang, dubbed 'The Tiger Killer', said:

> It's not like you're in an octagon where you're fighting against Tiger and he's going to bite you, or swing at you with his 9-iron. The worst that I could do was just lose to Tiger. So, I really had nothing much at stake.

Yang further commented:

> At first when I saw the tee time, I was just really happy to be the last group on the final day of a major. For a split second that was the first thought. And then second, my heart nearly pounded and exploded being so nervous, actually. I tried to go to sleep a bit early yesterday, ended up watching a lot of golf TV and a lot of myself on TV. It was really exciting.

Tiger killers—indeed.

*** *

The Big Easy

Ernie Els hasn't always been a fan of the 'Big Easy' nickname because it's not always true and perhaps doesn't reflect how much he puts into his golf. He does get upset on the course on occasion, he just does well not to show it.

In that regard he's like fellow South African, Bobby Locke who did everything slowly and refused to get upset. Like Locke, Els walks to a rhythm only he can hear, an internal soundtrack, a cool inner dialogue. Yet while Locke was not a favorite of his fellow tour pros, Els is more liked than Tom Hanks.

With a couple of mates, I followed Els for 18 holes in the first round of the 1997 Buick Classic at Westchester Country Club in New York. He was the world number one, had won the US Open at Congressional Country Club the week before, and was defending champion in this tournament. But because every other knucklehead was out watching Tiger Woods chop his way to 72 (and finish 3-over the tournament, 19 shots behind Els), we had The Ernie Show almost to ourselves. And it was magnificent.

We'd position ourselves where his second-shot was likely to be, and watch the man hit six-irons 200 metres. High, long, straight. It was unbelievable. We'd watch him laser-beam 3-irons. We'd watch him waft— no other word for it —sand-wedge from bunkers with the glorious soft hands of a surgeon. It was just all so effortless and 'easy'.

Because you haven't seen graceful power until you've seen Ernie Els swing a golf club.

And 'swing' is the word. The balance and tempo and rhythm of that golf swing, only Freddie Couples, for mine, exudes the same languid power. Nick Faldo once said if you want to work on tempo, say 'Ernie' on your backswing, 'Els' coming back.

Theodore Ernest 'Ernie' Els was born in Johannesburg on 17 October 1969. He grew up playing golf at Germiston Golf Club and was a scratch marker at the age of 14. He won the World Junior Championship in the 13–14 age group (the same year David Toms won the 15–17s and Tiger Woods won the 9–10s). Els won the South African Amateur at 17 breaking Gary Player's record, and when he was 19 as well.

He did military service in the Air Force—where he played a lot of golf and gave lessons to generals—and turned pro in '89.

In '91 he won on the South African Sunshine Tour. In '93 he ran T5 in the Open Championship at Muirfield. In the '93 US Open he shot 1-under and finished T7 at Baltusrol. And in the Open Championship of 1993 at Royal St George's he shot 68–69–69–68 to finish 6-under, seven behind champion Greg Norman.

Els began '94 by winning the Dubai Desert Classic (by six shots from Norman). The Shark had carded 68–69–68–69. Els's numbers were similar apart from the first round when he shot 11-under 61, a course record at Emirates Golf Club which still stands.

He was T8 in the '94 Masters (seven shots behind José María Olazábal) and T24 in the Open Championship (won by Nick Price). And going into the US Open at Oakmont Country Club, he was being lauded as the next big thing. Price compared him to Seve Ballesteros. Gary Player compared him to Sam Snead. And Arnold Palmer compared him to none other than Arnold Palmer.

It was 1994 and Els was 24 years old, long and lean, and could hit the ball a mile. The conventional wisdom was that he wasn't accurate enough to win the US Open held at Oakmont Pennsylvania that year, such is the thick rough protecting narrow fairways. Els scotched that theory with rounds of 69–71–66 and led the championship by two.

After 71 holes he needed par on 18 to win his first major. But believing he needed birdie—he had deliberately not looked at a scoreboard—he went hard at his drive and hooked it onto 15. Next one had to go under a tree to get on the correct fairway, which it did, but the ball rolled into a sand-filled divot. His approach hit the green, and he two-putted for bogey. And a date with Colin Montgomerie and Loren Roberts in the 18-hole play-off.

And then Oakmont really showed its teeth.

Wrote Rick Reilly in *Sports Illustrated*:

> Oakmont was about as much fun as the gout featuring fairways so narrow a man with wide feet might have to walk heel-toe down them to keep from snagging his laces on the weeds; rough five inches high and nasty; shirt-soaking, 90-something-degree heat that broke Pittsburgh records five days in a row; seasick, brown greens, harder than the Pennsylvania Turnpike, which divides the course in half; and dirty, rotten pin positions. In other words, the natural and classic horribleness that is a U.S. Open, times two.

Nick Faldo declared it: 'The hardest course I have ever seen'.

Montgomerie had four chunked chips and a 3-putt from four feet, and was shot out the cannon with a 78. Els and Roberts made matching 74s even with Els beginning his round with bogie, then triple-bogie. He would hit just six fairways and 11 greens all day but go around the last 16 holes one-under, including a clutch putt on 18 to force sudden death. Which Els won by parring the second play-off hole.

Gary Player said of Els:

> He showed me what I used to see in Jack Nicklaus. Jack could play badly and still get the ball in the hole and win. That to me is more impressive than long drives and all the other things that matter. He holed that putt on the last hole. The great ones don't miss 'em, and Ernie is going to be a great one.

Another great, Nicklaus, sang Els' praises:

> I have said for a long time that some guy is going to come along, big and strong, and have a touch. We might have one. He's already a very good player. But so darn young. He has a great opportunity, though. He is probably the golfer of the future.

Curtis Strange, winner of the championship in 1988 and '89, said of Ernie Els, 'I think I just played with the next god.'

Els went on to win the '97 US Open (again featuring a hard luck story for Montgomerie), the 2002 Open Championship (after a play-off with Stuart Appleby, Steve Elkington and Thomas Levet) and the 2012 Open Championship at Royal Lytham & St Anne's after he shot 4-under 30 on the back nine and overcame a six-shot deficit to reel in Adam Scott who bogied each of the last four holes.

In 2000 he was second to Vijay Singh in the Masters. In 2004 he was second to Phil Mickelson who stormed home with five birdies in the last seven holes. Els shot 5-under 67 but lost by a shot. He eagled 13, birdied 15 and had a bogey-free back nine. It's as close as he's been at Augusta.

In 96 major championships Els made the cut 77 times. He's been runner-up six times, third-placed five times and top-ten 35 times. He didn't miss a cut in majors from the 2000 Masters to the 2006 PGA. He has twice won the Dunhill Cup for South Africa ('97 and '98) and twice won the World Cup for South Africa ('96 and '01). He was world number one for nine weeks. And was inducted into the World Golf Hall of Fame in 2010.

And he made it look so easy.

✳✳✳

Henrik, Heir Jordan, J-Day and Danny Boy

Jordan Spieth won the Australian Open at the Australian Golf Club in Sydney in November 2014 with the most sublime golf one could see. In strong, gusty winds on a long, championship track that had known the hands of Carnegie Clark, Alister Mackenzie and Jack Nicklaus, this fresh-faced 21-year-old Texan blitzed it. He shot a course record 63 with eight birdies. Adam Scott battled to even par. Rory McIlroy ended one-over 72.

By April of 2015 Spieth had won the US Masters at Augusta National by four shots, and a new kid said hello to the world. How about him? First round he blitzed his way to 64, the best lead-off round at Augusta since The Shark's 63 in '96. Round two he smoked 'em again with 66 and extended his lead to five. Round 3 was a stock-standard two-under 70 and a lead of four from Justin Rose. Phil Mickelson was five back, Charley Hoffman six, and then a four-shot chasm of space where nobody could hear Tiger Woods scream.

Nobody came close. Mickelson had an eagle on 15 and was still five back. Rose shot 71. Hoffman had 74, finished 10 back. And Jordan Spieth equalled Woods 272-shot 4-round record, smashed the record for most birdies (28) and slipped into a green jacket proffered by big Bubba of Baghdad.

Then he won the US Open at bumpy old Chambers Bay at 21. He was the youngest man in the 92 years since Bobby Jones had won the 1923 US Open at Inwood Country Club.

And so over to the United Kingdom of Great Britain for the 144th Open Championship on the Old Course, St Andrews. Spieth contended yet again needing a putt on the 72nd to drop to get into a play-off. Jason Day needed the same putt to drop. They missed. Both watched Zach Johnson beat Louis Oosthuizen and Marc Leishman in the four-hole play-off.

Back onto the western edge of the Atlantic Ocean and Jason Day broke his major duck when he won the PGA Championship at Whistling Straits, Wisconsin. So well did Day play that he chunked a wedge on the 9th and still made par. When he smoked a 4-iron on the par-5 16th, Jordan Spieth (contending yet again, what a year he had) stood back and applauded.

There was nothing Spieth could do. 'It was Jason's day' Spieth said. 'He played like he'd won seven or eight majors. He took it back. He wailed on it. It was a stripe show.'

Spieth was then crowned world number one and won the Fed Ex Cup and $10 million while Henrik Stenson ($3 million), Jason Day ($2 million), Rickie Fowler ($1.5 million) and Bubba Watson ($1 million) filled the top-5. The tendrils of the Global Financial Crisis of 2008 obviously did not overly-affecting the multi-national companies, Barclays, Deutsche Bank and BMW, that sponsored the four tournament play-off series.

After nine holes of the 2016 Masters Jordan Spieth was leading by five and cruising to another green jacket. Then he bogied 10. Then he bogied 11. Then he walked onto the tee at 12 and hit a high but effete 9-iron that faded away and fell into Rae's Creek. He walked to the drop zone and took out a wedge, which he chunked in the manner of a 20-handicapper from Hull. Or Hell. The ball fell, went into Rae's Creek too. He chopped the next one into the back bunker. Got up and down, and wrote down quadruple-bogey 7.

And that was all she wrote for Jordan Spieth.

Soon enough Danny Willett's name was written in history while his funny brother PJ Willett wrote funny things on the Twitter including: 'Speechless. I once punched that kid in the head for hurting my pet rat. Now look.'

Dustin Johnson won the 2016 US Open at Oakmont Country Club, a tournament memorable for Shane Lowry of Ireland shooting 65 in round three to lead by four and 76 in the fourth, and Johnson putting out on 18 and winning by three and kissing Wayne Gretzky's daughter (his wife, Paulina) and their baby girl. And that's it.

Henrik Stenson is the amazing long and strong man of Europe. When he's on, there's a relentless, dead-eyed Terminator look about him. The man is a machine. But not like a Faldo or Hogan who'd just grind away and wear you down—Stenson hits golf shots like marksman from space with a space laser, and destroys. In England for the Open Charmpionship in 2016, the cracking final round was a head-to-head battle for the famous old claret jug between the ice-eyed Swedish Terminator Stenson and the flexible and super-skilful superstar Phil Mickelson. And what a match it was.

On that final day at Troon he'd have utterly destroyed anyone but Phil Mickelson. Because Stenson just kept on playing. Kept on hitting driver, attacking, lobbing his wedges, wafting putts close. He never went away.

Stenson shot 63, equalling Johnny Miller's final round 63 at Oakmont in '73.

Stenson began the day leading by one. Mickelson birdied the first and Stenson bogied, and they swapped positions. Stenson had five birdies in the next eight holes. Mickelson eagled 4, birdied 6, and they both shot 32 out.

Back nine, boom! They both birdie 10. Stenson bogies 11 and it's all square. They come to 14 and Stenson blitzes his opponent. Four birdies the last five holes. Mickelson had one. And came second. He'd shot 65, a brilliant final round score in one of the great head-to-head duels in the history of major championship golf.

***

Phil The Thrill

Phil Mickelson (and Ernie Els and Vijay Singh, at a pinch) would likely reside in the pantheon of all-time greats—sitting alongside Hogan, Nelson, Snead, Nicklaus, Palmer Player, Watson, Sarazen, Hagen, Jones, Vardon and Young Tom Morris—had Earl Woods never fought in Vietnam and married Kutilda and sired a son whom he taught to play golf. Such are fate's fickle fingers.

Instead dear old Earl did all those things and the world of golf has been awed by the golf of Tiger Woods. So Tiger does exist. And as such you'd suggest Mickelson rests on the second line of betting in terms of golfing immortality, along with Norman, Trevino, Ballesteros, Casper, Locke and Peter 'Thommo' Thomson. You could throw Henry Cotton in. Taylor and Braid. Cary Middlecoff? Not so much. But knock yourself out.

Best shot I've ever seen Mickelson hit—possibly one of the best ever—was that 6-iron from the pine straw on 13 at Augusta in the final round of the 2010 US Masters. How about *that* for a piece of happy golf action?

He's surveyed the land, there's the option to run the ball flat down the hill, give himself a flat lie for a little chip. But not our Phil. He takes his 6-iron on shaky ground and goes full swing at it. And hits it pure. You could hear the purity of it. You can't spank that puppy better. The ball soared high and straight at it, landed soft, rolled to five feet. What a shot! Nick Faldo called it 'The greatest shot of his life.'

His best round arguably—because he's had a few—was his head-to-head go with Henrik Stenston at Royal Troon in the 2016 Open Championship. How about that? Two giants of the sport, no quarter given or taken, thrashing away with supreme skill under pressure. Well, that's it really.

Mickelson has won five majors, 42 PGA Tour wins which puts him 9th all time, three behind Walter Hagen. He's played in 11 Ryder Cups and 11 Presidents Cups. His numbers are among the greatest there has ever been.

But it's not numbers that define Phil Mickelson, it's thrills. For truly Mickelson belongs in the swashbuckling class with Hagen, Norman and Ballesteros. Call it a sub-pantheon. No room for Player or Palmer. Ben Hogan? Tell your story walkin', Robot Man. This is the 'Land of Thrills'.

Mickelson won the Open Championship of 2013 with a brilliant 66 at a wet and windy Muirfield. He'd started the round five shots behind Lee Westwood, with Adam Scott, Tiger Woods, Hunter Mahan, Angel Cabrera and a certain Henrik Stenson all in contention. And Mickelson smoked them all. He birdied 13 and 14. He made a fine 7-footer for par on 16. On the par-5 17th he hit a 3-wood and said, 'Go, baby! Come on!' and the ball obeyed, rolled to mid-green. Two-putt bird. On 18 he wafted a 6-iron to ten feet, and rolled in the slow, right-to-left downhill putt and held his arms above his head like Muhammad Ali. He knew he had it. He was three shots clear. He'd smoked 'em all.

In tour events, he's a one-man show reel. He's hit the ball off a wall of plants. He's nipped them off the cart path, got up and down. On downhill lies in fluffy rough he's flopped them close. He once got up and down from 150 yards' dead under a tree with a low punchy-sliced three-wood. He was plugged in a bunker, sunk it. He hit a shot from a fairway bunker through a gap in some trees no bigger than a standard household door, onto the green. He hit a green he couldn't see from the synthetic carpet of a hospitality tent.

In a hail storm at the Grayhawk Golf Club in the 2000 Williams World Challenge, with the green completely covered in ball-bearing-sized pellets of frozen hail, Mickelson took his lob-wedge, on the green, and chipped in for birdie.

-CHAPTER THIRTEEN-

WHAT NOW?

◆◦◆———◆◦◆

That's it then, a short history of golf, so far. Not everything, mind, for no mere paper bound book could hold it all. And besides there is a medium that holds 'everything' and that's the great all-seeing infinite encyclopaedia in the sky, the Internet. Google responsibly.

This book, rather, has been one man's slightly subjective take on what constitutes the great game's history. Your take would differ from mine, and from everybody else's. *Vive la différence, que sera, sera* and pass the beer nuts.

So where is golf now? And where is it going? I'm no all-seeing one-eyed spider god. But I can have a stab at the future based on the past and predict that for one, technology will continue to advance—because technology always has—and allow us to hit the ball longer and straighter.

This should please all the mug amateurs with a penchant for the latest gleaming whacking sticks. But it mightn't please the purists who see professional players—almost to a man long, strong muscle-men with computer-aided swing planes—verily emasculating the world's most storied and greatest golf links with their prodigious length off the tee and everywhere else.

If history tells us anything, it's that money never sleeps, carries a big stick, and is the largest and loudest stakeholder, and a few other things like that. And you'd suggest the golf industry would win any argument about advances in technology, if there even is an argument given the 'industry' and 'golf' are almost one and the same.

Technology? The golf ball has evolved from a rock to a funny bit of kit stuffed with a top-hat full of feathers to Titleist's Next Generation 2.0 ZG Process Core with 'thin, responsive ionomeric casing layer' and 'soft Urethane Elastomer cover' and 'spherically-tiled 352 tetrahedral dimple design'.

And yet when one hits the thing into the woods, it's no easier to find. So surely someone will invent GPS ball-tracking technology that finds lost balls. If advances in military technology mean spies can put a little bit of paint on a target and know where that target is, ball-finding GPS can't be far away.

And as for clubs, there was once no bag limit. A player could heft around a whole host of mashies, niblicks, cleeks, spoons and so on. The limit was lowered to 14 where it sits today. Could it go lower again? Consider Bryson DeChambeau, the 'eccentric' young PGA Tour professional, who has wowed world golf by playing with irons all the same length. Take that idea an alternate direction and manufacturers could one day invent one single iron to replace the bagful, a wonder-stick which one could adjust in length (or not, in Bryson's case) and club-face angle to be anything from 2-iron to wedge, depending how far and high one wants to hit the ball. You can bet they're working on it. Man on the moon, and all that.

And as to course design, it's hoped that course architects and designers will continue to work out that 'playability' should be paramount in course design given, you know, people play the blessed game, and it should be fun. Indeed the term, playability, should always go hand-in-glove with 'fun', and all golf course design types should follow and improve on the philosophies of Tom Doak and Mike Clayton, to name but two devotees of Dr Alister Mackenzie and Old Tom Morris, men who knew golf should be fun. Like Disneyland, make golf fun and the people will come. No brainer. And yet ...

It doesn't appear that the demands of modern life within the great machine of capitalism will grant us any more time to play the game. And so alternative game-play formats will arrive by dint of the forces of supply and demand. Be that 9- or 12-hole, or even 6-hole competitions, golf clubs will look to arrest falling membership numbers caused by people in their 30s and 40s quitting golf to focus on families and careers and hobby–sports that don't take six hours on a Saturday and cost a lot of money.

Jack Nicklaus has banged on about 12-hole golf. The R&A is looking for ways to speed the game up. Greg Norman has something up his sleeve and under his Akubra hat he reckons will 'revolutionize golf'.

In the magazine, *Golf*, Greg Norman talks about his plan to disrupt the golf world:

> We will tell you exactly how we're going to break this cast iron that's been wrapped around golf for so long. We're going to shatter it. The institutions (USGA, R&A, PGA of America, PGA Tour) will eventually buy into it because they will have to buy into it. They won't have a choice.

In the early 1990s Norman proposed a World Golf Tour (WGT), an idea that was howled down then—notably by Arnold Palmer, a stance that caused a temporary rift in the pair's friendship. Yet something similar exists today. While there isn't one formal global WGT per se, disparate tour events are co-operating. The PGA Tour has an event in Kuala Lumpur. The European Tour has tournaments in Johannesburg, Perth and Shanghai. The Euro Tour's season-ending event is the Race To Dubai. Co-sanctioning is the new black.

Save for another Great Recession, golf will expand ever more. Yet you would like to think that as the game spreads and grows through Asia and beyond that people from relatively impoverished backgrounds can join in. That they can perhaps follow the great golfers of the past—Ben Hogan, Lee Trevino, Seve Ballesteros—and forge careers from the ranks of caddies. In Asia today caddies are near-universally young women who don't appear to play golf but rather help older people play. Perhaps naïve, even (gasp) socialist—but the game should be for all.

For as the game continues its exponential expansion into Asia, India and the Sub Continent, the Middle East and other markets, you'd suggest players from those regions will start seriously competing in major open golf championships, and that flags of all nations will dot world leaderboards. The 'Asian Tiger Woods' hasn't turned up yet—might not ever. But there could be 50 'Brooks Koepkas' from Asia or India. If we're lucky, in our lifetimes, a giant man from the Sudan will pull on a XXXL green jacket.

Will we still have major open golf championships in the future? You'd suggest we will. They've been around since 1860 and continue to grow in popularity. Koepka pocketed $2.16 million when he won the 2017 US Open. When Willie Park Snr won the first Open Championship in 1860, he was given a belt while the three runners-up got the cash.

So the four Major championships should see out this century, you'd suggest. But there could be modifications. One modification that the powers of the golf world could have a stab is to hold the fourth major (the US PGA Championship) each year at different courses around the world on a rotating basis. One year Australasia, another year Asia, another in Africa, the Middle East, wherever said burgeoning markets are. And, yes, in the USA. This may not be popular in the USA. But in terms of the big picture for the game, it makes sense. And rotation works for the Olympics.

Speaking of which, golf will continue at the Olympics. Why? Because of money. People can make all the arguments they like that it shouldn't be in the Olympics, or that it shouldn't be a 4-round stroke competition like nigh-on every other generic PGA Tour event. But when NBC pays the good burghers of the International Olympic Committee $7.75 billion to broadcast their carnival then NBC is the major—just about only—stakeholder to decide what's on and when and who's allowed to play in it. And that's just it. There's no arguing with that whale—high ten-figure sums of cash will win every time.

And thus the glorious, imperfect but largely honourable game of golf rolls inexorably on. And long may it. In an often vexed world, the game's values, its honour system—both on course and how it honours its past—live on as something of a light on the hill. A system of fair play devised by Scotsmen—and perhaps even 12th century Chinese—is honoured by golfers today.

In 1925 Bobby Jones was praised for calling a penalty upon himself in the US Open. Jones replied that people may as well praise him for not robbing a bank. Old Tom Morris would have nodded along with respect. So would Jordan Spieth.

Long live golf.

REFERENCES

Apatow Productions, *Anchorman: The Legend of Ron Burgundy*, 2004.

Baker-Finch, Ian, interview with Matt Cleary, 3 February 2017.

Baker-Finch, Ian, cited in 'Driven mad' by Rick Reilly, *Sports Illustrated*, 23 February 1998: https://www.si.com/vault/1998/02/23/239208/driven-mad-after-winning-the-1991-british-open-ian-baker-finch-lost-his-game-and-in-a-desperate-effort-to-find-it-nearly-lost-his-mind (accessed 13 June 2017).

Ballard, Sarah, 'My, Oh Mize', *Sports Illustrated*, 20 April 1987: https://www.si.com/vault/1987/04/20/115242/my-oh-mize (accessed 13 June 2017).

Ballesteros, Severiano, cited in 'Mano A Mano on the Links', *Golf*. This article first appeared in the 25 July 1988 issue of *Sports Illustrated*: http://www.golf.com/tour-and-news/mano-mano-links (accessed 13 June 2017).

Ballesteros, Severiano, cited in 'Masterful' by Rick Reilly, *Sports Illustrated*, 18 April 1988: https://www.si.com/vault/1988/04/18/117515/masterful-with-a-dramatic-birdie-on-18-sandy-lyle-won-the-masters-by-one-stroke----and-the-green-jacket-bestowed-by-1987-champ-larry-mize (accessed 16 June 2017).

Ballesteros, Severiano, cited in 'The Open 2010: Severiano Ballesteros denied an emotional return to St Andrews' by Oliver Brown (9 July 2010), reprinted in *The Telegraph*, 15 June 2017: http://www.telegraph.co.uk/sport/golf/theopen/7880440/The-Open-2010-Severiano-Ballesteros-denied-an-emotional-return-to-St-Andrews.html (accessed 10 May 2017).

Barklow, Sam, 2010, *The One and Only Sam Snead*, Taylor Trade

Publishing: USA.

Bolt, Tommy, cited in 'Ben Hogan, Golf's Iron-Willed Legend, Dies at 84' by Larry Dorman, *New York Times*, 26 July 1997: http://www. nytimes.com/1997/07/26/sports/ben-hogan-golf-s-iron-willed-legend-dies-at-84.html (accessed 16 May 2017).

Boros, Julius, cited on Brainy Quote website: https://www. brainyquote.com/quotes/quotes/j/juliusboro234322.html (accessed 21 June 2017).

Boyette, John, 'History, drama that led to "Amen Corner"', *Augusta Cronicle*, 5 April 2017: http://www.augusta.com/masters/story/ news/2017-04-05/history-drama-led-amen-corner (accessed 16 May 2017).

Brown, Oliver, 'Carl Jackson captures The Masters essence but race is still a major issue at Augusta', *Daily Telegraph*, 8 April 2015: http:// www.telegraph.co.uk/sport/golf/mastersaugusta/11523855/Carl-Jackson-captures-The-Masters-essence-but-race-is-still-a-major-issue-at-Augusta.html (accessed 2 June 2017).

Bush, George W., cited on *CNN*, 23 May 2003: edition.cnn.com/ TRANSCRIPTS/0305/23/ip.00.html (accessed 5 July 2017).

Calcavecchia Mark cited in 'Masterful' by Rick Reilly, *Sports Illustrated*, 18 April 1988: https://www.si.com/vault/1988/04/18/117515/ masterful-with-a-dramatic-birdie-on-18-sandy-lyle-won-the-masters-by-one-stroke----and-the-green-jacket-bestowed-by-1987-champ-larry-mize# (accessed 2 June 2017).

Chirkinian, Frank cited in 'Behind the Scenes' by Tim Roseforte, *Golf Digest*, 19 December 2007: http://www.golfdigest.com/ story/200404behindscences (accessed 16 June 2017).

Chirkinin, Frank, cited in 'The Dawn Of Dominance: Oral History Of Tiger's '97 Win' by Peter McDaniel, *Golf Digest*, 4 April 2017: http://www.golfdigest.com/story/the-dawn-of-dominance-oral-history-of-tiger-woods-97-win (accessed 5 July 2017).

Cink, Stuart, cited in 'Cink honed his game on Irish links courses', *The Irish Times*, 21 July 2009: www.irishtimes.com/sport/cink-honed-his-game-on-irish-links-courses-1.1228194 (accessed 5 July 2017).

Clayton, Mike, interview with Matt Cleary, 13 January 2017.

Coody, Charles, cited in 'Masterful' by Rick Reilly, *Sports Illustrated*, 18 April 1988: https://www.si.com/vault/1988/04/18/117515/masterful-with-a-dramatic-birdie-on-18-sandy-lyle-won-the-masters-by-one-stroke----and-the-green-jacket-bestowed-by-1987-champ-larry-mize (accessed 16 June 2017).

Couples Fred, cited in 'Masterful' by Rick Reilly, *Sports Illustrated*, 18 April 1988: https://www.si.com/vault/1988/04/18/117515/masterful-with-a-dramatic-birdie-on-18-sandy-lyle-won-the-masters-by-one-stroke----and-the-green-jacket-bestowed-by-1987-champ-larry-mize (accessed 16 June 2017).

Crenshaw, Ben, cited in 'Golf/US PGA: Price shatters the spell of mediocrity: Double champion moves into the Watson class' by Tim Glover, *The Independent*, 15 August 1994: http://www.independent.co.uk/sport/golf-us-pga-price-shatters-the-spell-of-mediocrity-double-champion-moves-into-the-watson-class-1383950.html, (accessed 16 May 2017).

Crenshaw, Ben, cited in 'Masterful' by Rick Reilly, *Sports Illustrated*, 18 April 1988: https://www.si.com/vault/1988/04/18/117515/masterful-with-a-dramatic-birdie-on-18-sandy-lyle-won-the-masters-by-one-stroke----and-the-green-jacket-bestowed-by-1987-champ-larry-mize (accessed 16 June 2017).

Crockett, Andrew, 'Joe Kirkwood: Australia's "arger than life" golf icon', *Inside Golf*, 29 December 2015: issuu.com/insidegolf/docs/ig126_jan16_final/22 (accessed 6 July 2017).

Cutmore, Chris, 'Jacklin recalls his Muirfield meltdown with words

that will chill Westwood and Co', *mailonline*, 16 July 2013: http://
www.dailymail.co.uk/sport/golf/article-2364401/THE-OPEN-
2012-Tony-Jacklin-recalls-Muirfield-meltdown-words-chill-Lee-
Westwood-Co.html#ixzz4knSzNONr (accessed 23 June 2017).

Demaret, Jimmy, cited in *The Book of Golf Quotations* by Pat Sullivan,
2012, Random House.

Dobereiner, Peter, cited in 'Last bite at a green jacket for the Great
White Shark' by David Davies, *The Guardian*, 9 April 2002: https://
www.theguardian.com/sport/2002/apr/08/golf.comment (accessed
16 June 2017).

Dobereiner, Peter, 'The Enigma of Seve Balesteros: A penetrating
profile of the swashbuckling young man from Spain', *Golf
Digest*, 27 October 2008: http://www.golfdigest.com/story/
seve101980dobereiner (accessed 2 June 2017).

Dobson, James, *A Golfer's Life*, (co-author with Arnold Palmer),
Random House Publishing Group, 2000.

Dodson, James, *Ben Hogan: An American Life*, Broadway Books, New
York, 2005.

Drum, Bob, cited in 'The "Drummer" Marched to a Different Beat'
by Thomas Bonk, *Los Angeles Times*, 19 May 1996: articles.latimes.
com/1996-05-19/sports/sp-5964_1_golf-courses (accessed 5 July
2017).

Dye, Pete as cited in 'Pete and Alice Dye and their Pinehurst
connection' by Lee Pace, *Pinehurst Heritage Golf News*, 16 April
2015: www.pinehurst.com/news/live-let-dye-pinehurst-connection
(accessed 5 July 2017).

Dye, Pete, 1995, *Bury Me in a Pot Bunker*, Contemporary Books.

Dyer, Alfred (Rabbit), cited in 'Gary Player's Expo' by Dan
Jenkins, *Sports Illustrated*, 22 July 1974: https://www.si.com/
vault/1974/07/22/606566/gary-players-expo (accessed 12 June 2017).

Eisenhower D., cited in *Slovick Lyle, 2016, Trials and Triumphs of Golf's Greatest Champions: A Legacy of Hope*, Rowman and Littlefield Publishers Inc: London.

Elvy, Luke, interview with Matt Cleary, 28 December 2016.

Erskine, James, interview with Matt Cleary, 16 January 2017.

Faldo, Nick, cited in 'From Trouble to Triumph' by Rick Reilly, *Sports Illustrated*, 27 June 1994: http://www.golf.com/tour-and-news/trouble-triumph (accessed 16 June 2017).

Faldo, Nick, cited in 'In His Own Words: Nick Faldo on 1987 British Open win at Muirfield' by Gary Van Sickle, *Golf*, 4 July 2009: http://www.golf.com/tour-and-news/his-own-words-nick-faldo-1987-british-open-win-muirfield (accessed 16 June 2017).

Faldo, Nick, cited in 'The bold shot on 13 just Phil being Phil' by Scott Michaux, Old Augusta (website), 1 April 2011: http://old.augusta.com/stories/2011/04/01/mas_611047.shtml (accessed 23 June 2017).

Faldo Nick, with Bruce Gritchley, *In Search of Perfection*, London: Weidenfeld and Nicholson, 1994.

Fawcett, John, 'A brief history of the sand iron', T*he Long Game: Newsletter of the Golf Society of Australia,* January 2014: www.golf.org.au/newsdisplay/a-brief-history-of-the-sand-iron/79076 (accessed 5 July 2017).

Floyd, Ray, cited in 'Betting on Golf is a Natural Part of the Game, from $1 Skins to $100 Nassaus' by Jeff Williams, *Cigar Aficionado*, July 2003: www.cigaraficionado.com/webfeatures/show/id/Golf-Gambling-on-the-Greens_8315 (accessed 5 July 2017).

Frank Williams interview with Matt Cleary, 20 January 2017.

Carner, JoAnne, as cited in 'A New Force In The Game' by Jaime Diaz, *Sports Illustrated*, 10 August 2017: www.si.com/vault/issue/702721/72/2 (accessed 5 July 2017).

Glover Tim, 'Golf/US PGA: Price shatters the spell of mediocrity:

Double champion moves into the Watson class', *The Independent*, 15
August 1994: http://www.independent.co.uk/sport/golf-us-pga-
price-shatters-the-spell-of-mediocrity-double-champion-moves-into-
the-watson-class-1383950.html, accessed 16 May 2017.

Golf Channel Documentary, 2011, *Frank Chirkinian, The Master
Storyteller*, http://www.worldgolf.com/newswire/browse/67241-
Golf-Channel-celebrates-life-golf-television-pioneer-Frank-
Chirkinian-Master-Storyteller (assessed 15 June 2017).

Golf Digest, 12 August 2010: http://www.golfdigest.com/story/
myshot_gd0204 (accessed 16 May 2017).

Golf Grinder (website), 'Titleist unveils all-new 2017 ProV1, ProV1x
balls' 27 January 2017: http://www.golfgrinder.com/news/
equipment/titleist-unveils-all-new-2017-prov1-prov1x-balls/
(accessed 29 June 2017).

Golf, 'Mano A Mano on the Links': article first appeared in the 25 July
1988 issue of *Sports Illustrated* by Jacqueline Duvoisin: http://www.
golf.com/tour-and-news/mano-mano-links (accessed 15 June 2017).

Graham, David, cited in 'The Graham Simply Refused to Crack' by
Dan Jenkins, *Sports Illustrated*, 13 August, 1979: https://www.
si.com/vault/1979/08/13/823873/this-graham-simply-refused-to-
crack-unfazed-by-a-double-bogey-on-the-72nd-hole-david-graham-
sank-three-big-putts-in-sudden-death-to-beat-ben-crenshaw-for-the-
pga-title (accessed 16 June 2017).

Hagan Walter, his quote reproduced on website: http://quotes.
yourdictionary.com/author/walter-hagen/612852 (accessed 15 June
2017).

Hagen, Walter, cited in 'Eighty Years Later, Sarazen's Shot Heard
Round the World Still Resounds' by John Steinbreder on Masters.
com, 12 April, 2015: http://www.masters.com/en_US/news/
photos/2013-04-06/sarazen_deagle_82681517.html (accessed 5

July 2017).

Hagen, Walter, 2004 edition, *The Walter Hagen Story: By the Haig, Himself*, Rare Book Collections.

Hagen, Walter, cited in 'Fairway Queens and Rough Cats', *Esquire*, Volume 2, Issues 1–3, p. 89. https://books.google.com.au/boo ks?id=h80cAQAAMAAJ&q=Esquire,+Volume+2,+Issues+1-3&dq=Esquire,+Volume+2,+Issues+1-3&hl=en&sa=X&ved=0a hUKEwiszqizobLUAhVIxLwKHRj7D9IQ6AEIJjAA (accessed 16 June 2017).

Herbert, Ian, 'Masters 2015: Augusta and the great class divide—"We were proud that a black man had won. Very, very happy...", *The Independent*, 8 April 2015: http://www.independent.co.uk/sport/ golf/masters-2015-we-were-proud-that-a-black-man-had-won-verClayton, My-very-happy-10163612.html (accessed 16 June 2017).

Hoch, Scott, cited in 'Golf's leading men outraged at teeing off with a woman' by Adam Lusher, *The Telegraph*, 8 May 2003: www. telegraph.co.uk/news/worldnews/northamerica/usa/1430460/ Golfs-leading-men-outraged-at-teeing-off-with-a-woman.html (accessed 6 July 2017).

Hogan, Ben, cited in 'Ben Hogan's Secrets: What Drove Him, Who He Admired, and Why the Game So Thrilled Him' by George Peper, *Golf*, 13 August 2014: http://www.golf.com/tour-and-news/ben-hogan-golf-magazine-interview (accessed 22 June 2017).

Hogan, Ben, cited in *Moe and Me: Encounters with Moe Norman, Golf's Mysterious Genius*, by Lorne Rubenstein, ECW Press, 2014, p. 98.

Hogan, Ben, cited in 'Sanders reflects on a missed putt and missed boats' by Dermot Gilleece, *The Irish Times*, 2 September 1997: www. irishtimes.com/sport/sanders-reflects-on-a-missed-putt-and-missed-boats-1.102514 (accessed 6 July 2017).

Inglis, David, cited in 'Celebrating a "damn good idea"' by Peter Stone,

The Age, 27 November 2008: www.theage.com.au/news/sport/golf/celebrating-a-damn-good-idea/2008/11/26/1227491635633.html (accessed 6 July 2017).

Inglis, David cited in 'Foresight: How the Masters was born', *Sydney Morning Herald*, 22 November 2008: http://www.smh.com.au/news/sport/golf/foresight-how-the-masters-was-born/2008/11/21/1226770739116.html (accessed 6 July 2017).

Jackson, Carl cited in 'Carl Jackson captures The Masters essence but race is still a major issue at Augusta' by Oliver Brown, Daily Telegraph, 8 April 2015: http://www.telegraph.co.uk/sport/golf/mastersaugusta/11523855/Carl-Jackson-captures-The-Masters-essence-but-race-is-still-a-major-issue-at-Augusta.html (accessed 2 June 2017).

Jackson, Carl, cited in 'Carl Jackson: A history told through golf' by Meredith Anderson, *WRDW–TV*, posted 7 April 2015: http://www.wrdw.com/home/headlines/Carl-Jackson-A-history-told-through-golf-298846551.html (accessed 2 June 2017).

Jenkins, Dan, 'Eyes Right...But Wrong', *Sports Illustrated*, 24 June 1968: http://www.golfdigest.com/story/lee_trevino (accessed 9 June 2017).

Jenkins, Dan, 'ADIOS, AMIGOS!' , *Sports Illustrated*, 30 July 1979, excerpt https://www.si.com/vault/1979/07/30/823827/adios-amigos-on-the-murderous-back-nine-at-royal-lytham-and-st-annes-seve-ballesteros-of-spain-came-charging-out-of-the-rough-to-say-so-long-to-his-us-challengers# (accessed 2 June 2107)

Jenkins, Dan, 'All Yours, Billy Boy', *Sports Illustrated*, 20 April 1970: https://www.si.com/vault/1970/04/20/610815/all-yours-billy-boy (accessed 2 June 2017).

Jenkins, Dan, 'The Bogey That Won The Open', *Sports Illustrated*, 26

June 1978: https://www.si.com/vault/1978/06/26/822755/the-bogey-that-won-the-open-andy-north-knew-he-didnt-need-par-on-the-awesome-18th-one-over-would-suffice--and-two-high-pressure-shots-got-it-for-him (accessed 13 June 2017).

Jiminez, Miguel Angel, cited in 'A Conversation With Golf's Most Interesting Man: Miguel Angel Jimenez' by Shipnuck Alan, *Golf,* 30 April 2015: http://www.golf.com/tour-and-news/conversation-miguel-angel-jimenez (accessed 16 May 2017).

Kelley, Brent, 1980 US Open: Jack is Back', *Thought Co,* updated 8 July 2015: https://www.thoughtco.com/1980-us-open-jack-is-back-1564939 (accessed 15 June 2017).

Kimber Jarrod, 'Swimming With The Shark', *The Cauldron,* 12 April 2016: https://the-cauldron.com/swimming-with-the-shark-ee638a40da31 (accessed 5 July 2017).

Lang, Andrew, *The Early Days of Golf,* Read Country Books, 1904.

Latimer, Clay, 'Mark McCormack Transformed Sports As First Superagent', *Investors Business Daily,* 26 May 2015: http://www.investors.com/news/management/leaders-and-success/mark-mccormack-was-godfather-of-sports-marketing/ (accessed 15 June 2017).

Leach, Henry, cited in 'Remembering Ouimet: Why Vardon and Ray?' by Al Tays, *Golf Channel,* Golf Central blog, 5 June 2013: www.golfchannel.com/news/golftalkcentral/remembering-ouimet-why-vardon-and-ray (accessed 5 July 2017).

Leadbetter, David, cited in 'Profile: Driven by the green effect: Nick Price' by Robert Green, *The Independent,* 27 February 1994: http://www.independent.co.uk/sport/profile-driven-by-the-green-effect-nick-price-1396699.html (accessed 16 June 2017).

Longhurst, Henry quoted from television coverage of Open Championship, 12 July 1970: www.youtube.com/

watch?v=aYR6ZyS0lf8 (accessed 6 July 2017).MacKenzie, A, 1920,
Golf Architecture: Economy in Course Construction and Greenkeeping,
London: Simkin, Marshall, Hamilton, Kent and Co.

MacLeod, Connor, quote from *Highlander* (1986): web source http://
www.quotes.net/mquote/42982 (accessed 16 June 2017).

McKenzie, Alister, *Golf Architecture: Economy in Course Construction
and Greenkeeping*, 1920: books.google.com.au/books/about/Golf_
Architecture.html?id=hYOFCgAAQBAJ&redir_esc=y (accessed 6
July 2017).

McPherson, J.G., 'Braid's Marvelous Recovery for the Open
Championship', *The Golfers Magazine*, Crafts Wright Higgins,
January 1908, p. 226.

Manning, George, cited in 'Iron Byron: Repeat after me' by Jason Sobel,
Golf Channel website, 13 March 2012: www.golfchannel.com/news/
jason-sobel/iron-byron-repeat-after-me (accessed 5 July 2017).

Mickelson, Phil, cited in 'Golf's leading men outraged at teeing off
with a woman' by Adam Lusher, *The Telegraph*, 18 May 2003: www.
telegraph.co.uk/news/worldnews/northamerica/usa/1430460/
Golfs-leading-men-outraged-at-teeing-off-with-a-woman.html
(accessed 5 July 2017).

Morris, Tom (Old), cited in 'Golf's Founding Father and Son' by Fergus
Bisset, *Golf Monthly*, 20 August 2015: http://www.golf-monthly.
co.uk/features/the-game/golfs-founding-father-and-son-79840
(accessed 10 May 2017).

Nelson, Byron, cited in 'Ben Hogan and Byron Nelson Dueled in a
Masters Playoff for the Ages in 1942' by John Garrity, 8 March 2012,
Golf: http://www.golf.com/tour-and-news/1942-ben-hogan-and-
byron-nelson-dueled-masters-playoff-ages (accessed 21 June 2017).

New York Times (1902) obituary of Dr Robert Adams Paterson,
reprinted on lorespot.com/lore-moment/2013/2/25/reveren-

paterson-invents-the-gutta-percha-ball-1848 (accessed 10 May 2017).

Nicklaus, Jack, cited in 'Arnold Palmer: Sport's first television superstar' by Camilla Tait, *skysports.com*, Last updated: 10 May 2016: http://www.skysports.com/golf/news/12176/10593782/arnold-palmer-sports-first-television-superstar (accessed 18 May 2017).

Nicklaus, Jack, cited in 'Golf: Forget Finesse, Remember a Name: Els Wins Open' by Larry Dorman, *New York Times*, 21 June 1994: http://www.nytimes.com/1994/06/21/sports/golf-forget-finesse-remember-a-name-els-wins-open.html (accessed 5 July 2017).

Nicklaus, Jack, cited on *World Golf Hall of Fame*, http://www.worldgolfhalloffame.org/clifford-roberts/ (accessed 12 May 2017).

Norman, Greg, cited in 'My, Oh Mize' by Sarah Ballard, *Sports Illustrated*, 20 April 1987: https://www.si.com/vault/1987/04/20/115242/my-oh-mize (accessed 13 June 2017).

Norman, Greg, 'Greg Norman Has a Secret Plan to Disrupt the Golf World', *Golf*, 11 December 2016: http://www.golf.com/tour-and-news/greg-norman-has-secret-plan-disrupt-golf-world (accessed 29 June 2017).

Norman, Greg, interview with Matt Cleary, 21 January 2017.

Norman, Greg, Phillips, Donald T., 2007, *The Way of the Shark*, Random House Australia.

Norman, Greg, Press conference before 1986 US Open. Sourced from: http://www.golf.com/tour-and-news/guts-grit-and-grandeur-raymond-floyd-wins-1986-us-open (accessed 15 January 2017).

Norman, Greg; Peper George, 1989, *Shark Attack: Greg Norman's guide to aggressive golf*, Simon and Schuster.

Norman, Moe (website), 'When Moe Norman Played Augusta' by Tim O'Connor, 16 December 2016: https://moenorman.org/2016/12/16/when-moe-norman-played-augusta/ (accessed 21

June 2017).

Norman, Moe, cited in 'Memories of Moe Norman' by Rob Doster, *Athlon Sports & Life*, 26 July 2012: https://athlonsports.com/golf/memories-moe-norman (accessed 21 June 2017).

Norman, Moe, cited in 'My Shot: Moe Norman', by Guy Yocum, *Golf Digest*, 7 July 2007: http://www.golfdigest.com/story/myshot_gd0411 (accessed 16 May 2017).

Norman, Moe, cited in 'The Legend of Moe Norman: The Man With the Perfect Swing', by Andrew Podnieks, Arcturus Publishing, 2015.

Norman, Moe, quoted from ESPN documentary by Chris Connelly, 10 April 2005 www.youtube.com/watch?v=w8bphcoEGc4 (accessed 7 July 2017).

North, Andrew cited in 'The Bogey That Won The Open' by Dan Jenkins, *Sports Illustrated*, 26 June 1978. https://www.si.com/vault/1978/06/26/822755/the-bogey-that-won-the-open-andy-north-knew-he-didnt-need-par-on-the-awesome-18th-one-over-would-suffice--and-two-high-pressure-shots-got-it-for-him: (accessed 13 June 2017).

Okamoto, Ayako, cited in 'A New Force In The Game' by Jaime Diaz, *Sports Illustrated*, 10 August 2017: www.si.com/vault/issue/702721/72/2 (accessed 5 July 2017).

Palmer, Arnold, cited in 'Golf Channel Celebrates the Life of Golf Television Pioneer in Frank Chirkinian, The Master Storyteller', Bunkershot.com: http://www.bunkershot.com/post/5194969488/golf-channel-celebrates-the-life-of-golf (accessed 16 June 2017).

Palmer, Arnold, cited on World Golf Hall of Fame, http://www.worldgolfhalloffame.org/clifford-roberts/ (accessed 12 May 2017).

Parnevik, Jesper, cited in 'Strokes of Genius' by Rick Reilly, *Sports Illustrated*, 21 April 1997: www.si.com/vault/1997/04/21/225867/strokes-of-genius-overpowering-a-storied-course-and-a-stellar-field-tiger-woods-heralded-a-new-era-in-golf-with-an-awesome-12-shot-victory-in-the-masters (accessed 5 July 2017).

Peale, Norman Vincent, *The Power of Positive Thinking*, New York: Prentice-Hall, 1952.

Perry, Kenny, cited in 'Golf's leading men outraged at teeing off with a woman' by Adam Lusher, *The Telegraph*, 8 May 2003: www. telegraph.co.uk/news/worldnews/northamerica/usa/1430460/ Golfs-leading-men-outraged-at-teeing-off-with-a-woman.html (accessed 6 July 2017).

Peskin, Hy, photo of Ben Hogan, 1950 US Open: see http://www. historicgolfphotos.com/store/hogan-ben-pictures-photographs-prints-art/product/hogan-1-iron-at-merion-1950-us-open-the-underdog/ (accessed 5 July 2017).

Pittsburgh Post-Gazette, 5 April, 1937, headline 'Ralph Guldahl, loser'.

Player, Gary, cited in 'Gary Player: In 1955 I slept in the dunes. I wanted to win so badly' by Chris Medland, *The Independent*, 17 July 2009: http://www.independent.co.uk/sport/golf/gary-player-in-1955-i-slept-in-the-dunes-i-wanted-to-win-so-badly-1751455.html (accessed 17 May 2009).

Player, Gary, cited in 'Golf Gets a Look at the Real World' by Dan Jenkins, *Sports Illustrated*, 25 August 1969: https://www.si.com/ vault/1969/08/25/609890/golf-gets-a-look-at-the-real-world# (accessed 12 June 2107).

Player, Gary, cited in 'Golf: The paradox that is Gary Player' by Tim Glover, *The Independent*, 15 July 1996: http://www.independent. co.uk/sport/golf-the-paradox-that-is-gary-player-1329010.html (accessed 12 June 2017).

Player, Gary, cited in 'Golf's greatest taboo makes an unwelcome return', *The Scotsman*, 19 September 2003: http://www.scotsman. com/sport/golf/golf-s-greatest-taboo-makes-an-unwelcome-return-1-664613 (accessed 12 June 2017).

Player, Gary cited in 'Greats of Golf at Insperity Invitational Press Conference', 6 May 2017, on Nicklaus (website): http://www. nicklaus.com/news/greats-golf-insperity-invitational-press-conference/ (accessed 21 June 2017).

Player, Gary, cited in 'My Shot: Gary Player' by Guy Yocom, *Golf Digest*, August 12, 2010: http://www.golfdigest.com/story/myshot_gd0308 (accessed 12 May 2017).

Player, Gary, cited in *The Daily Mail* (Australia), article by Derek Lawrenson, 30 October 2015: http://www.dailymail.co.uk/sport/golf/article-3295850/Gary-Player-80-Sunday-does-1-300-sit-ups-day-never-shoots-age-No-wonder-gets-kick-life.html (accessed 16 June 2017).

Player, Gary, Thatcher, Floyd, 1974, *Gary Player: World Golfer*, Waco Texas: Word Books.

Podneiks, Andrew, 2015, *Golf's Greatest Collapses*, London: Arcturus Publishing Limited, (source for anonymous quote about Bobby Jones).

Povich, Shirley, from the Povich Center for Sports Journalism, 1 May 1942: http://povichcenter.org/slammin-sammy-snead-goes-to-war/ (accessed 2 June 2017).

Price, Nick, cited in 'The Great Masters' by Dan Jenkins, *Golf Digest*, 17 December 2007: http://www.golfdigest.com/story/198606greatestmasters (accessed 17 May 2017).

Price, Nick, cited in 'Trampled Roots' by Barry Havenga, *Golf Digest*, 24 September 2013: http://www.golfdigest.com/story/gwar-zimbabwe-nick-price-0930 (accessed 16 May 2017).

Price, Nick, 'My Shot I lost a brother, and golf lost one of its true ambassadors, when Lewie died', *Sports Illustrated*, 16 July 2001: https://www.si.com/vault/2001/07/16/307530/my-shot-i-lost-a-brother-and-golf-lost-one-of-its-true-ambassadors-when-lewie-died (accessed 16 May 2017).

Reilly, Rick 'From Trouble to Triumph', *Sports Illustrated*, 27 June 1994: http://www.golf.com/tour-and-news/trouble-triumph (accessed 16 June 2017).

Rice, Grantland, cited in 'Greatest shot in Masters history? Revisit Sarazen's "shot heard round the world"' by Matt S. Craig, PGA website, 7 April 2017: http://www.pga.com/news/masters/greatest-shot-in-masters-history-revisit-sarazens-shot-heard-round-world (accessed 12 May 2017).

Roberts, Clifford, cited in 'Treasure of Golf's Sad Past, Black Caddies Vanish in Era of Riches' by Karen Crouse, *New York Times*, 2 April 2012.

Rotella, Bob, 1995, *Golf is Not a Game of Perfect*, Simon and Schuster.

Russell, James, 2012, David Graham: *From Ridicule to Acclaim*, Random House.

Sanders, Doug, cited in 'My Shot: Doug Sanders' by Guy Yocom in *Golf Digest*, 12 August 2010: http://www.golfdigest.com/story/myshot_gd0308 (accessed 11 June 2017).

Sanders, Doug, cited in 'The Open 2015: Remembering Doug Sanders' St Andrews pain', *National Club Golfer*, 8 July 2015: http://www.nationalclubgolfer.com/2015/07/08/the-open-2015-doug-sanders-st-andrews-pain/ (accessed 13 June 2017).

Selcraig, Bruce, 'The Man with the Perfect Swing', *Reader's Digest*, December 1999: moenormangolf.com/man-perfect-swingdec-1999-readers-digest (accessed 6 July 2017).

Shipnuck Alan, 'A Conversation With Golf's Most Interesting Man: Miguel Angel Jimenez', *Golf*, 30 April 2015: http://www.golf.com/tour-and-news/conversation-miguel-angel-jimenez, accessed 16 May 2017.

Singh, Vijay, cited in 'Golf's leading men outraged at teeing off with a woman' by Adam Lusher, *The Telegraph*, 8 May 2003: www.telegraph.co.uk/news/worldnews/northamerica/usa/1430460/Golfs-leading-men-outraged-at-teeing-off-with-a-woman.html (accessed 6 July 2017).

Slovick Lyle (2016) Trials and Triumphs of Golf's Greatest Champions: A Legacy of Hope, Rowman and Littlefield Publishers Inc: London.

Snead, Jack, cited in 'Golf: Sam Snead's son tells stories of his father, and Naples' Oak Grill & Tavern' by Greg Hardwig, *Naples Daily News*, 1 February 2016: archive.naplesnews.com/sports/golf/golf-sam-sneads-son-tells-stories-of-his-father-and-naples-oak-grill--tavern-2a682721-dfb0-190c-e053-367100821.html (accessed 6 July 2017).

Snead, Sam, cited in 'My Shot: Sam Snead', by Guy Yocom, *Golf Digest*, 12 August 2010: http://www.golfdigest.com/story/myshot_gd0204 (accessed 16 May 2017).

Snead, Sam, Pirozzolo, Fran, 1997, T*he Game I Love: Wisdom, Insight, and Instruction from Golf's Greatest Player*, Random House, New York.

Sorenstam, Annika, 'Letter to My Daughter', *Players Tribune*, 30 March 2016: www.theplayerstribune.com/annika-sorenstam-golf-letter-to-my-daughter (accessed 6 July 2017).

Spieth, Jordan, cited in 'Jason Day wins his first major with victory over Jordan Spieth in US PGA Championship', *The Daily Telegraph*, 17 August 2015: http://www.dailytelegraph.com.au/sport/golf/2015-pga-championship-can-jason-day-hold-off-jordan-spieth-and-win-his-first-major/news-story/994a94bb71bea7d143d650733a23565d (accessed 6 June 2017).

Spieth, Jordan, cited in 'Jordan Spieth on U.S. Open's 18th: "The dumbest hole I've ever played in my life'" by Luke Kerr-Dineen, *USA Today*, 19 June 2015: http://ftw.usatoday.com/2015/06/jordan-spieth-on-u-s-opens-18th-hole-the-dumbest-hole-ive-ever-played-in-my-life (accessed 5 July 2015).

Sports Illustrated, 12 April 1999. cover 'David Duval is On Fire'.

Stephenson, Jan cited in *The Book of Golf Quotations* by Pat Sullivan, 2012, Random House: original quote from Playboy.

Stone, Peter, 'Celebrating a "damn good idea"', *The Age*, 27 November 2008: www.theage.com.au/news/sport/golf/celebrating-a-damn-good-idea/2008/11/26/1227491635633.html (accessed 6 July 2017).

Strange, Curtis, cited in 'From Trouble To Triumph' by Rick Reilly, *Sports Illustrated*, 27 June 1994: https://www.si.com/vault/1994/06/27/131530/from-trouble-to-triumph-south-africas-ernie-els-strayed-all-over-oakont-but-ended-up-in-clover-as-he-won-a-three-way-playoff-for-the-us-open-title (accessed 6 July 2017).

Thomson Peter, cited in 'An open discussion with Peter Thomson' by Andrew Crockett, *Inside Golf*, 15 July 2015: http://www.insidegolf.com.au/feature-articles/an-open-discussion-with-peter-thomson/ (accessed 11 June 2017).

Thomson, Peter, cited in 'Von Nida blazed trail' by Trevor Grant, *Herald Sun*, 22 May 2007: http://www.heraldsun.com.au/sport/golf/von-nida-blazed-trail/news-story/6340b18a66b0415fc4a3ca256db13016?sv=524b901ad7978251e8c3f78c76bd1c0 (accessed 15 June 2017).

Thomson, Peter, 2013, *A Life in Golf: Inspirations & Insights From Australia's Greatest Golfer*, The Slattery Media Group.

Titleist (website), 'Titleist Introduces the New 2017 Pro V1 and Pro V1x Golf Balls' By Rick V., Team Titleist, 25 January 2017: https://www.titleist.com.au/teamtitleist/au/b/weblog/archive/2017/01/25/

titleist-introduces-the-new-2017-pro-v1-and-pro-v1x-golf-balls (accessed 20 June 2017).

Trading Places, Cinema Group Ventures/Eddie Murphy Productions, 1983.

Trevino, Lee, cited in 'Lee Trevino Talks About the Masters' by Phil Stukenborg, *The Commercial Appeal*, 8 April 2015: http://archive. commercialappeal.com/sports/golf/Lee-Trevino-talks-about-the-Masters-375030641.html/ (accessed 2 June 2017).

Trevino, Lee, cited in 'Q&A With Lee Trevino' by Jaime Diaz, *Golf Digest*, 20 October 2009: http://www.golfdigest.com/story/lee_trevino (accessed 16 June 2017).

Trevino, Lee, talking to Matt Adams on the *Golf Channel* (ms p. 132)

Trevino, Lee to Jack Nicklaus at Augusta 1970 (ms p. 116)

Uihlein, Wally, cited in 'Moe Norman: Greatest Striker Ever? Remembering the eccentric, brilliantly accurate Canadian' by Jeff Neuman, *Wall Street Journal*, 25 July 2014: http://moenormangolf. com/wall-street-journal-article-moe-norman-golfs-greatest-ball-striker/ (accessed 15 June 2017).

United States Golf Association, 1929 (first edition), *The Rules of Golf*, 32nd edition published 2012.

Van Pelt, Scott, interview with Matt Cleary, 23 March 2017.

Vardon, Harry, *The Complete Golfer*, first published 1902 by Library of Alexandria, 2017 edition published by Createspace Independent Publishing Platform, United States.

Von Nida, Norman, 2014, *The Von: Stories and Suggestions from Australian Golf's Little Master*, University of Queensland Press.

Von Nida, Norman, Von Nida's story of 2-blow fight with American pro', *The Argus* (Melbourne), 16 February 1948, p. 3: recreated on http://trove.nla.gov.au/newspaper/article/22534925 (accessed 2 June 2017).

Walt Disney Pictures, *The Greatest Game Ever Played*, 2005.

Warner Bros., *Superman II*, 1980.

Watson, Tom, cited in 'Regrets? I've Had a Few', by the editors, *Golf Digest*, 14 May 2012, excerpt: http://www.golfdigest.com/story/ mulligans (accessed 17 May 2017).

Watson, Willie, cited in *The Cronicle of Golf*, 2000, by Ted Barrett, Carlton Books Ltd, p. 81.

Watson, Tom, cited in 'The Open 2009: Soldier's appreciation helps ease Tom Watson's Turnberry pain' by Oliver Brown, *The Telegraph*, 21 July 2009: http://www.telegraph.co.uk/sport/golf/ theopen/5881097/The-Open-2009-Soldiers-appreciation-helps-ease-Tom-Watsons-Turnberry-pain.html (accessed 16 June 2017).

Weiskopf, Tom, cited in 'His First Hurrah' by Dan Jenkins, *Sports Illustrated*, 23 July 1973: https://www.si.com/ vault/1973/07/23/615663/his-first-hurrah (accessed 17 May 2017).

Weiskopf, Tom, cited in 'Julius Boros, 74, a Pro Golfer Known for His Masterly Touch' by Herbert Warren Wind, *New York Times*, 30 May 1994: http://www.nytimes.com/1994/05/30/obituaries/julius-boros-74-a-pro-golfer-known-for-his-masterly-touch.html (accessed 17 May 2017).

Weiskopf, Tom, cited in 'The Masters' by Ewan Murray, *The Observer*, 9 April 2017: https://www.pressreader.com/uk/the-observer-sport/20170409 (accessed 16 June 2017). See also: http://www. golf.com/photos/augusta-we-have-problem/martha-burk-masters (accessed 16 June 2017).

Wethered, Joyce, cited in 'Joyce Wethered', *Golf Bible*, 16 November 2015. https://golfbible.co.uk/2015/11/16/joyce-wethered (accessed 9 June 2017).

Wilson, Enid, cited in 'Golf and the Women' by Herbert Warren Wind, *Sports Illustrated*, 23 July 1956: https://www.si.com/

vault/1956/07/23/582320/golf-and-the-women# (accessed 16 Jue 2017).

Wind, Herbert Warren, 'The Doc Shows the Masters How', *Sports Illustrated*, 18 April 1955: https://www.si.com/vault/1955/04/18/621625/the-doc-shows-the-masters-how (accessed 17 May 2017).

Wind, Herbert Warren, 'Julius Boros, 74, a Pro Golfer Known for His Masterly Touch', *New York Times*, 30 May 1994: http://www.nytimes.com/1994/05/30/obituaries/julius-boros-74-a-pro-golfer-known-for-his-masterly-touch.html (accessed 17 May 2017).

Woods, Tiger, cited in 'Back to the future Big internal trouble brewing for...' by Steve Rosenbloom, *Chicago Tribune*, 28 October 1996: http://articles.chicagotribune.com/1996-10-28/sports/9610280062_1_tiger-tales-quad-city-classic-flack (accessed 5 July 2017).

Wright, Mickey, cited in *The Illustrated History of Women's Golf*, by Rhonda Glenn, Taylor Publishing Company, 1991.

Wright, Mickey, cited in 'Patty Berg, Champion and Pioneer in Golf, Is Dead at 88' by Richard Goldstein, *New York Times*, 11 September, 2006: http://www.nytimes.com/2006/09/11/sports/golf/patty-berg-champion-and-pioneer-in-golf-is-dead-at-88.html (accessed 17 May 2017).

Yale Harvey W., cited in 'Nida in Golf Course Scene—Blows Struck', *Valley Morning Star*, Harlingen, Texas, 15 February 1948: http://trove.nla.gov.au/newspaper/article/18061138 (accessed 15 June 2017).

Yang Y.E., cited in 'Yang achieves a major moment in authoritative fashion' by T.J. Auclair, *PGA Championship*, 2009: http://www.pga.com/pgachampionship/2009/news/yang_081609.html (accessed 14 June 2017).

Yang Y.E., cited in ,PGA Champion Y.E. Yang Comeback Story Has Its Roots in Weight Room' by Barry Svrluga, *Washington Post*, 17 August 2009: http://www.washingtonpost.com/wp-dyn/content/article/2009/08/16/AR2009081602411.html (accessed 13 June 2017).

Zoeller, Frank (Fuzzy), cited in 'Masterful' by Rick Reilly, *Sports Illustrated*, 18 April 1988: https://www.si.com/vault/1988/04/18/117515/masterful-with-a-dramatic-birdie-on-18-sandy-lyle-won-the-masters-by-one-stroke----and-the-green-jacket-bestowed-by-1987-champ-larry-mize (accessed 16 June 2017).

ACKNOWLEDGEMENTS

Time is money, they say, but I could never repay the following folks for the great generosity of their time. So, it's my shout for a beer in perpetuity to: Greg Norman, David Graham, Luke Elvy, Bernie McGuire, Andrew Crockett, Gary Player, Bruce Young, Stephanie Ridley, Mike Clayton, Nick O'Hern, Paul 'The Singing Caddie' Stevens, James Erskine, Ian Baker-Finch, Frank Williams and Scott Van Pelt.

A shout-out to golf writers Dan Jenkins and Rick Reilly who don't write history so much as paint it. I turned to their evocative tales often. As I did to the old boys: Andrew Lang, Bernard Darwin, O.B. Keeler, Grantland Rice, Herbert Warren Wind, Bob Drum. These people not only painted history they decided what it would be.

Thanks to Brendan 'BJ' James of *Golf Australia* magazine for tipping New Holland onto a baggy-arsed freelancer. Thanks to *Inside Sport* editors, Graem Sims, Jeff Centenara and the late, great Greg Hunter for the mentorship.

And to Frances, who kept telling me the book would be good because I'm good at writing, and brought me cups of tea and chocolate muffins. Thanks sweetheart, love you. And to my boys Charlie, George and Henry—I'm free for footy in the backyard, champions.

ABOUT THE AUTHOR

Matt Cleary is a sports, travel and lifestyle writer who contributes to such journals as: *The Guardian*; *Inside Sport*; *Golf Digest*; *Inside Golf*; *Luxury Travel*, *Men's Health*; *Men's Fitness*; *Bleacher Report*; *Robb Report*; *Big League*; *The Roar*; *Inside Rugby*; several in-flight magazines; and others.

He has played golf in Tahiti, Tasmania and Thailand. He shot 81 on the Old Course at St Andrews, a round he can still remember shot for shot. He once spent four months driving 25,000 kilometres (16,000 miles) for a 12-month series of stories in *Golf Digest*.

Matt was Internet famous for about a fortnight when a live blog he wrote for *The Guardian* about Jarryd Hayne's first game for San Francisco 49ers went viral.

Memorably, *ESPN*'s Scott van Pelt interviewed Matt about the blog on *SportsCenter*, then 18 months later Matt interviewed Scott for this very book (Scott's a fellow golf nut and a confidante of Tiger Woods).

Matt enjoys travelling the world writing golf stories, Four Pines Pale Ale, and hitting little white balls around a golf course—any golf course. He also runs golf tours because they're fun.

He has three young boys and an understanding wife.

First published in 2017 by New Holland Publishers
London • Sydney • Auckland

The Chandlery, 50 Westminster Bridge Road, London SE1 7QY, United Kingdom
1/66 Gibbes Street, Chatswood, NSW 2067, Australia
5/39 Woodside Avenue, Northcote, Auckland 0627, New Zealand

newhollandpublishers.com

A record of this book is held at the British Library and the National Library of
Australia.

ISBN: 9781742579771

Group Managing Director: Fiona Schultz
Publisher: Alan Whiticker
Project Editor: Susie Stevens
Designer: Andrew Quinlan
Production Director: James Mills-Hicks
Printer: Hang Tai Printing Company Limited

10 9 8 7 6 5 4 3 2 1

Keep up with New Holland Publishers on Facebook
facebook.com/NewHollandPublishers

US: $19.99
UK: £14.99